Research-Based Strategies for Improving Outcomes in Academics

David J. Chard
Southern Methodist University

Bryan G. Cook
University of Hawaii

Melody Tankersley
Kent State University

PEARSON

Boston   Columbus   Indianapolis   New York   San Francisco   Upper Saddle River
Amsterdam   Cape Town   Dubai   London   Madrid   Milan   Munich   Paris   Montreal   Toronto
Delhi   Mexico City   São Paulo   Sydney   Hong Kong   Seoul   Singapore   Taipei   Tokyo

Vice President and Editorial Director: Jeffery W. Johnston
Executive Editor: Ann Castel Davis
Editorial Assistant: Andrea Hall
Vice President, Director of Marketing: Margaret Waples
Marketing Manager: Joanna Sabella
Senior Managing Editor: Pamela D. Bennett
Project Manager: Sheryl Glicker Langner
Senior Operations Supervisor: Matthew Ottenweller
Senior Art Director: Diane C. Lorenzo

Cover Designer: Candace Rowley
Cover Image: Background: © Lora liu/Shutterstock;
Photo: © kali9/iStockphoto
Full-Service Project Management: S4Carlisle
Publishing Services
Composition: S4Carlisle Publishing Services
Printer/Binder: Edwards Brothers Malloy
Cover Printer: Lehigh-Phoenix Color/Hagerstown
Text Font: Times LT Std

Credits and acknowledgments for material borrowed from other sources and reproduced, with permission, in this textbook appear on the appropriate page within the text.

Photo Credits: Chapter-opening photo: © kali9/iStockphoto. Design images (from left to right): © Orange Line Media/Shutterstock; © kali9/iStockphoto; © Nailia Schwarz/Shutterstock; © iofoto/Shutterstock; © Jaren Jai Wicklund/Shutterstock.

Every effort has been made to provide accurate and current Internet information in this book. However, the Internet and information posted on it are constantly changing, so it is inevitable that some of the Internet addresses listed in this textbook will change.

Library of Congress Cataloging-in-Publication Data is available upon request.

10 9 8 7 6 5 4 3 2 1

ISBN 10:   0-13-702990-X
ISBN 13: 978-0-13-702990-7

Dedication

We dedicate this to our families, who help us remember what life is really about.

To Richard, Cecilia, Madeleine, and James. – DJC

To Lysandra, Zoe, and Ben. – BC

To Bebe and Jackson. – MT

Preface

Research-Based Strategies for Improving Outcomes in Academics was born of discussions over many years between special education practitioners and researchers regarding the need for a reliable and practical guide to highly effective, research-based practices in special education. Providing this type of information is a primary focus of the Council for Exceptional Children's Division for Research (CEC-DR), which the Division has pursued in many ways—sometimes with considerable success, sometimes with disappointment. At a meeting of the Executive Board of CEC-DR, then President Dr. Robin A. McWilliam suggested that the division consider producing a textbook to meet this need that would be unique in its emphasis on research-based practices. And so began concrete discussions that led to the book you are now reading.

You have probably read or heard something about the research-to-practice gap in special education—when practice is not based on research and, although less often emphasized in the professional literature, when research is not relevant to practice. This gap is not unique to special education; it occurs in general education and many other professional fields, including medicine. It is unlikely that the gap between research and practice will ever disappear entirely; indeed, it may not be desirable to thoroughly commingle the worlds of special education research and practice. However, when the gap between research and practice becomes a chasm, with practice being dictated more by tradition and personal trial-and-error than reliable research, the outcomes and opportunities of students suffer unnecessarily. Simply stated, special educators need to use the most effective instructional practices so that students with disabilities can reach their potentials; all too often, that does not occur.

We believe that this text is made all the more timely and important given the recent explosion of information on the Internet. The wealth of information available on the Internet (as well as from other, more traditional sources of recommendations on instructional practices such as professional development trainings, textbooks, and journals) can be an important asset in helping determine what works. However, much of the information on the Internet and other sources is not research based and therefore is often inaccurate. Thus, although having thousands of pieces of information about various teaching techniques at one's fingertips may seem wonderful, it often has a stultifying effect, leaving many educators drowning in a sea of information overload, without the time or necessary information (i.e., research findings) to determine what is truly credible and what is not. Rather than unsubstantiated promotion of scores of techniques, special educators need in-depth information on the practices shown by reliable research to be most effective for improving important outcomes of learners with disabilities, which is our aim in this text. By focusing on practices with solid research support, such as those featured in this text, special educators can feel confident that they are implementing approaches that are most likely to work for learners with disabilities.

It is important to realize, though, that research support is not an iron-clad guarantee of effectiveness for each and every student. Even the most effective, research-based practices do not work for everyone (there are nonresponders to every practice); and contextual factors (e.g., school and classroom environments, student characteristics) found in practice seldom align perfectly with the research studies supporting most practices. Therefore, teachers will have to rely on their professional wisdom to select and adapt the research-based practices targeted in this text to make them work in their classrooms, for their students. Nonetheless, having practices identified as effective on the basis of sound research, knowing what the research says about those practices, and understanding how those practices work are critical first steps in achieving effective special education practice.

We believe that *Research-Based Strategies for Improving Outcomes in Academics* will be counted as one of the considerable successes of CEC-DR because it provides researchers, teacher trainers, policy makers, practitioners, family members, and other stakeholders information about research-based practices shown to generally produce desirable outcomes in the core area of academics for instructing learners with disabilities.

Acknowledgments

Very little is accomplished in isolation, and that was certainly true for this text. It is important for us to acknowledge the many professionals whose hard work is responsible for this text. We first acknowledge the chapter authors. We were fortunate to have the participation of the foremost authorities in the topics of focus in this work. We thank them for sharing their expertise and working so diligently and agreeably with us throughout the entire process. We thank Ann Davis, our editor at Pearson, for her unflagging support and insightful assistance. We also express our appreciation to Dr. Christine Balan, Dr. Lysandra Cook, Luanne Dreyer Elliott, and Norine Strang for their excellent and professional editing. Thank you to our reviewers: Mary E. Cronin, University of New Orleans, and E. Paula Crowley, Illinois State University. And most importantly, we acknowledge our families, without whose support and forbearance this work could not have been accomplished.

David J. Chard
Southern Methodist University

Bryan G. Cook
University of Hawaii

Melody Tankersley
Kent State University

Contents

CHAPTER 1

Introduction to Research-Based Practices for Increasing Behavioral Outcomes

Bryan G. Cook | *University of Hawaii*

Melody Tankersley | *Kent State University*

This is not a typical introductory textbook in special education that provides brief overviews of a large number of student characteristics and instructional practices. Textbooks with this focus serve important purposes. For example, individuals who are just beginning to explore the field of special education need to understand the breadth of student needs and corresponding instructional techniques that have been and are being used to teach students with disabilities. This text addresses a different need—the need for extensive information on selected, highly effective practices in special education. Stakeholders such as advanced preservice special educators, practicing special education and inclusive teachers, administrators, parents, and many teacher-educators are more directly involved with the instruction and learning of children and youth with disabilities and as a result need in-depth treatments of the most effective practices that they can use to meaningfully impact and improve the educational experiences of children and youth with and at risk for disabilities.

In this textbook we provide extensive (rather than cursory) information on selected, highly effective practices (rather than on many practices, some of which may be less than effective) in special education. This endeavor begs an important question: What are the most highly effective practices identified in special education?

That is, how do we tell "what works" for children and youth with and at risk for disabilities?

Traditionally, special educators have relied on sources such as personal experience, colleagues, tradition, and experts to guide their instructional decision making (e.g., Cook & Smith, in press). These resources have served teachers well in many ways. Special education teachers are skilled professionals who learn from their personal experiences and refine their teaching accordingly. Traditions and custom represent the accumulated personal experiences of whole groups and cultures and therefore can be imbued with great wisdom. And experts most often know of which they speak (and write) and make many valid recommendations. Yet, just as in other aspects of life, the personal experiences that lie at the root of these sources of knowing are prone to error and can lead special educators to false conclusions about which practices work and should be implemented with students with disabilities.

Limitations of Traditional Methods for Determining What Works

Chabris and Simons (2010) described five everyday illusions documented in the psychological literature (i.e., illusions of attention, memory, confidence, knowledge, and cause) that cast doubt on whether teachers can use personal experiences (their own, or those of their colleagues) to determine reliably whether practices work for their students. Chabris and Simons noted that although people assume that they attend to everything within their perceptual field, in reality many stimuli—especially those that contrast with one's expectations—"often go completely unnoticed" (p. 7). That is, people tend to focus their attention on what they expect to happen. Moreover, even when people actively attend to phenomena, their memories are unlikely to be wholly accurate and also are biased by their preconceptions. "We cannot play back our memories like a DVD—each time we recall a memory, we integrate whatever details we do remember with our expectations for what we should remember" (p. 49). Moreover, people tend to hold false illusions of confidence (e.g., most people think of themselves as above-average drivers) and knowledge (e.g., people tend to falsely believe that they know how familiar tools and systems work). Finally, "Our minds are built to detect meaning in patterns, to infer causal relationships from coincidences, and to believe that earlier events cause later ones" (p. 153), even though many patterns are meaningless, many associations are coincidental, and earlier events often simply precede rather than cause later occurrences.

Special education teachers—just like other people in their professional and day-to-day lives—may, then, not attend to events in a classroom that they do not expect (e.g., when using preferred practices, teachers may be more likely to focus on students who are doing well but not recognize struggling students); may construct memories of teaching experiences that are influenced by their preconceptions of whether a practice is likely to work; may be more confident than warranted that a favored instructional approach works when they use it; may believe that they fully understand why and how a practice works when they do not; and may believe that a practice causes positive changes in student outcomes when it does not. We are not suggesting that special educators are more gullible or error prone than anyone else. Nonetheless, these documented illusions show that using one's perceptions of personal experiences is an error-prone method for establishing whether instructional practices cause improved student outcomes.

Traditional wisdom shares many important traits with scientific research (e.g., refining understanding based on empirical input over time; Arunachalam, 2001). Indeed, many traditional practices are shown to be valid when examined scientifically (Dickson, 2003). Yet, tradition and custom often are based on incomplete science or consist of inaccurate superstition and folklore. History is replete with examples of traditional thinking that science subsequently has shown to be incorrect—from

the flat-earth and geocentric models of the solar system to the direct inheritability of intelligence and ineducability of individuals with various disabilities. Accordingly, although many traditional instructional practices for students with disabilities may be effective, others have been passed down through generations of teachers even though they do not have a consistently positive effect on student outcomes. Basing instruction on the individual learning styles of students with disabilities, for example, is an accepted, traditional teaching practice despite the lack of supporting evidence (see Landrum & McDuffie, 2010).

As with personal experience and tradition, expert opinion is often faulty. Indeed, a common logical fallacy is the appeal to authority, in which one argues that a statement is true based on the authority of who said it. Not surprisingly, so-called authorities such as new-age gurus and celebrities often support less than effective products. But experts more commonly considered credible, such as textbook authors, also frequently provide inaccurate guidance. "The fact is, expert wisdom usually turns out to be at best highly contested and ephemeral, and at worst flat-out wrong" (Freedman, 2010, p. 7). In special education, "experts" have a long history of advocating for ineffective practices such as avoiding immunizations, facilitated communication, colored glasses or prism lenses, and patterning (e.g., Mostert, 2010; Mostert & Crockett, 2000). Thus, special educators need to be wary of basing instructional decisions on unverified expert recommendation.

Unlike their nondisabled peers, who often experience success in school while receiving mediocre or even poor instruction, students with disabilities require the most effective instruction to succeed (Dammann & Vaughn, 2001). As Malouf and Schiller (1995) noted, special education serves "students and families who are especially dependent on receiving effective services and who are especially vulnerable to fraudulent treatment claims" (p. 223). It appears, then, that those who teach and work with students with disabilities need a more reliable and trustworthy method for determining what works than personal experience, tradition, or expert opinion. Scientific research can provide a meaningful guide to special educators and other stakeholders when making decisions about what and how to teach learners with disabilities.

Benefits of Using Research to Determine What Works

It is the professional and ethical duty of special educators to implement the instructional techniques most likely to benefit the students they serve. Indeed, the Council for Exceptional Children's (CEC) standards for well-prepared special education teachers specify that special educators should keep abreast of research findings and implement

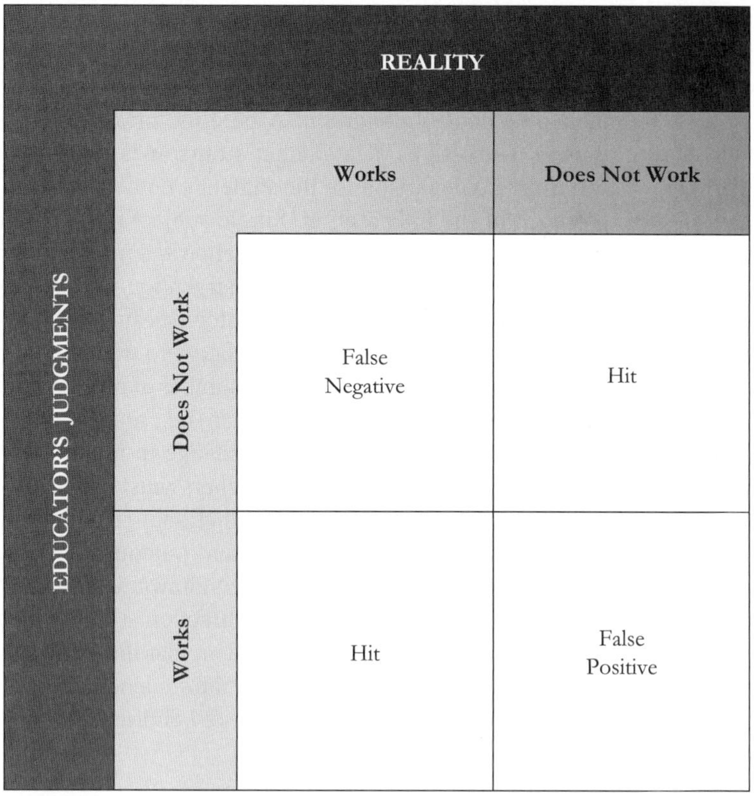

Figure 1.1 Relation between educator's judgments and reality regarding the effectiveness of instructional practices.

research-based practices with their students (CEC, 2009). Moreover, the No Child Left Behind Act and the Individuals with Disabilities Education Act of 2004 both place considerable emphasis on practices that are supported by scientifically based research (e.g., Hess & Petrilli, 2006; A. Smith, 2003; H. R. Turnbull, 2005). Using research as the preferred method to determine what and how to teach makes sense because research can address many of the shortcomings of other traditional approaches for identifying what works.

False Positives and False Negatives

When examining a practice's effectiveness, four possibilities exist to represent the relation between reality (Does the practice actually work for the children in question?) and educators' judgments (Do I believe that the practice works?) (see Figure 1.1). Educators can be right, or hit, in two ways: they can conclude that the practice (a) works, and it actually does, or (b) does not work, and it actually does not. They can also be wrong, or miss, in two ways. First, educators can commit a false positive by concluding that the practice works when it actually *is not* effective. Second, educators can commit a false negative by concluding that the practice does not work, when it actually *is* effective. The goal of any approach to determining what works is to maximize the number of hits while minimizing the likelihood of false positives and false negatives.

As discussed in the previous section, using personal experience, colleagues, tradition, and expert opinion leaves the door open to false positives and false negatives, which results in ineffective teaching and suboptimal outcomes for students with disabilities. Sound scientific research reduces the likelihood of false positives and false negatives in a number of ways, such as (a) using credible measures of student performance, (b) involving large and representative samples, (c) using research designs that rule out alternative explanations for change in student performance, and (d) engaging in the open and iterative nature of science (Lloyd, Pullen, Tankersley, & Lloyd, 2006).

Safeguards in Scientific Research

Credible Measures

Teachers' perceptions of students' behavior and academic performance are often based on subjective perceptions and unreliable measures and therefore do not correspond strictly with actual student behavior and performance (e.g., Madelaine & Wheldall, 2005). In contrast, sound scientific research uses trustworthy methods for measuring phenomena. Whether using direct observations of behavior, formal assessments, curriculum-based measures, or standardized rating scales, high-quality research utilizes procedures and instruments that are both reliable (i.e., consistent) and valid (i.e., meaningful) to accurately gauge student behavior and performance.

Large and Representative Samples

Educators typically interact with a limited number of students, whose performance and behavior may differ meaningfully from other students. Consequently, personal experience (as well as the experiences of colleagues or experts) may not generalize to other students. That is, just because a practice worked for a few students does not mean that it will work for most others. In contrast, research studies typically involve relatively large and often representative samples of student participants across multiple environments and educators. When research has shown that a practice has been effective for the vast majority of a very large number of students, the results are likely to generalize to others in the same population. It is true, however, that most single-subject research studies and some group experimental studies involve a relatively small number of participants. In these cases, confidence in research findings is obtained across a body of research, when multiple studies with convergent findings show that an intervention works for a substantial number of students within a population.

Ruling Out Alternative Explanations

When educators informally examine whether a practice works, they might implement the technique and observe whether students' outcomes subsequently improve. If outcomes do improve, it might seem reasonable to conclude that the intervention worked. However, this conclusion might be a false positive. The students may have improved because of their own development, or something else (e.g., a new educational assistant, a change in class schedule) may be responsible for improved outcomes. Group experimental and single-subject research studies are designed to rule out explanations for improved student outcomes other than the intervention being examined. In other words, causality (i.e., an intervention generally *causes* improved outcomes) can be inferred reasonably from these designs (B. G. Cook, Tankersley, Cook, & Landrum, 2008).

Group experimental research incorporates a control group (to which participants are randomly assigned in true experiments) that is as similar as possible to the experimental group. Ideally, the control and experimental groups comprise functionally equivalent participants and the only differences in their experiences are that the experimental group receives the intervention whereas the control group does not. Under these conditions, if the experimental group improves more than the control group, those improved

outcomes must logically be ascribed to the intervention (e.g., L. Cook, Cook, Landrum, & Tankersley, 2008).

In single-subject research studies, individuals provide their own control condition. A baseline measure (e.g., typical instruction) of a student's outcomes over time serves as a comparison for the student's outcomes in the presence of the intervention. Single-subject researchers strive to make conditions in the baseline and intervention phases equivalent, except for the intervention. Of course, it is possible that the student's outcomes improved in the presence of the intervention relative to the outcome trend during baseline because of a number of phenomena outside the control of the researcher (i.e., not the intervention; e.g., new medication, a change in home life). Accordingly, single-subject researchers must provide at least three demonstrations of a functional relationship between the intervention and student outcomes. When the intervention is introduced or withdrawn and student outcomes change in the predicted direction at least three times, educators can then be confident that the intervention was responsible for changes in the student outcomes (e.g., Tankersley, Harjusola-Webb, & Landrum, 2008).

Open and Iterative Nature of Science

Although many safeguards exist at the level of individual studies to protect against false positives and false negatives, scientific research is inevitably an imperfect enterprise. No study is ideal, and it is impossible for researchers to control for all possible factors that may influence student outcomes in the real world of schools. Furthermore, researchers can and sometimes do make mistakes, which may result in reporting misleading findings. The more general process and nature of scientific research protects against spurious findings in at least two additional ways: public examination of research and recognizing that knowledge is an iterative process.

When reporting a study, researchers must describe their research (e.g., sample, procedures, instruments) in detail. Additionally, before being published in a peer-reviewed journal (the most common outlet for research studies), research studies are evaluated by the journal editors and blind-reviewed (the reviewers' and authors' identities are confidential) by a number of experts in the relevant field. Authors also must provide contact information, which readers can use to make queries about the study or request the data for reevaluation. These processes necessitate that published research undergoes multiple layers of scrutiny, which are likely to (a) weed out most studies with serious errors before being published and (b) identify errors that do exist in published studies.

Finally, it is critical to recognize that research is an iterative process in which greater confidence in a practice is accrued as findings from multiple studies converge in its support. Even with the safeguard of peer review and public scrutiny of research, published studies do sometimes report inaccurate findings. However, the iterative nature of science suggests that conclusions are best examined across entire bodies of research literature made up of multiple studies. For truly effective practices, the possible erroneous conclusions of one or two studies will be shown to be incorrect by a far larger number of studies with accurate findings. Thus, in contrast to relying on personal experience or on expert opinions, science has built-in self-correction mechanisms for identifying spurious results (Sagan, 1996; Shermer, 2002).

Caveats

Research-based practices represent powerful tools for improving the educational outcomes of students with disabilities, yet special educators need to understand a number of associated caveats and limitations. Specifically, research-based practices (a) will not work for everyone, (b) need to be implemented in concert with effective teaching practices, (c) must be selected carefully to match the needs of targeted students, and (d) should be adapted to maximize their impact.

Special educators cannot assume that a practice shown by research to be *generally* effective will be automatically effective for *all* of their students. No number of research participants or studies translates into a guarantee that a practice will work for each and every student, especially for students with disabilities who have unique learning characteristics and needs. Nonresponders, or treatment resistors, will exist for even the most effective instructional approaches. Therefore, although research-based practices are highly likely to be effective and special educators should therefore prioritize these practices, special educators should also always systematically evaluate the effects of these practices through progress monitoring (e.g., Deno, 2006).

Furthermore, research-based practices do not constitute good teaching but represent one important component of effective instruction. Research on effective teaching indicates that effective instruction is characterized by a collection of teacher behaviors, such as pacing instruction appropriately, emphasizing academic instruction, previewing instruction and reviewing previous instruction, monitoring student performance, circulating around and scanning the instructional environment to identify learner needs, recognizing appropriate student behavior, exhibiting enthusiasm, displaying "withitness" (an awareness of what is happening throughout the classroom), and using wait time after asking questions (Brophy & Good, 1986; Doyle, 1986). When educators implement research-based practices in the context of generally *ineffective* instruction—instruction

that occurs in the absence of these hallmarks of effective teaching—the practices are unlikely to produce desired outcomes. As such, research-based practices cannot take the place of and should always be applied in the context of good teaching (B. G. Cook, Tankersley, & Harjusola-Webb, 2008).

Another important caveat is that a practice demonstrated by research studies to be effective for one group may not work for others. It is therefore important that special educators are aware of the student group for which a practice has been demonstrated to be effective when selecting instructional and assessment practices to use with their students. For example, although a practice may have been shown by research studies to be effective for elementary students with learning disabilities, it may not work or even be appropriate for high school students with autism. However, highly effective practices tend to be powerful and their effects robust, and as such, they typically work for more than one specific group of children. For example, the use of mnemonic strategies has been shown to be effective for nondisabled students, students with learning disabilities, students with emotional and behavioral disorders, and students with intellectual impairments at a variety of grade levels (Scruggs & Mastropieri, 2000). Therefore, when reading about a practice that has been validated by research as effective with, for example, students with learning disabilities, special educators working with children and youth with other disabilities should not simply assume that the practice will be similarly effective for their students. But neither should they automatically assume that the practice will be ineffective. Rather, we recommend that special educators use their unique insights and knowledge of their students to evaluate the supporting research, underlying theory, and critical elements of a practice to determine the likelihood that a research-based practice will work for them.

Furthermore, special educators will need to consider whether and how to adapt research-based practices to meet the unique needs of their students. Although implementing a practice as designed is important (e.g., if a practice is not implemented correctly, one cannot expect it to be as effective as it was in the supporting research), recent research has indicated that overly rigid adherence to research-based practices may actually reduce their effectiveness (e.g., Hogue et al., 2008). It appears that teachers should adapt research-based practices to match the unique learning needs of their students and make the practice their own (McMaster et al., 2010). Yet they must do so in a way that preserves the integrity of the essential elements of the research-based practice to avoid rendering it ineffective.

These caveats notwithstanding, because of its many safeguards protecting against false-positive and false-negative conclusions regarding what works, scientific research is the best method available for special educators to identify effective instructional practices. By making decisions about how to teach on the basis of collective bodies of peer-reviewed research studies, special educators can identify with confidence practices that are likely to work for their students.

The Research-to-Practice Gap in Special Education

"Educational research could and should be a vital resource to teachers, particularly when they work with diverse learners—students with disabilities, children of poverty, limited-English speaking students. It is not" (Carnine, 1997, p. 513). The research-to-practice gap describes the commonplace occurrence of children and youth being taught with unproven practices while practices supported through research are not implemented. It is a complex phenomenon with many underlying causes that defies simple solutions. Kauffman (1996) suggested that the research-to-practice gap may be particularly extreme in special education, illustrating that an inverse relationship may actually exist between research support and degree of implementation for instructional practices in special education.

Despite reforms and legislation supporting the role of research in education, research findings indicate that the gap between research and practice continues to persist. For example, special educators reported using research-based practices no more often than ineffective practices (Burns & Ysseldyke, 2009; Jones, 2009). Jones also observed that some special education teachers over-reported their use of research-based practices, suggesting that the actual implementation rate of research-based practices may be even lower than reported. To make matters worse, when special educators do implement research-based practices, they often do so with low levels of fidelity (or not as designed; e.g., B. G. Cook & Schirmer, 2006)—potentially rendering the practices ineffective. Furthermore, many special educators report that they do not trust research or researchers (Boardman, Arguelles, Vaughn, Hughes, & Klingner, 2005) and find information from other teachers more trustworthy and usable (Landrum, Cook, Tankersley, & Fitzgerald, 2002, 2007).

The research-to-practice gap has clear and direct implications for the educational outcomes of students with disabilities. Using practices shown to have reliable and positive effects on student outcomes is the most likely way to improve student performance. Using research-based practices should, therefore, be a professional and ethical imperative for educators. This is true for all teachers. But as Dammann and Vaughn (2001) noted, whereas nondisabled students may perform adequately even in the presence of less than optimal instruction, students

with disabilities require that their teachers use the most effective instructional practices to reach their potentials and attain successful school outcomes.

This Textbook and Addressing the Research-to-Practice Gap

Bridging the research-to-practice gap in special education represents a significant challenge. Many issues will have to be addressed, such as improving teachers' attitudes toward research, providing ongoing supports for teachers to adopt and maintain research-based practices, and conducting high-quality research that is relevant to special education teachers (see B. G. Cook, Landrum, Tankersley, & Kauffman, 2003). But perhaps the most fundamental issues for bridging the research-to-practice gap are (a) *identifying* those practices that are research-based in critical areas of special education and (b) *providing the relevant information* (e.g., supporting theory, critical elements of the research-based practices, specific information on the supporting research studies) necessary to guide special educators in deciding whether the practice is right for them and their students and how to implement it. Without these critical first steps of identifying and providing special educators relevant information about research-based practices, the field of special education is unlikely to make significant progress in bridging the gap between research and practice.

Turning to original reports of research is an unsatisfactory alternative for the vast majority of special educators. Most teachers do not have the training to critically analyze technical research reports that often are geared for audiences with advanced training in statistics and research (Greenwood & Abbott, 2001). And even for those educators with advanced training in these areas, their full-time teaching jobs should and typically do occupy their time. It is simply not realistic for teachers to read through, synthesize, and critically analyze entire bodies of research literature for every instructional decision with which they are faced.

Textbooks focused on methods of instruction and assessment seem an ideal place to provide educators with useful information on research-based practices that can be used to bridge the research-to-practice gap. Unfortunately, much of teacher education—both preservice and inservice—is based on expert opinion and the personal experiences of those conducting the training or writing the training materials (e.g., textbooks). For example, textbook authors frequently recommend practices with little justification. Discussion of supporting research, if provided at all, is often too brief and incomplete for educators to make informed decisions about the appropriateness of the recommended practice for their classrooms. For example, Dacy, Nihalani, Cestone, and Robinson (2011) analyzed the content of three teaching methods textbooks and found that when prescriptive recommendations for using practices were supported by citations, authors predominantly cited secondary sources (e.g., books, positions papers) rather than provide discussions of original research from which their readers might arrive at meaningful conclusions regarding the effectiveness of the practices.

To address special educators' need for trustworthy, detailed, and teacher-friendly summaries of the research literature regarding what works in special education, the chapters in the complete, four-part text (Cook & Tankersley, 2012) text provide thorough synopses of the research literature supporting research-based practices in core areas of special education: academics, behavior, assessment, and targeted groups of learners. Specifically, in this volume on improving the academic outcomes of students with disabilities, chapter authors, who are documented experts on the topics of focus, address how to improve the outcomes of students with disabilities in critical academic content areas: early literacy, reading fluency, reading comprehension, vocabulary, mathematics computation, mathematics reasoning, written expression, the content areas (e.g., social studies, science), and co-taught classrooms. Chapter authors discuss and recommend practices and approaches based on

supporting research. Chapter authors also provide readers with descriptions of the underlying theory supporting the practices; supporting research studies, including information such as the research designs, the number and type of participants, and the degree to which the recommended practices positively affected student outcomes; and the critical elements of each research-based practice. Using this information, special educators can (a) make informed decisions about which research-based practices best fit their needs and (b) begin to implement the practices and improve the educational outcomes of their students with disabilities.

Conclusion

Special educators clearly want to use the most effective practices to enhance the educational outcomes and opportunities of the students they teach. However, given traditional methods for determining what works and the rapid proliferation of information on teaching techniques on the Internet (Landrum & Tankersley, 2004), much of which is misleading, it is increasingly difficult and complicated to know what works, what doesn't, and how to know the difference. Research is the most trustworthy method for determining what works in special education. This text provides readers with a wealth of information on specific research-based practices for academic outcomes in special education.

CHAPTER 2

Strategies for Improving Student Outcomes in Emergent Reading: *Advances in the Field of Early Literacy Instruction*

Jill H. Allor | *Southern Methodist University*

Stephanie Al Otaiba | *Florida State University*

*F*ar too many children do not learn to read within the primary grades and consequently have limited opportunities for future education and employment. Recent statistics from the National Assessment of Educational Progress (NAEP; National Center for Educational Statistics, 2007) show that nearly a third of all fourth graders and about half of students from minority backgrounds do not read on grade level. Over two decades ago, Juel (1988) showed that roughly 90% of children would remain poor readers if they were poor readers at the end of first grade. Ten years later, the seminal work *Preventing Reading Difficulties in Young Children* (Snow, Burns, & Griffin, 1998) presented a synthesis of research and identified three areas of difficulty that negatively impact early reading development: (a) the inability to acquire and apply the alphabetic principle, resulting in dysfluent and inaccurate word reading

skills; (b) poor verbal knowledge and comprehension strategies; and (c) poor initial motivation or the failure to develop an appreciation for the benefits of reading.

More recently, three seminal reviews of the research on reading have emphasized the importance of preventing reading difficulties through effective early literacy instruction (e.g., National Early Literacy Panel [NELP], 2008; National Reading Panel [NRP], 2000; Sweet & Snow, 2002). Converging evidence from these reviews has identified five critical early literacy intervention components: phonemic awareness, phonics, fluency, vocabulary, and comprehension. Evidence indicates that these components should be taught explicitly and systematically in order to prevent most reading difficulties. However, researchers have shown that a small number of students who do not learn to read despite having received comprehensive instruction need (and benefit from) more

This work was supported by (a) Mental Retardation and Reading Center Grant H324K040011-05 from the Institute of Education Sciences in the U.S. Department of Education, and by (b) Multidisciplinary Learning Disabilities Center Grant P50HD052120 from the National Institute of Child Health and Human Development.

intensive help that is individualized according to their needs (for review see Al Otaiba & Torgesen, 2007).

This knowledge about what works and the need for early intervention provided in layers of increasing intensity to match students' assessed needs is incorporated into new educational policy. Response to Intervention (RtI) is an important aspect of the Individuals with Disabilities Act (IDEA, 2004). RtI is a focus Burns and Scholin's examination of school-wide prevention of academic difficulties (2012). In this chapter, we briefly describe RtI to help readers think about how each of the interventions we discuss might be used.

In RtI, Tier 1 is primary reading instruction (and assessment to inform instruction including screening and progress monitoring) and is the foundation for all children. If Tier 1 is not successful, extra tiers of supplemental intervention are provided by classroom teachers, by well-trained and supervised nonteacher tutors, or by interventionists. Students with the most persistent challenges will require instruction provided by more highly trained interventionists. Methods for increasing intensity include reducing the group size, increasing the length and/or frequency of instructional sessions, and individualizing instruction based on student needs. Frequent progress monitoring is used to ensure that students are responding to additional tiers and to guide decisions regarding whether students should need to receive more or less intense and individualized instruction. Typically, specialists such as special educators, reading coaches, and highly-trained teachers provide Tier-3 instruction.

In the present chapter, we highlight three research-based early literacy interventions: Peer-Assisted Learning Strategies, Sound Partners, and Early Interventions in Reading. We describe the research base for each program and teachers can deliver the program to improve reading outcomes. These programs vary in their intensity and individualization and so are useful resources or tools for schools and teachers to implement at different tiers within RtI. Although these programs are research-based, we emphasize they have been successful when implemented *as intended*. This is a very important consideration because, if programs are not implemented with fidelity, they will not be as effective as they could be (Al Otaiba & Fuchs, 2006). For example, a school may decide to implement an intervention program that was shown by research to be successful when implemented 4 days a week, but if the intervention is only provided twice a week, it will likely not be as successful (Al Otaiba, Schatschneider, & Silverman, 2005). Thus, we provide guidelines for ensuring implementation fidelity. Finally, we discuss suggestions for implementation of these three programs within RtI contexts in the primary grades.

Before discussing each of these three programs, we describe our theoretical framework for emergent literacy development.

Theoretical Framework

Our theoretical framework for this chapter is the Simple View of Reading, in which Gough (1996) described reading comprehension as dependent on two broad sets of skills: (a) accurate and fluent word recognition and (b) language comprehension. Research is clear that good readers fully process print, meaning that they attend to internal structures (i.e., complete spellings) of words as they read (Adams, 1990; Ehri, 2002; Torgesen, 1998). They do this quickly and effortlessly. Once readers learn to recognize words with automaticity, they can shift the majority of their attention to the meaning of text (Torgesen, 1998). The underlying processes of comprehension are more complex, depending on a variety of factors including listening comprehension, linguistic abilities, relevant knowledge, understanding of story structure, and the ability to monitor comprehension (Perfetti, Landi, & Oakhill, 2005). In sum, good readers effortlessly recognize words and build mental representations of the message of the text, which in turn adds to their overall knowledge.

Owing to years of research and current technological advances, particularly those enabling researchers to examine brain activity, we are rapidly increasing our knowledge about underlying reading processes. Learning to read is a remarkable, complex process that requires students to connect experiences cracking the alphabetic code with oral language and background knowledge. In spite of this complexity, researchers agree that most individuals progress through predictable stages as they learn to read (Chall, 1983; Ehri, 2002). Early on, phonological awareness, print awareness, and expressive and receptive oral language skills develop. Later, decoding skills—including morphographic knowledge, or understanding the meaning of different word parts such as prefixes, suffixes, and roots—increase. Finally, students quickly and effortlessly retrieve both the pronunciation and meaning of individual words from long-term memory, enabling them to read fluently with deep understanding. Stage theories recognize that reading is an integrated process and that instruction at all stages focuses on development in multiple areas. For example, vocabulary and general knowledge are addressed in all stages of reading development, with early instruction focused on oral activities and later instruction focused on print-based activities. The Simple View of Reading and theory about how reading develops undergird the rationale for the early interventions presented in the remainder of this chapter.

Peer-Assisted Learning Strategies (PALS)

What Is PALS, and How Does It Work?

Converging findings from more than two decades of research demonstrate the efficacy of class-wide peer-tutoring interventions as a strategy for improving reading outcomes in the primary grades (Greenwood, Carta, & Hall, 1988). For the purposes of this chapter, we focus on one of the most widely researched peer-tutoring programs, Peer-Assisted Learning Strategies (PALS; see McMaster, Fuchs, & Fuchs, 2007). PALS is recommended as a supplement to classroom core reading programs and typically takes between 20% to 25% of a 90-minute reading block (i.e., approximately 30 minutes, three times per week).

During PALS lessons, dyads of higher- and lower-performing readers work together to practice critical skills including word recognition, fluency, and comprehension. Kindergarten and first-grade PALS include practice with phonological awareness and word recognition, as well as basic comprehension strategies. The classroom teacher introduces these components in a systematic and explicit fashion, and includes PALS activities that are designed to incorporate cumulative review and practice. The components and design reflect stage theories of reading development (Ehri, 2002) and the recommendations of the NELP (2008) and NRP (2000) as students are first taught the internal structure of words and then systematically apply those skills in increasingly difficult lesson passages and trade books. Comprehension strategies are incorporated into all PALS programs, but PALS for grades 2 and higher emphasizes building fluency and engaging in structured dialogue about text (i.e., discussing main ideas and predictions). The comprehensive nature of PALS assists students in integrating skills so that they can comprehend text more fully, which is also consistent with our theoretical framework recognizing the complexity of reading with deep comprehension. Both higher- and lower-performing readers take turns being the reader and being the coach, so that each student in the pair has an opportunity to practice key skills. A typical PALS lesson is described in Table 2.1, and sample lessons are available online (http://store .cambiumlearning.com and http://kc.vanderbilt.edu/pals).

The structure of PALS enables teachers to efficiently increase the amount of reading practice and provide differentiated instruction during a manageable whole-class activity. During PALS, students receive increased opportunities to respond as compared to typical instruction, thereby increasing the amount of practice with important early literacy skills. Simply put, students spend more time practicing key skills during PALS, because at all times half

Table 2.1   Overview of Typical First-Grade PALS Lesson

Activity	Brief Description
1. What sound?	Teacher presents new letter–sound correspondences, and pairs of students practice identifying them.
2. Sound it out and say it fast.	Teacher models decoding words, and students practice.
3. What word?	Teacher models sight–word reading, and students practice.
4. Story reading	Students practice reading simple stories composed of previously taught decodable and sight words.
5. Story sharing	Students "pretend read" a picture book, looking at the pictures and telling what is happening. Students "read aloud" the storybook two or more times. Students "retell" the events in the story, using the pictures as needed.

of the students are reading or practicing key reading skills while the other half of the students are coaches whose job is to follow along, assisting the reader and discussing the text. Thus, students are more actively engaged during PALS than typical instruction. Active engagement that increases opportunities to use literacy skills, time spent reading, and opportunities to engage in structured dialogue about stories have all been associated with long-term positive effects for students who are English Language Learners (ELLs) (A. W. Graves, Gersten, & Haager, 2004).

Although all students within the classroom follow the same structure, PALS allows teachers to tailor instruction to meet individual needs by assigning texts and lessons at levels appropriate for each pair. For example, a teacher may choose a specific text for a student who is an ELL, ensuring that it is of the appropriate difficulty level and includes content the student is likely to comprehend based on the student's current level of English proficiency. PALS provides students with opportunities to engage in meaningful conversation with their peers, and it also enables teachers to move around the classroom, monitoring student performance and providing brief feedback as needed. For example, as students discuss whether a new prediction is reasonable, the teacher is free to listen to these discussions and guide pairs to discuss why a prediction is reasonable or not. In these ways, teachers provide instructional support, or scaffolds, for different learner types. Scaffolded instruction and increased opportunities to engage in dialogue about text are particularly important for struggling readers and for students who are ELLs. Thus, PALS can assist teachers as they address linguistic diversity within their classrooms by ensuring the meaning of stories is understood by students who are ELLs and the needs of students who are native English speakers are also met.

PALS Research Base

An impressive line of rigorous empirical research has demonstrated that participating in PALS three to four times per week for 16 to 20 weeks improves reading achievement for students in kindergarten through 12th grade (D. Fuchs & Fuchs, 2005; D. Fuchs et al., 2001; D. Fuchs, Fuchs, Mathes, & Simmons, 1997; Mathes & Babyak, 2001; Mathes, Howard, Allen, & Fuchs, 1998; D. C. Simmons, Fuchs, Fuchs, Mathes, & Hodge, 1995). Furthermore, across these studies, researchers have carefully documented that teachers and students can implement PALS with a high degree of fidelity, meaning that they successfully follow PALS procedures as designed. Teachers have been surveyed to show that they enjoy PALS, agree that it is easily implemented, and that they attribute student gains to the PALS activities.

A series of experimental studies show that participating in PALS led to improved reading outcomes for first graders who were high, average, and low achieving (Mathes & Babyak, 2001; Mathes et al., 1998). In these studies, researchers compared students engaged in PALS to a control group who received typical reading instruction. Students in PALS consistently showed statistically greater gains on measures of phonological awareness and word reading. Across these studies, effect sizes, which explain the degree of difference between PALS and control students, indicate that students engaged in PALS outperformed the control group by a 0.5 standard deviation or greater. For example, Mathes and colleagues (1998) reported an overall average effect size (ES) of 0.55, and Mathes and Babyak (2001) reported an ES of 0.60 for high-achieving, 0.94 for average-achieving, and 0.67 for low-achieving students. In other words, the differences between the PALS and control groups were large and meaningful.

The effect of PALS was also tested in kindergarten, when formal reading instruction begins (D. Fuchs et al., 2001) and a subsequent study followed student progress through third grade (Al Otaiba & Fuchs, 2006). Researchers randomly assigned 33 kindergarten teachers in eight culturally diverse urban schools to a control group or to one of two treatments in order to compare the efficacy of (a) a teacher-directed phonological awareness intervention, Ladders to Literacy (or Ladders; O'Connor, Notari-Syverson, & Vadasy, 1998) (totaling 15 hours), or (b) a combination of Ladders activities and Kindergarten Peer-Assisted Learning Strategies (K-PALS; D. Fuchs et al., 2001) (totaling 35 hours). On average, students receiving this combined approach outperformed controls on a variety of measures. The differences among low-achieving

students were moderate to large on phonological awareness measures (blending and segmenting), with effect sizes ranging from 0.45 to 1.27, and were small to large on reading and alphabetic measures, with effect sizes ranging from 0.28 to 1.28. Differences were even larger for average-achieving students, with effect sizes ranging from 1.97 to 2.10 on phonological measures and 0.73 to 1.42 on reading and alphabetic measures. The following year, researchers randomly assigned all first-grade teachers in the same eight schools to first-grade PALS or control conditions. First graders in the PALS condition outperformed controls across most measures of reading achievement, and notably large effects favored students with the weakest initial skills at the start of the study.

At the end of the 2-year study, D. Fuchs and colleagues (2001) examined the degree to which students had benefited from PALS. Encouragingly, only about 2% of students had word-attack skills below the 30th percentile on a standardized reading measure, and only 4% had similarly low word-identification scores. In addition, Al Otaiba and Fuchs (2006) examined the characteristics of "less-responsive" students and reported that those students made less growth in phonological and early reading skills than the sample average. These less-responsive students began kindergarten with significantly weaker vocabulary, rapid letter naming, and verbal memory, and had relatively more teacher-rated problem behaviors than their peers. Thus, an important cautionary implication is that even well-implemented PALS was not intensive or individualized enough to prevent reading problems for some children with very low vocabulary, with phonological processing deficits, or who experienced serious attention and behavior issues. An examination of less-responsive students' school records at the end of third grade revealed that all but one student was receiving special education services in reading. Therefore, these studies suggest that well-implemented peer tutoring can be incorporated into Tier-1 instruction to reduce the number of students who might need more intensive intervention.

Another smaller-scale experimental study (Calhoon et al., 2006) shows the promise of PALS as a strategy for improving reading outcomes for Hispanic students who have varying degrees of English proficiency. The study was conducted in six predominately Hispanic Title I first-grade bilingual classrooms in a U.S./Mexico border town. Nearly 80% of the 76 participating students were Hispanic; of these, 24 were identified as ELLs. Thus, in addition to examining the overall impact of PALS on students' reading scores, researchers also explored the degree of student responsiveness on various measures depending on English proficiency. Consistent with other first-grade PALS studies, statistically significant differences favored students in the PALS condition over the control condition on measures of phoneme segmentation and nonsense word fluency. Students who were English proficient and participating in PALS showed greater growth on phoneme segmentation and oral reading fluency, with large effect sizes of 0.85 and 0.56, respectively. However, the performance of students who were ELLs in PALS was more similar to controls', with negative to very small effect sizes on these same measures (i.e., ES = −0.60 on phoneme segmentation and 0.03 on oral reading fluency). By contrast, effect sizes for students who were ELLs in PALS were 1.29 on nonsense word fluency and 1.15 on letter naming fluency; whereas, students who were English proficient in PALS performed similarly to controls on these two measures. These different patterns of findings appear related to students' oral language proficiency in English, but could also be explained by the initial weak skills in phonological and alphabetic awareness among the students who were ELLs. This finding is consistent with two reviews of responsiveness to early literacy interventions that were conducted predominantly with native English speakers (Al Otaiba & Fuchs, 2002; Nelson, Benner, & Gonzalez, 2003).

How Is PALS Implemented?

Preparation and Planning

Preparing and planning to implement PALS is straightforward, and all materials (except trade books) are provided with PALS programs, including detailed manuals describing how to implement programs. The first step is to select the appropriate program for the participating classrooms. Some PALS programs are available commercially (Mathes, Torgesen, Allen, & Allor, 2001; Mathes, Torgesen, & Clancy-Menchetti, 2001), and others are available through Vanderbilt University (D. Fuchs, Fuchs, Svenson, et al., 2000; D. Fuchs, Fuchs, Thompson, et al., 2000; kc.vanderbilt.edu/pals/). All PALS programs are fairly inexpensive and have research support, so selecting the appropriate program should generally be based on how well the scope and sequence matches the current needs of students. Obviously, the range of ability level varies from classroom to classroom, so it is more important to consider students' skills rather than their actual grade level. For example, one kindergarten classroom may need a version of PALS designed for kindergarten, and another classroom, especially at the beginning of the spring semester, may need a version of PALS designed for first grade.

After obtaining materials, teachers should receive training similar to that provided to teachers who participated in the research studies. Researchers usually incorporate a one-day workshop for teacher participants, with informal assistance provided to them occasionally throughout the year. In workshops conducted during research studies, teachers observed while professional development staff modeled each activity and then participated in role-plays and practice of each PALS activity. Experts familiar with PALS, many of whom participated in the research studies, are available to conduct workshops. Alternatively, because the PALS materials are detailed and complete, an experienced and knowledgeable reading specialist can be effective in providing this training. The manual provides clear directions about how to implement the program, including pairing students, placing students in appropriate lessons, and preparing materials. Scripts to teach students how to conduct PALS are also provided. Costs for materials are nominal. Black-line masters are provided, and no special texts or other materials are needed.

Key Implementation Issues

As we have emphasized, positive outcomes for students may be jeopardized if programs are not implemented in the same manner as they were conducted in research studies. Monitoring the quality and intensity of implementation is therefore important. For example, to ensure high fidelity of implementation across the PALS studies, research assistants (typically experienced teachers) visited classrooms to provide ongoing support, answer questions, and offer corrective feedback (e.g., D. Fuchs et al., 1997). Thus, teachers followed scripted lessons that included teacher presentation, student practice, and teacher feedback to students. Typically, within these published studies, researchers assessed treatment fidelity by direct observations using an observational checklist to record whether teachers and students implemented PALS components correctly. The fidelity scores for K-1 PALS implementation are typically high (on average, above 90%).

One distinct advantage of PALS is that ongoing planning is straightforward and requires relatively little teacher time. However, it is very important that the skills being practiced during PALS match the needs of the students. Although this recommendation seems self-evident, student needs are moving targets and always challenging to determine, particularly in general education classes with many students with varying needs. We strongly recommend the involvement of a reading specialist or coach in monitoring the implementation of PALS. Specialists should ensure that students are following procedures accurately and that teachers are regularly moving among the pairs of students, listening carefully (though briefly) to each pair of students, providing needed scaffolding and feedback as well as praise and reinforcement for appropriate behaviors. PALS provides a great opportunity for teachers to provide brief (1 to 2 minutes) assistance to individual pairs of students. PALS is also an excellent vehicle for differentiated instruction, because all pairs do not need to be reading from the same text or lesson sheet; however, some teachers may require the encouragement and assistance of a reading coach or specialist to differentiate effectively.

In summary, PALS has been shown to be an effective technique in helping teachers adapt instruction for students with different levels of achievement (i.e., high, average, low, with learning disabilities; D. Fuchs et al., 1997; D. Fuchs, Fuchs, Thompson, et al., 2001; Mathes et al., 1998) and for students with different levels of English proficiency. However, students who show a poor response to PALS are likely to require more intensive individualized reading instruction.

We next describe two programs that can be used to intensify instruction for struggling students: Sound Partners and Early Interventions in Reading.

Sound Partners

What Is Sound Partners and How Does It Work?

Sound Partners (Vadasy et al., 2004) is a code-oriented (phonics-based), structured, supplemental tutoring program designed for struggling readers in kindergarten through second grade. Intended to be implemented by volunteers or para-educators for 30 minutes, four times each week, the program consists of 100 scripted, code-oriented lessons that follow a structured routine and include learning letter–sound correspondences, decoding words with familiar sounds or from common word families, practicing sight words, demonstrating fluency on decodable text, and monitoring comprehension. Although vocabulary is not specifically addressed, tutors are encouraged to address vocabulary during lessons as the need arises. Sound Partners provides instruction and practice that proceeds from early decoding skills to fluent passage reading and is consistent with stage theory of reading development (Ehri, 2002). Tutors are trained and supervised by a reading coach, reading teacher, or special education teacher. The goal of the program is to improve student outcomes so they can read grade-level text and participate successfully in the core reading program. A typical Sound Partners lesson is described in Table 2.2, and sample lessons are available on the Internet (http://store.cambiumlearning.com).

Several program characteristics are key to successful implementation of Sound Partners. First, although Sound Partners is specifically designed to be implemented by nonteachers with relatively limited training, tutors do need some training and regular support. This training is minimal when compared to typical professional development for reading teachers. The program is well organized, and lessons are scripted and easy to implement. Second,

Table 2.2 Overview of Typical Sound Partners Lesson

Activity	Brief Description
1. Say the Sounds (and Write Sounds)	Student says the sounds for all letters printed in the lesson. Student writes letters that represent the sounds the tutor says.
2. Segmenting	Student orally breaks words into parts.
3. Word Reading (and Spelling)	Student sounds out and says fast words that are printed in the lesson book. Student spells selected words from the list.
4. Sight Words	Student reads and orally spells high-frequency words that are printed in the lesson book.
5. Sentence Reading	Student reads sentences that are printed in the lesson book.
6. Book Reading	Student reads books orally.
7. Letter–Sound Dictation	Student writes the letters for the sounds the teacher says.
8. Sounding Out	Student sounds out words that are printed in the lesson book.
9. Connected Text	Student reads text orally that is printed in the lesson book.

the instructional design of the program is consistent with research-based reading instruction and incorporates multiple elements of effective instruction including explicit modeling, scaffolding and feedback, cumulative review, and application of skills to text, making it consistent with the Simple View of Reading (Gough, 1996) and recommendations of the NRP (2000). Third, it is individually administered, providing supported intensive practice of key skills at an appropriate level of difficulty for each student. The program has a proven track record when it is implemented fully by tutors who are provided with appropriate (though not extensive) training and ongoing support to ensure accurate implementation of lessons that are at the appropriate difficulty level.

Sound Partners Research Base

Since 1993, Sound Partners has been actively field tested and validated through a program of research studies (e.g., Jenkins, Vadasy, Firebaugh, & Profliet, 2000; Vadasy, Jenkins, Antil, Wayne, & O'Connor, 1997; Vadasy, Jenkins, & Pool, 2000; Vadasy, Sanders, & Abbott, 2008; Vadasy, Sanders, & Peyton, 2006). Multiple studies have demonstrated that Sound Partners can be an effective tool for improving the reading performance of at-risk students in the early grades. In each of these studies, Sound Partners was implemented by nonprofessional tutors who had participated in training and were paid to tutor. In some of these studies, community members were recruited, including parents, grandparents, college students, and high school students. In other studies, schools identified para-educators to serve as tutors. Participants in the studies were students at risk for developing reading problems and included students with special education, Title I, or ELL status. In the following paragraphs, we describe three studies in detail. We selected these to demonstrate the effectiveness of the program with kindergarten through second grade, as well as to discuss factors that predicted students for whom the intervention would be most effective and students who would likely need additional support.

Vadasy et al. (2006) found that Sound Partners was effective when provided by para-educators to at-risk kindergarten students identified in the middle of their kindergarten year. In this study, Vadasy et al. selected students from schools with high minority enrollment, as well as large numbers of students who were from high-poverty backgrounds. More than half of the students received Title I, ELL, or special education services. Researchers identified students as at risk based on scores on several measures and randomly assigned them to groups, with the final sample including 36 students in the treatment group and 31 students in the control group. Para-educators participated in an initial 4-hour training session and received ongoing assistance provided by the researchers. The para-educators tutored participants four times each week for 30 minutes per session, for an average of approximately 27 hours of individual instruction per student.

Students who received the tutoring outperformed those who did not receive tutoring, demonstrating gains in reading and spelling at the end of kindergarten. The largest differences between the groups were for reading accuracy (ES = 1.02) and oral reading fluency (ES = 0.81). Differences were moderate for reading efficiency (ES = 0.61) and developmental spelling (ES = 0.57). Average reading accuracy and efficiency scores were at the 45th and 32nd percentiles at the end of kindergarten, as compared to the 25th percentile for the control group. Approximately one fourth of the tutored students were considered to be no longer at risk by the end of kindergarten based on performance on phoneme fluency and nonsense word fluency. All of the students in the control group were considered to be at risk according to these measures. The authors concluded that para-educators can effectively implement supplemental Sound Partners instruction, thereby reducing the number of students at risk for reading failure. However, Vadasy et al. (2006) caution that the level of intensity provided in their study is not sufficient to bring all students to adequate levels of performance. Further, this type of instruction could

assist schools in identifying students who require more intensive and typically more expensive intervention.

The second study we chose to highlight was conducted by the same research group and found Sound Partners to be effective for at-risk first graders who were followed through spring of second grade (Vadasy et al., 2000). Researchers selected at-risk first-grade students based on teacher recommendation and pretest scores. The authors then randomly assigned the resulting sample of 46 students to either the treatment or control group. Approximately two thirds of the students were members of minority groups, and almost half were eligible for free or reduced-price lunch. Tutors in this study were nonprofessionals recruited from the community (primarily parents) and paid a nominal hourly rate. Tutors received 8 hours of training before tutoring and 6 hours across the school year. Tutors were also observed and assisted by an experienced, certified special education teacher who provided expert feedback.

The results strongly supported the effectiveness of Sound Partners when implemented by nonteacher tutors to at-risk first graders. Students who were tutored performed better on all measures, with very large and statistically significant differences on all but one measure. Effect sizes ranged from 0.42 to 1.24, with the smallest effect size for reading in context and the largest effect size for nonword reading. By the spring of second grade, the tutored group continued to outperform the control group on measures of phonics and spelling, but not word recognition or fluency.

The third study we describe followed students through third grade with 79 students participating in Sound Partners in first grade and a subgroup of these students also receiving tutoring in second grade (Vadasy et al., 2008). Although this study did not compare treatment students to a control group, its findings provide key information about (a) the long-term reading outcomes that are likely for at-risk students who receive the Sound Partners intervention from nonteacher tutors for 1 or 2 years and (b) which students are likely to require more intensive interventions. In first grade, students were assessed on measures that in other studies have been found to be predictive of later reading ability, including receptive language, phoneme segmentation, and rapid letter naming. Researchers collected outcome measures in the fall and spring of first grade and then in the spring of both second and third grade. These measures included decoding (word attack/nonword reading), word reading (real-word identification), spelling, fluency, and comprehension.

Primary conclusions were that (a) benefits of Sound Partners were evident through the third grade and (b) receptive language and rapid letter naming in the first grade were important predictors of third-grade outcomes.

For each outcome measure, researchers calculated average predicted scores indicating that the typical student participating in first-grade tutoring would earn scores at the 48th percentile on decoding, the 42nd percentile on word reading, the 30th percentile in spelling, and the 37th percentile in comprehension. Additionally, a score of 129 words correct per minute on passage reading was predicted, which corresponds to a percentile rank estimated to be between the 50th and 75th percentiles. Considering students in this study were performing near the 20th percentile at the beginning of first grade when the study began, these long-term gains are impressive. The second primary finding of the study was that rapid letter naming and receptive language were the best predictors of long-term reading performance. This finding informs practice by providing schools with some guidance in determining who may require more intensive intervention, that is, students who demonstrate significant weaknesses on measures of rapid letter naming and receptive language.

How Is Sound Partners Implemented?

Preparation and Planning

The Sound Partners program includes all materials needed for implementation, including an implementation manual, lesson book, and tutor handbook, as well as sets of decodable books for use during lessons. The implementation manual provides detailed information about the organization of the program, as well as how to train tutors. The program thoroughly describes all routines, which are easily implemented by individuals with little or no knowledge or experience tutoring struggling readers.

The first step in preparing for the implementation of Sound Partners is determining who will be the supervisor. This person may be a reading coach, reading teacher, reading specialist, or special education teacher who will oversee the tutoring. Although this individual certainly may delegate many tasks related to implementation, it is key that someone knowledgeable about teaching reading is responsible for the tutoring program. In addition to being knowledgeable about reading instruction, this individual should have strong interpersonal and organizational skills and be able to share knowledge (e.g., modeling procedures, providing feedback to tutors) effectively and positively. The amount of time a supervisor will need to devote to a tutoring program depends on the number of students being tutored, the number of different tutors, and the experience and skills of the tutors.

Even enthusiastic teachers are likely to be unable to allocate sufficient time to this task, unless they are released from some of their teaching responsibilities. Primary duties include recruiting and training tutors, determining which students should be tutored, collaborating with teachers and tutors to schedule tutoring sessions, providing technical assistance on instructional and management problems, and monitoring students' success and progress. In research studies, Sound Partners was typically implemented four times each week in 30-minute sessions. It is important that a supervisor has time to recruit, train, and monitor tutors. In research studies tutors were provided with approximately 2 to 6 hours of initial training and approximately the same amount of follow-up training, in addition to assistance during tutoring sessions.

Selecting students who are in need of tutoring should be linked to screening and assessment procedures already used by the school. Generally, measures of phonemic awareness, rapid letter naming, and language should be used to identify students who are likely to struggle learning to read. Students with the lowest scores on these measures should be monitored carefully. If they respond slowly to Sound Partners tutoring provided by a paraprofessional, other more intensive interventions, particularly those provided by a specialist, should be considered. Of course, these decisions must be made based on the resources available to the school.

In research studies, Sound Partners has been implemented by a variety of people, including community-based tutors (e.g., parents, college students) and para-educators. The educational backgrounds of the para-educators in the Sound Partners studies averaged 14 years (e.g., high school plus 2 years), which is similar to current No Child Left Behind (NCLB, 2001) requirements for para-educators. Fortunately, the cost of nonteacher tutors is relatively small, and the evidence is clear that employing them as tutors can result in long-term gains for many students.

Key Implementation Issues

The supervisor should monitor tutoring sessions regularly. First and foremost, the supervisor should monitor whether sessions are being implemented according to the schedule. We recommend the use of monitoring forms so the supervisor can quickly determine who is being tutored, by whom, and for how long. If the sessions are not occurring on a regular basis, the supervisor should determine the cause of the problem and identify possible solutions (e.g., changing the schedule, contacting a parent regarding excessive absences, assisting a tutor with time management). Second, through direct observation, the supervisor should determine whether the lessons are being implemented effectively. Supervisors can also learn about the appropriateness of tutoring by tutoring students themselves occasionally, either substituting for an absent tutor or providing additional sessions. By tutoring, supervisors quickly learn whether the lesson is at the right difficulty level and whether students can participate in lessons successfully and apply strategies. Finally, supervisors should monitor student progress. If lessons are being implemented appropriately, yet students are making slow progress toward grade-level reading ability, other more intensive interventions should be considered. Options would be simply increasing the length or number of sessions provided each week or placing the student in an additional or separate intervention taught by a reading specialist (e.g., reading specialist provides tutoring two times each week, and para-educator provides tutoring three times). One program to consider for those needing more intensive intervention is Early Interventions in Reading, described in the following section.

Early Interventions in Reading

What Is Early Interventions in Reading and How Does It Work?

Early Interventions in Reading—Level 1 (EIR; Mathes & Torgesen, 2005) is a comprehensive, structured small-group reading intervention designed for struggling readers in grades 1 and 2; it is consistent with the recommendations of NELP (2008) and NRP (2000), providing for explicit and systematic instruction in multiple strands, including phonemic awareness, letter knowledge, word-recognition fluency, connected text fluency, vocabulary, and comprehension. The program consists of 120 highly detailed lesson plans that are constructed so that each of the critical strands are practiced daily in 7 to 10 short, interrelated activities, including application of skills in context. Lessons progress in a manner consistent with stage theory of reading development (Ehri, 2002), as students proceed from foundational skills to automaticity and fluency with connected text. For most struggling readers, a complete lesson can be implemented in one session, but when necessary, lessons can continue from one session to the next. Lesson plans provide teachers with concise language to model, practice, scaffold, and reinforce critical skills facilitating the delivery of explicit, highly interactive instruction. Many activities require students to respond in unison followed by brief individual practice. Other activities require students to write in a workbook or read to a partner. Although a second level of the intervention is also available to address more advanced skills, our focus in this chapter is on Level 1. A typical lesson early in Level 1 is described in Table 2.3, and sample lessons are available on the Internet (www.sraonline.com).

Table 2.3   Overview of Typical Early Interventions in Reading Lesson

Activity	Brief Description
1. Tricky Words/ Story-Time Reader	Students read high-frequency irregular words from flashcards and then read a decodable book in unison. Students make predictions before reading and check predictions after reading.
2. Letter–Sound Introduction	Teacher presents new letter sound and students practice new sound.
3. Thumbs Up– Thumbs Down	Teacher says words beginning or ending with the new sound and students put their thumbs up if the word begins with the new sound or thumbs down if it ends with the new sound.
4. Letter–Sound Review	Students say the sounds for all letters printed in the presentation book.
5. Stretch and Blend	Students orally repeat words and then stretch words by saying them one sound at a time.
6. Writing the Letter	Students write the new letter, saying its sound each time they write it.
7. Letter–Sound Dictation	Students write the letters for the sounds the teacher says.
8. Sounding Out	Students sound out words that are printed in the presentation book.
9. Connected Text	Students read text orally that is printed in the presentation book.

As is the case with PALS and Sound Partners, EIR is consistent with current theory of reading development and scientifically based reading instruction. When implemented with sufficient intensity, the program is effective in improving the performance of even extremely challenged learners, including students who are at risk, are ELLs, or have intellectual disabilities (Allor, Mathes, Roberts, Jones, & Champlin, 2010; Mathes et al., 2005; Vaughn, Cirino, et al., 2006). Its effectiveness is a result of very careful instructional design, as well as careful, intense implementation in small groups. The program closely follows principles of the theory of instruction or Direct Instruction model (Engelmann & Carnine, 1982; Coyne, Kame'enui, & Simmons, 2001). Lesson plans provide teachers with tools to minimize student confusion and maximize practice opportunities. The lesson activities provide for extensive cumulative review, systematic introduction of increasingly more complex skills, and specific instruction in applying skills to more complex skills and to connected text (e.g., letter-sound knowledge is quickly applied to sounding out words, which is in turn applied to connected text). Students are taught to become flexible decoders (using decoding skills to produce a pronunciation that is close enough to the actual word to figure it out) and to approach comprehension strategically. Effective implementation requires initial teacher training (i.e., approximately 2 days of workshops) and ongoing professional development, particularly when teaching extremely challenging students.

Early Interventions in Reading Research Base

The research base for EIR provides evidence of its effectiveness for greatly reducing the number of students who experience significant difficulty learning to read. It has been found to be effective for first graders who are at risk for reading difficulty and typically not identified as learning disabled at this early age (Mathes et al., 2005; Mathes, Kethley, Nimon, Denton, & Ware, 2009). It has also been found to be effective for first graders who are ELLs and also at risk for reading difficulty (Vaughn, Cirino, et al., 2006; Vaughn, Mathes, et al., 2006), as well as students with mild or moderate intellectual disabilities (i.e., mental retardation: Allor, Mathes, Roberts, Cheatham, & Champlin, 2010; Allor, Mathes, Roberts, Jones, et al., 2010). Following, we highlight studies with first-grade students.

In the first study, Mathes and colleagues (2005) compared the reading performance of students participating in one of two intensive interventions, EIR and Responsive Reading, to students receiving typical instruction alone. In this large-scale study (252 participants), students in both interventions significantly outperformed the students in the control condition on measures of phonological awareness, word reading, and passage fluency. Effect sizes were moderate to large.

Importantly, by the end of first grade, only 7% of the Responsive Reading intervention students and 1% of the EIR students were still below the 30th percentile on basic reading skills, compared to 16% of the students in the typical classroom condition. This sample was drawn from students performing in the lowest 20th percentile at the beginning of first grade, and it therefore demonstrates that the total number of poor readers would likely be less than 1% of the broader student population if interventions such as EIR were routinely and appropriately implemented.

When effect sizes for each intervention (relative to the typical classroom condition) were compared, the effect sizes for EIR were somewhat higher on measures related to decoding, including phonological awareness, timed and untimed nonword reading, and untimed word reading. In contrast, effect sizes for Responsive Reading (relative to classroom condition) were somewhat higher on oral reading fluency. Another difference was

that fewer students in the EIR condition remained at or below the 30th percentile on basic skills.

Research studies have also supported the effectiveness of an enhanced version of EIR with first-grade students who were ELLs and at risk for developing reading difficulties (Vaughn, Cirino, et al., 2006; Vaughn, Mathes, et al., 2006). In these studies, 10 minutes of focused oral language and vocabulary practice were added to each EIR lesson. Language support was also incorporated throughout the EIR lessons. Language supports varied and included the use of instructional scripts with pictures, use of gestures, additional explanations of vocabulary, explicit instruction in English language usage, and opportunities to give elaborated responses. In both studies, students were randomly assigned to either the treatment group who received enhanced EIR in small groups of three to five students or to a control group that participated in instruction typically provided by the schools. Although the Vaughn, Cirino, et al. (2006) study included a sample of students who were learning to read in Spanish, discussion in this chapter is limited to the sample of students who were learning to read in English.

The findings in these studies were similar; students participating in the intervention significantly outperformed students in control groups on multiple measures. Effect sizes were found to be substantively important, according to What Works Clearinghouse (2006). In the Vaughn, Mathes, et al. (2006) study, the treatment and control groups performed similarly on measures of picture vocabulary and oral reading fluency; however, the effect sizes on all other measures showed positive and meaningful gains for the treatment group, ranging from a modest 0.26 (listening comprehension) to a strong 1.24 (phonemic awareness). Differences on seven of these measures were statistically significant. In the Vaughn, Cirino, et al. (2006) study, the treatment and control groups performed similarly on rapid letter naming, letter-word identification, and oral language measures, but the treatment group outperformed the control group on other measures, with effect sizes ranging from 0.36 (letter-sound identification) to 0.42 (word attack). These differences were statistically significant on four measures.

How Is Early Interventions in Reading Implemented?

Preparation and Planning

The EIR program includes all materials needed for implementation, as well as professional development materials to ensure that teachers are fully prepared to implement EIR. In addition to a staff development guide, teacher's editions with detailed lessons, and an assessment guide, a Teaching Tutor CD-ROM is also provided that details the teaching techniques with explicit instructions and video examples. The first step in implementing EIR is determining which students would most likely benefit from the program and identifying teachers to provide instruction. Generally, students who exhibit weaknesses on measures that predict future reading performance will benefit from EIR. Moreover, EIR is particularly appropriate for students who do not respond to less-intensive interventions. In a recent study analyzing the effectiveness of EIR when implemented on a large scale by school districts, the importance of both the quality and quantity of intervention implementation was documented (Mathes et al., 2009). This finding points to the importance of administrators' ensuring that teachers (a) provide instruction that is high quality, implementing EIR as it was designed, and (b) provide a "full dose" of the intervention (daily lessons across the entire first-grade year). In addition to providing teachers with training on effective implementation of EIR, administrators must allocate adequate teacher time for the intervention and plan ways to ensure that this time is uninterrupted.

Key Implementation Issues

Teacher implementation and student performance should be monitored throughout the school year to ensure that instructional and behavioral techniques critical to the success of EIR lessons are effective. Teachers benefit from the assistance and support of reading coaches or specialists, particularly when teaching students who experience significant difficulty learning how to read. The scripted and straightforward lessons allow teachers to model skills clearly and focus on responding to students appropriately; however, teachers must make many decisions as they implement EIR lessons, including pacing and how to respond to student errors. The program calls for unison responses to increase opportunities for students to practice, but it is critical that teachers also require frequent individual responses in order to assess students adequately. Quick pacing and positive reinforcement are also important to keep students actively engaged. For students who have low IQs, including those with intellectual disabilities, teachers should take particular care to pace EIR lessons according to student needs. Mastery of content may require repeating lessons or sets of lessons multiple times and specifically teaching students to transfer skills learned during EIR lessons to connected text. For further information about implementing EIR with this type of student, see Allor, Mathes, Champlin, and Cheatham (2009) and Allor, Mathes, Jones, Champlin, and Cheatham (2010).

Discussion

A strong, well-developed research base supports understanding why students have difficulty learning to read and which methods can help prevent most reading difficulties. In this chapter, we focused on beginning reading stages and described three specific emergent literacy interventions: PALS, Sound Partners, and EIR. Our discussion illustrated how educators can use these research-based programs to teach all students to read, specifically within an RtI model, and we drew from our own research to provide some helpful procedural guidelines and to describe some potential challenges with implementation. Next, we suggest some adaptations for using these programs with students who are ELLs and students with intellectual disabilities. Finally, we conclude with directions for future research.

Using PALS, Sound Partners, and EIR within a Multitier RtI Model

The three programs we reviewed, PALS, Sound Partners, and EIR, have been rigorously tested; beginning readers made educationally important reading gains when the programs were implemented faithfully at the intended intensity. Consistent with the recommendations of NELP (2008) and the NRP (2000), each program incorporates explicit instruction and practice applying the alphabetic principle to support decoding, as well as reading connected text to build reading vocabulary and develop comprehension strategies. In addition to increasing instructional time, the programs also incorporate, albeit to varying degrees, motivation and behavioral supports. These programs also complement one another in that they use a similar direct instruction approach. Thus, although the programs' scopes, sequences, and specific activities differ, they are similar enough that students could transfer skills learned in one program to another.

Within Tier 1 of an RtI model, PALS is particularly effective as a supplement to core instruction, because it is a manageable method for greatly increasing practice time on critical beginning reading skills that would be taught in any core reading program consisting of NRP-recommended components (NRP, 2000). Further, the entire class participates, and teachers may use the text from the core reading program during PALS, allowing time for all students to read assigned text within a structure that is proven to be effective. Although teachers report that time is a frequent barrier to sustaining research-based practices (Gersten, Chard, & Baker, 2000), PALS could replace some of the independent seat work or independent center time activities typically conducted during a language arts block. Because PALS is conducted with the entire class, the teacher moves throughout the room to ensure all students are on task and that their lessons are at the appropriate instructional level. Effective PALS teachers ensure that the entire class actively participates by frequently providing positive reinforcement, including praise and awarding points to pairs of students that are engaged, helpful to one another, and showing good effort. To further keep all students motivated, teachers have an option to divide students into teams that compete to earn the most points. Keep in mind that in the research studies, the PALS intervention was supported by weekly or biweekly visits by research staff; thus, a reading coach or even a trained para-educator could be similarly helpful, at least during the initial training of students in following PALS procedures. Another important consideration is that research has shown that students who responded less well to PALS had lower levels of language, relatively weaker initial skills, and relatively more attention and behavior issues (Al Otaiba & Fuchs, 2006).

Another delivery option would be for a para-educator to monitor the whole-class implementation of PALS. This option would free the teacher up during PALS time to provide additional teacher-directed small-group intensive and individualized instruction to the lowest-performing students receiving Tier-2 and Tier-3 services. Another similar option is for pairs of teachers to combine students and co-teach. For example, one teacher conducts PALS with a large group, and the second manages a small group of students in Tier 2. It is vital that teachers regularly monitor how students respond to PALS to identify individual students who are not making adequate gains relative to their peers (see Lembke, Hampton, & Hendricker, 2012)) and may, therefore, require more intensive supports associated with Tiers 2 and 3 of a typical RtI model.

Sound Partners could be appropriate as a Tier-2 intervention for students who did not fully benefit from Tier 1 (whether Tier 1 involved PALS, or just well-implemented classroom instruction). Typically, Tier-2 intervention is provided in small groups by someone other than the classroom teacher. Sound Partners is specifically designed to be implemented by individuals with little knowledge or experience with tutoring struggling readers, meaning that it is carefully scripted to support fidelity of implementation and may be implemented by a variety of individuals. In our own research, we have enlisted high school students participating in service learning, college students, retired teachers, Ameri-Corps members, parents, or other community members. However, Vadasy and co-workers' (2006) use of para-educators may be an easier solution for many schools. Similarly, teachers or reading specialists could also implement Sound Partners to students with the greatest need. This flexibility makes Sound Partners highly feasible as a Tier-2 intervention.

As we have learned from experience, it can be challenging to ensure that programs implemented by someone other than the classroom teacher (as is common in Tier-2 interventions) are well-supervised and that tutors understand the balance between following a program and individualizing that program. For instance, some students need a slower pace and more frequent repetition and scaffolding; others benefit from a faster pace. Training and ongoing supervision to ensure that tutors provide positive reinforcement for on-task behavior is vital. Inattention and behavioral problems may co-occur with reading problems, but we have observed these problems are exacerbated when tutors move too quickly or too slowly within a program. Going too fast can prevent children from mastering and applying skills. For example, if a tutor moves too quickly, students may not master reading a sound, which will then compromise their ability to read that sound in a word, which in turn makes it unlikely that they will read that word correctly in connected text. In contrast, going too slowly can be boring and lead to off-task behavior.

Because EIR is the program demonstrated to succeed with students who experience the most significant learning challenges, it is appropriate for students with the greatest need. Thus, it can be used as a Tier-2 or -3 intervention for students who have not succeeded with other, less-intensive and less-individualized interventions. The hallmark of Tier-3 instruction is that it is delivered by an expert teacher who provides highly tailored instruction designed to meet the specific needs of individual students who are experiencing severe learning challenges. When implemented appropriately, instructors pace EIR lessons according to student needs and repeat lessons or lesson components until students have fully mastered content. Because EIR is implemented in small groups (or individually), experienced and knowledgeable teachers can provide both individual instructional and behavioral support in the form of explicit modeling, expert feedback, and reinforcement. For EIR to succeed with the most challenging students, interventionists would ideally be the most carefully trained in terms of initially placing students on an appropriate lesson, pacing, individualizing, supporting behavior, matching books to students' instructional levels, and managing grouping assignments. Teachers or tutors ideally should instruct small groups of three to four children, and groups need to be carefully monitored and adjusted. Paraprofessionals or less-experienced teachers can be successful with EIR as well, if adequate professional development is provided. However, students with more severe learning difficulties (e.g., children in Tier 3) are likely to require instruction or support from a reading specialist with extensive expertise in individualizing reading instruction.

Adaptations for Learners with Limited Language and other Special Needs

Classrooms in America are rapidly changing. First, demographics are changing, and an increasing number of students are learning English while learning to read (Kindler, 2002). Second, more students with disabilities participate in general education than ever before, and RtI is recognized as a tool for improving collaboration between general education and special education (Gersten, Compton, et al., 2008). Therefore, we emphasize that interventions used within RtI will likely also be provided to a diverse student population. Generally speaking, considerable evidence shows that well-implemented reading instruction for all students should include both code- and meaning-focused components, as well as fluency components. For learners who are learning English as a second language, instruction may initially include a relatively strong focus on building vocabulary so that words that are sounded out are meaningful and immediately linked to meaning. Similarly, reading passages should include extensive discussion of meaning to support comprehension. For many students with higher IQs and stronger first-language skills, these needs are likely to be met through a combination of Tier-1 and English as a second language (ESL) strategies. However, as we described earlier in this chapter, an emerging research base supports the efficacy of both PALS and EIR with students who are ELLs.

Students identified with intellectual disabilities are also likely to benefit from the three programs we have reviewed, although they likely will need individualized pacing to ensure mastery of skills. EIR has been demonstrated to be effective with students with intellectual disabilities, although extensive practice over a much longer period of time is needed for students to acquire skills (Allor, Mathes, Roberts, Cheatham, et al., 2010; Allor, Mathes, Roberts, Jones, et al., 2010). For these students, it is vital to begin reading familiar words and to ensure mastery learning through a slow pace and cycle of cumulative review and practice.

Conclusion and Directions for Future Research

Research on early reading instruction provides educators with strategies that produce strong outcomes when implemented as designed. More research and refinement of techniques are needed for students with low language levels, such as students who are ELLs and students with low IQs, including those with intellectual disabilities. Further research is also needed with regard to how to use these interventions and similar interventions in a coordinated fashion to prevent and greatly minimize reading failure. The current national focus on prevention and early intervention brings fresh optimism to efforts to teach all children to read.

CHAPTER 3

Strategies for Improving
Students' Reading Fluency

Beth Harn | *University of Oregon*

David J. Chard | *Southern Methodist University*

Reading fluency, a neglected aspect of reading instruction for many decades, has received increased attention over the past few years (Rasinski, Rueztel, Chard, & Linan-Thompson, 2010). More and more, discussion and promotion of reading programs, assessments, and standards includes expectations that students will achieve measureable growth in reading fluency as part of their overall reading development. Many researchers have argued that fluent reading is critical to understanding text and to motivating readers to read more and, subsequently, is key to success in school and beyond (e.g., Logan, 1988; Therrien, 2004). Clearly, the most important point about this renewed emphasis on reading fluency is that it is directly related to *understanding* what is read.

Theoretical Framework

A significant and positive relationship exists between oral reading fluency and reading comprehension (Pinnell et al., 1995). For example, T. Harris and Hodges (1985) described fluency as the "freedom from word identification problems that might hinder comprehension" (p. 85). Several studies and reviews of research have emphasized the connection between fluency and meaning

by describing *fluency* as simultaneously being able to process text while reflecting on the syntax and semantic features of the text and attending to its meaning (Chard, Pikulski, & McDonagh, 2006; Hudson, Mercer, & Lane, 2000; LaBerge & Samuels, 1974; Perfetti, 1985). The relationship between fluency and comprehension is complex, however, with research seeming to suggest that they contribute to one another in a reciprocal manner (Stecker, Roser, & Martinez, 1998). This reciprocity led Pikulski and Chard (2005) to develop a comprehensive definition of reading fluency that acknowledges the relationship of fluency to comprehension and all of its dimensions.

> Reading fluency refers to efficient, effective word recognition skills that permit a reader to construct the meaning of text. Fluency is manifested in accurate, rapid, expressive oral reading and is applied during, and makes possible, silent reading comprehension. (p. 3)

Pikulski and Chard's (2005) definition emphasized that fluency is part of a developmental process of building oral language and decoding skills that ultimately support reading comprehension. Described as a "deep construct view" (p. 40), this definition explicates four specific dimensions of fluency: rate, accuracy, and quality of oral reading, as well as reading comprehension. This deep construct view promotes the explicit connection between the development of early reading skills, including oral language, phonemic awareness, alphabetic principle, and decoding to the development of comprehension. Despite the increased instructional attention placed on reading fluency and the recognition that it is intimately related to comprehension development, evidence suggests that many children still struggle to develop fluent reading, particularly students with learning disabilities (LDs) (Therrien, 2004; Vellutino et al., 1996).

Perhaps what is most important about ensuring that students develop reading fluency in the early elementary grades is the benefits it affords readers as they progress through school. For example, fluent readers can synchronize their skills of decoding, knowledge of vocabulary, and comprehension strategies to focus their attention on understanding the text (Stanovich, 1986). In addition, they can read with sufficient speed and accuracy so that what results sounds like language. Finally, because they are more facile with reading, they are better able to interpret text and make connections between the ideas in the text, ideas in other texts, and the world around them. In contrast, students who have not achieved fluency focus their attention almost entirely on decoding and accessing meanings of individual words. In addition, their reading is slowed by frequent errors, resulting in few cognitive resources being available to dedicate to comprehension (R. G. Nathan & Stanovich, 1991).

Torgesen, Rashotte, and Alexander (2001) identified five factors that impact a child's ability to read fluently:

1. *The proportion of recognized words in text.* Reading words as orthographic chunks (i.e., word parts such as *ing*, *igh*, etc.) increases word-recognition speed, thereby allowing the reader to focus on text meaning. Rapid word recognition is strongly related to reading rate in connected texts (Torgesen et al., 2001).

2. *Variations in speed of sight-word processing.* Depending on the number and quality of exposures to words, students vary in the speed with which they process sight words (Ehri, 1997; Logan, 1988). Difficulty processing smaller orthographic units (e.g., letters, word parts) results in slower processing of larger orthographic units (e.g., words) (Wolf, Bowers, & Biddle, 2000).

3. *Speed of identifying novel words.* Reading new words requires careful analysis including decoding, recognizing familiar word parts, and guessing from the context or meaning of the passage (Torgesen et al., 2001). All aspects of this process slow reading.

4. *Use of context to increase word identification.* Fluent readers do not rely on context for word identification, but struggling readers and beginning readers do (Pressley & Afferbach, 1995). Relying on passage context during reading likely contributes to slow, effortful reading and may be less helpful than accurate word identification in supporting comprehension (I. L. Beck, McKeown, & Kucan, 2002).

5. *Speed with which word meanings are identified.* When students can accurately decode and identify the meaning of a word while reading connected text, they can maintain speed, and comprehension can occur. If students cannot recognize the meaning of a word rapidly and must actively reflect on word meanings while reading, both fluency and comprehension will decline (Torgesen et al., 2001).

In light of these factors, it seems straightforward that the development of fluency for struggling readers should encompass instruction and practice in multiple skill areas, including phonemic awareness, decoding, vocabulary, oral language, and connected text reading. Instruction across these multiple skills has the potential to positively impact both independent text reading fluency and comprehension and should be considered when planning, scheduling, and providing instructional and practice opportunities to struggling readers including students with disabilities.

In this chapter, we review two practices that are commonly used in classrooms to improve reading fluency for struggling readers including students with disabilities: repeated reading and a multidimensional approach to fluency. We provide an overview of each practice, discuss critical instructional elements required for each practice, detail the theoretical underpinnings of each practice, and describe the available research with regard to its impact on student fluency development.

Repeated Reading

Repeated reading has been defined in a number of ways based on theoretical orientation or program emphasis, but a definition across approaches is that repeated reading requires students to "read passages in connected text or word lists more than once" (Chard, Ketterlin-Geller, Baker, Doabler, & Apichatabutra, 2009, p. 266). This definition emphasizes both word-level and sentence- or passage-level fluency as recommended within factors that impact fluency development (Torgesen et al., 2001). Although numerous approaches and programs emphasize repeated reading, they can be grouped by the manner in which they are delivered: (a) by the teacher directly or (b) within a peer-tutoring approach. A common research-based program that is teacher-delivered is Read Naturally (Hasbrouck, Ihnot, & Rogers, 1999). The most common research-based peer-tutoring approaches are Classwide Peer Tutoring (CWPT; Arreaga-Mayer, Terry, & Greenwood, 1998) and the more recent and widely implemented Peer-Assisted Learning Strategies (PALS) by Fuchs and colleagues (D. Simmons, Fuchs, Fuchs, Pate, & Mathes, 1994). We review both Read Naturally and PALS in this chapter; first we present the critical features these repeated reading interventions share.

Critical Elements of Repeated Reading Interventions

Therrien (2004) completed a meta-analysis of published repeated reading interventions studies conducted between the 1990s and early 2000s. From this review, Therrien identified essential intervention features in effective repeated reading interventions: (a) having students read to an adult, (b) ensuring students were explicitly told that becoming a more fluent reader will help them understand what they are reading, (c) establishing an explicit student-specific goal, (d) providing corrective feedback, and (e) having students repeatedly read a passage three to four times. Each of these components can be found in the repeated reading interventions discussed in this chapter (i.e., Read Naturally and PALS). We provide specific examples of each in the following descriptions and emphasize these examples in the respective research reviews.

Read Naturally

An experienced Title 1 teacher developed Read Naturally (RN; Hasbrouck et al., 1999) for use in her elementary school setting. The initial version of the program was designed to be implemented in small groups (i.e., 3 to 10 students) three times a week for about 30 minutes each time. Read Naturally was designed to supplement a more comprehensive reading intervention by providing students systematic opportunities to practice rereading carefully selected and developed reading passages. The general approach of RN has the teacher determine a student's instructional level when reading connected text (i.e., reading passages students can read with about 90% accuracy) within the RN passages. The RN program does note that teachers should use their judgment and past experience with the student in determining the level at which they should be placed to build fluency. The program has developed at least three sets (20 passages per set) of nonfiction passages per grade level that have been grouped to be of comparable difficulty based on common readability formulae (i.e., Spache readability formula and Fry Graph readability formula; see A. Harris & Jacobson, 1980). After determining a student's instructional level, the teacher

assigns that student to the appropriate set of instructional materials.

Read Naturally provides standard steps for reading each passage. The student begins by completing a "cold" reading of the passage to the teacher. This reading is referred to as "cold" because it is not previously practiced. During this phase the student reads the unfamiliar passage independently and the teacher determines the number of words read correctly in 1 minute and notes quantity of errors and trends in the types of errors made. The teacher then provides the student corrective feedback on the errors and provides practice on new sight words that are in the passage. Next, the teacher determines a fluency goal for the student based on the "cold" reading. The goal is typically to improve on the cold reading by reading 30% more words correctly in 1 minute after completing the remaining steps of the intervention. Students graph their "cold" reading time, visually see their goal, and then move to the repeated reading aspect of the intervention.

A unique aspect to RN is the process of listening and reading along with a recorded model of expressive and fluent reading. The student reads along (audibly subvocalizing) with a recording that models reading with good prosody (i.e., reading with accuracy and natural conversational expression). The read-along model is done three times, with each consecutive reading paced more quickly than the previous. The final reading sounds like a proficient reader. After these multiple models, the student conducts a self-timing for 1 minute, reading the passage independently to determine if the goal is reached.

In general, students will reach the goal within two to four repeated readings. After achieving the predetermined goal, the student answers the associated comprehension questions and writes a brief retell about the passage (i.e., one to two sentences summarizing what the student remembered). The comprehension questions are designed to measure both inferential and literal aspects of the passage as well as the main idea and vocabulary specific to the topic of that passage. After completing the independent comprehension step, the student rereads the passage again while being timed by the teacher to determine the number of words read correctly in 1 minute. The student then graphs her score on the chart to determine if she met her goal. The teacher and the student review and discuss the student's answers to the comprehension section, and the student practices words that she missed. The program provides guidelines about how many passages in a row a student should "pass" before either increasing the student's goal or moving on to more difficult passages.

As mentioned, the original version of RN was developed for use with audiotapes. More recently, the modeled readings have been provided on compact discs. The passages are designed to be of high interest to students, present factual information across a range of topics, and vary in length from about 100 words (first-grade level) to 300 words (grades 5 and up). More recent passages have been developed with a range of multicultural themes as well as some passages developed in Spanish. In addition, a computerized version of RN has been developed. Research findings published on each of these versions will be reviewed.

Research on Read Naturally

The initial study of RN completed by Hasbrouck et al. (1999) included 25 third-grade students, both at risk for and identified as having LD, within an urban school setting in Minnesota. Students received their general education instruction in a traditional core reading program that was supplemented with small-group phonics and fluency building with RN three times a week. Results indicated that all students demonstrated significant improvements in reading fluency across the duration of intervention (i.e., an average improvement of more than two words read correctly per week). Although this was not an experimental study (i.e., no random assignment of students to RN or a control group), it does provide initial support for the intervention and was published in a peer-reviewed research journal. However, because the students all received instruction that included more than RN, it is difficult to determine how much of the improvement in reading fluency was directly tied to RN or the other intervention components.

Although the publisher's Web site provides numerous "case studies" documenting the efficacy of RN in a range of different settings (e.g., rural, large urban schools), grade levels, and student populations (i.e., English Language Learners [ELLs]), none of these case studies are designed to support the notion that the RN program alone caused improved reading fluency. The program has been widely used in schools for decades with strong support from educators as to its utility; however, the body of peer-reviewed research on the program is extremely limited. More information is available from the publisher's Web site, http://www.readnaturally.com/.

Read Naturally—Software Edition (RN-SE) was developed around 2005 to provide a computer-delivered version of the program. The computer automates many of the steps of the original RN program. The teacher still determines the instructional level of the student, but the program provides a suggested goal for the student. The teacher can modify as needed. When the student logs on to the system, the computer matches the instructional level to the student, and the student chooses the story he prefers from the set. During the "cold," timed reading step, the software prompts the student to begin reading

and click on words that are difficult or unfamiliar. The program pronounces highlighted words at the end of the timing. Next, the computer presents the key words to the student visually and orally, reviews words the student indicated were difficult, and prompts the student to write a prediction. Similar to the original version, the student then reads along with the model of good fluency and prosody, with each successive model increasing its pace. The student then proceeds to answer the comprehension questions, writes a retell, and signals to the teacher that he is ready for the final check out or "hot timing." The program presents the student an automated graph of both the cold and hot timings on that story as well as a history of prior repeated reading practices.

At this writing, no peer-reviewed study of the RN-SE program has been published. However, the RN Web site provides a study completed by Christ and Davie (2009) from the University of Minnesota (http://www .readnaturally.com/company/news_seStudyUMn.htm). The authors report that the monies used to complete the study were provided by the publishers of RN. In the reported study, researchers randomly assigned 109 low-performing third-grade students from six elementary schools to either the RN-SE or the control (business as usual) condition and monitored reading performance for 10 weeks. Students in the RN-SE condition received the computerized intervention for 20 minutes daily across the intervention. Results indicated that students who received the RN-SE program performed significantly better on multiple measures of fluency (i.e., word and connected text) and on one measure of word accuracy, although effect sizes were small. No significant differences were found between conditions on multiple measures of comprehension. Although this is an experimental study, it has not been published in a peer-reviewed journal and must be viewed within that context.

Peer-Assisted Learning Strategies

Peer-Assisted Learning Strategies (PALS; D. Simmons et al., 1994) was initially designed as a strategy for use in general education classrooms to supplement comprehensive reading programs by increasing student opportunities to read aloud, receive feedback, and practice answering comprehension questions (D. Simmons et al., 1994). Since its inception, it has been modified across grade levels (preschool, elementary, middle and high school), content areas (reading and math), and student populations such as students with LD (D. Fuchs & Fuchs, 1998; D. Simmons, Fuchs, & Fuchs, 1995) and students who are ELLs (Sáenz, Fuchs, & Fuchs, 2005). Across each of these areas, the general steps and method of implementation are the same and will be discussed next, with more specific research findings following.

The theoretical basis for PALS is found in the research on the effectiveness of reciprocal teaching developed by A. L. Brown and Palincsar (1987) and the practical basis is the CWPT approach (Arreaga-Mayer et al., 1998) previously mentioned.

The general process of implementing PALS requires the teacher to create student pairs that vary in reading skill level. The higher performer is called the "coach" and the lower performer is the "player." Within these dyads both students receive structured and efficient opportunities to practice reading letter sounds, words, or both (depending on grade/skill level); reading connected texts; and identifying and discussing the main ideas and essential information to develop comprehension. The teacher trains the coach and player how to interact (training materials provide explicit scripts for students to follow) while moving through the teacher-selected materials (i.e., each dyad has individually chosen instructional materials), and the teacher supervises and supports implementation through each of the phases of practice.

The developers designed PALS to be implemented two to three times a week in 20- to 30-minute sessions (D. Fuchs, Fuchs, & Burish, 2000). Implementation can occur in small-group or whole-group situations. After the teacher trains the students on the specific approach of moving through the phases of PALS, the teacher signals the coach to begin the first phase (Partner Reading), and the coach reads the words/passage while the player watches. It is assumed that the coach will have sufficient skills to complete the task accurately and will be a successful model for the player. They then switch roles, and the player reads the words/passage with the coach providing feedback as needed. This reciprocal approach (coach and player taking turns and discussing) is used across the three phases of PALS: Partner Reading, Paragraph Shrinking, and Prediction Relay. For each phase, the teacher provides initial training on the essential steps and expectations in each phase. After training the teacher typically will be the timer and facilitator to ensure students are successful and on track.

The first phase of PALS is Partner Reading, which the coach begins by reading a passage for 5 minutes while the player follows along. The player then rereads the same section. The coach uses specific error-correction procedures when the player makes an error or does not know a word (e.g., "Can you figure it out?" If not, the coach provides the word and has the player reread the sentence). After the reread is complete, the player provides a 2-minute retell. Within the retell, the coach prompts the player to answer the following questions: "What did you learn first?" "What did you learn next?" "What did you learn next?" To keep motivation high for students, the dyad earns points for successful reading and accurate retell.

Next, the pair moves to the second phase, called Paragraph Shrinking. In this phase, students continue to read the material a paragraph at a time to practice identifying the main idea and important information. The coach goes first and does this for 5 minutes; they switch roles, and then they repeat. After finishing a paragraph the listener (either the coach or player) prompts the reader to achieve the following: identify the main point/person (who or what), identify the most important thing about the "who or what," and then summarize the main idea in less than 11 words. If the coach and player succeed, they earn additional points for their team.

The final phase is the Prediction Relay, in which students predict what will happen in the next section and earn points for being correct. Instead of going a paragraph at a time as in the prior phase, the Prediction Relay covers larger chunks of material (e.g., half a page). After reading half the page, the nonreader asks the student to predict what may happen next. When they finish the page, the nonreader then asks, "Did your prediction come true?" and then they switch roles for the next page. Students take turns making and confirming predictions about the text. If dyad members don't agree about the accuracy of the prediction or are wrong, they are expected to go back to that paragraph and use the Partner Reading activities to clarify.

Students are also trained to administer a traditional timed oral reading fluency (ORF) assessment, which is an assessment of the number of words read correctly in 1 minute. They administer an ORF to each other and graph scores to monitor progress at the end of each session. In addition, the teacher completes ORF assessments at least twice a month to formally evaluate progress. D. Simmons et al. (1994) suggested that teachers modify dyad pairings every 4 to 6 weeks to keep things fresh and interesting for the students.

Research on PALS

Numerous published research articles demonstrate PALS's efficacy across grade levels for students who are at risk, have LD, have behavior disorders (BDs), and who are ELLs (D. Fuchs, Fuchs, & Burish, 2000). For this review, we focus only on research involving students included in general education classrooms who have LDs, emotional and behavioral disorders (EBDs), and students who are ELLs. In one of the initial studies using PALS, 118 students in grades 2 to 5 in five elementary schools participated. The authors reported that 58 of the students were identified as having LD, 27 were below average readers, and the remaining 33 were average readers. All students received explicit reading instruction, but half were randomly assigned to explicit teaching plus PALS for the 14-week intervention. Because this was the initial study measuring the efficacy of PALS, there were four conditions that students were randomly assigned to, including the current prescribed PALS steps previously described. Results indicated that students who received the full PALS condition performed significantly better on a measure of fluency (medium effect size) and comprehension (large effect size) when compared to the control condition. Within this study the researchers also demonstrated the efficacy of the comprehension discussion steps that students completed (i.e., shrinking and prediction), because these students showed the most growth on comprehension during the study.

An early version of the PALS intervention was also used with students who not only had significant reading delays but also corresponding attention and behavioral difficulties. Locke and Fuchs (1995) used a single-subject withdrawal design to measure the impact of on-task behavior of three fifth- and sixth-grade boys by implementing PALS. After baseline was established, students had 5 days of PALS intervention, then 4 days of withdrawal, and then 4 more days of PALS, followed by a corresponding withdrawal phase. Results indicated that on-task behavior improved markedly across all students during the PALS reading in comparison to typical reading instruction. This study did not measure reading performance but demonstrates how the PALS approach may also provide the structured experience that some students need to maximize instructional time.

The utility of using PALS with students who are ELLs was investigated in a study completed by Sáenz et al. (2005). All students ($n = 132$) were native Spanish speakers in grades 3 through 6 including students who were LD, as well as low-, typical-, as well as high-achieving readers. The teachers were randomly assigned to use PALS three times a week for 15 weeks, and student performance was contrasted with the reading performance of comparable classrooms during this same time. Results indicated that although the overall growth between PALS and the control condition were similar at the average class-level on the fluency measure, the students with LD demonstrated significantly more growth across the PALS condition (large effect size) than students with LD in the control condition. All students in the PALS condition performed significantly better on a measure of comprehension than the control group, with all learner types displaying large effect sizes.

Whereas PALS was initially developed for use with elementary-aged students, it has also been extended for use in high schools. L. S. Fuchs, Fuchs, and Kazdan (1999) completed a study in which they randomly assigned special education and remedial reading teachers to use PALS two to three times a week within their traditional reading instruction and compared fluency, comprehension development, and student attitudes to

comparable classrooms that did not use PALS. The students who were monitored across the study included some students with reading disabilities but also any students who were reading below the sixth-grade level. PALS was implemented for 16 weeks with only a minor adjustment to the typical PALS steps. The intervention included the typical steps of partner reading, paragraph shrinking, prediction relay, and use of points for motivation. The modifications included changing partners at least weekly as well as daily tangible reinforcement for successful completion of activities. Researchers believed this would make the intervention more palatable and motivating for high school students. Results indicated that although growth on fluency measures was comparable across conditions, the PALS condition demonstrated significantly larger improvements in reading comprehension than students in the control classrooms, with a medium effect size reported. When compared to students who did not receive PALS, students in the PALS condition indicated that they were more likely to enjoy working collaboratively with their peers and reported a greater sense of self-efficacy in their approach to reading (e.g., "In this class, I have worked hard to improve my reading skills").

As previously mentioned, numerous studies document the efficacy of PALS across grade levels and disability types (i.e., LD, BD), as well as ELLs. We have provided just a summary of key articles documenting the range of empirical studies. PALS has been reviewed by the What Works Clearinghouse and found to have positive effects at improving not only fluency but also word analysis/phonics and comprehension skills (see review at http://ies.ed.gov/ncee/wwc/reports/beginning_reading/pals/).

Multidimensional Approach to Improving Reading Fluency: RAVE-O

A more recent approach to fluency development for students with LD in reading has been developed by Maryanne Wolf and colleagues (Wolf, Barzillai, et al., 2009). This approach takes a multidimensional approach to developing fluency. In contrast to the repeated reading approach that emphasizes successful, accurate rereading of connected text, Wolf et al. asserted that students need more practice and opportunities across all reading dimensions (i.e., semantic, or word meaning; orthographic, or print; morphologic, or meaningful word parts; phonologic, or sounds; and syntactic, or word order). Wolf and her colleagues have developed a reading intervention called Retrieval, Automaticity, Vocabulary, Engagement with Language, and Orthography (RAVE-O) that has primarily been used with struggling readers in second and third grade. The 60-minute intervention has two components and is delivered in small groups of one to four students through computer-assisted instruction. The first 30 minutes focus on developing phonological awareness, letter-sound understanding, and phonological recoding to support word-reading development using an explicit, systemic intervention called Phonological Analysis and Blending (PHAB; Lovett, Steinbach, & Frijters, 2000). Using this as the base, the second 30 minutes includes a systematically integrated approach to developing students' semantic, orthographic, morphologic, and comprehension skills through the use of unique teacher- or computer-delivered activities. The intervention is implemented over 70 total hours, and the research on its efficacy is just emerging (Morris et al., 2010; Wolf, Barzillai, et al., 2009).

Critical Elements of RAVE-O

Wolf and colleagues developed the RAVE-O program using theoretical perspectives from cognitive psychology, neuroscience, and linguistics that view reading disabilities as a breakdown across a range of dimensions (Wolf & Katzir-Cohen, 2001). One of the hallmark characteristics for students with reading disabilities is dysfluent reading, which these researchers believe to be influenced not only by deficits in phonological processing (as many reading interventionists do), but also by deficits in cognitive and linguistic processing. They believe that successful reading "depends on the integrity, speed, and automatic connections" across each of these subprocesses (Wolf, Barzillai, et al., 2009, p. 86). This approach is influenced by work on the "Double-Deficit" hypothesis initially developed by Wolf and Bowers (1999), which indicated that the most significantly impaired readers have deficient skills not only in phonological processing but also in rapid automatized naming (i.e., the ability to quickly name colors, letters, or objects under timed conditions). According to this approach, all aspects of reading (e.g., semantic, orthographic, phonologic) are important and intertwined to support the efficient cognitive processing of reading for understanding. Therefore, RAVE-O strives to provide students with daily, repeated, and varied practice with linguistic stimuli that will improve the efficiency of the connections across all subprocesses to support reading development. It is theorized that this multidimensional approach will improve fluency development more effectively and efficiently than interventions that focus primarily on phonologic processing or repeated reading separately.

As previously mentioned, the first 30 minutes of RAVE-O instruction consists of the PHAB intervention, which uses explicit and systematic approaches to teach phonological awareness, word analysis, some orthography, and connected text reading. Skills are sequentially organized and systematically delivered using careful wording, corrective feedback, and active pacing. After completing the PHAB, students move into the RAVE-O activities that link to the skills taught in the PHAB. Recent publications have also used other explicit and systematic phonics-based interventions for this first 30-minute intervention time (Morris et al., 2010). Each RAVE-O lesson has several major dimensions that are linked to one another to provide students repeated and varying approaches to developing the subprocesses by addressing the critical elements discussed previously.

In the RAVE-O lesson, several core words are introduced. For example, core words for the -*it* rime may be *fit, sit, split*. The meanings of the words are discussed, and then the words are taught on rime cards with separable, color-coded onsets. Students are taught to segment and combine onsets (e.g., /f/, /s/, /sp/) and rimes (e.g., /it/) for about five words each week while learning to recognize other words containing the same rime. They also play a computerized game and engage in other activities to increase automaticity. These activities are combined with writing to enhance automaticity with decoding and word recognition. Finally, multiple meanings of core words are taught. To help students to retrieve the word meanings, they engage in multimodal activities and cognitive monitoring activities. The core words were carefully selected and sequenced to teach critical phonologic, semantic, and orthographic principles of reading. The words were also specifically chosen to link to the skills taught in the PHAB, teach the most essential letter sounds, and have multiple meanings (i.e., ram=animal, physical act, or computer processor). Teachers introduce a group of core words each week of the intervention and use and review these words across the duration of the intervention. These core words are the base to which all additional activities are strategically linked to support students' understanding of the multiple dimensions involved in reading (Wolf, Barzillai, et al., 2009; Wolf, Miller, & Donnelly, 2000).

The core words are used in activities to develop *semantic* skills through the use of (a) pictures to teach and demonstrate the words' multiple meanings, (b) word webs showing varying linkages to words of similar meaning, (c) a computer activity prompting students to use specific strategies to discover the missing word in a game called "Sam Spade Detectives," and (d) "minute stories" that integrate the words within connected text during a repeated reading activity. *Orthographic* skills are addressed through the daily use of a computer game called "Speed Wizard" to systematically provide practice and increase the speed of retrieval of common orthographic patterns. For example, if students were learning the word part *-ight,* the student would have multiple exposures to words of this type but the computer would expect them to recognize/identify it more quickly through each round to spur retrieval efficiency. *Morphologic* skills are developed through activities demonstrating how changing specific aspects of words change their meaning in a game-like activity called "Ender Benders." *Phonologic* skills are taught through activities such as dice and cards with high-frequency spelling patterns on them that students use to build words; high-frequency word drill practice; and "sound sliders" that have onsets, rhymes, and blends on word strips for word building. *Syntactic* skills are taught within the context of sentence and paragraph reading where students are shown how varying morphemes can change the grammatical role of a word within the passage.

So, for example, one of the core words is *jam.* The teacher explicitly teaches students how to phonologically segment the word (/j/ /a/ /m/) and then link it to meaning (semantics) and discusses its syntactic variations as a noun (jam you eat) or a verb (to be in a jam). Additionally, students are shown how adding different morphemes (i.e., *ing, ed, s*) changes the root word meaning. The goal of this multicomponent approach is to provide students multiple and differential exposure to all processes involved in reading to provide a greater depth of reading for meaning (Wolf, Gottwald, & Orking, 2009). The core words are systematically introduced and used across the entire intervention and in each domain to develop an integrated approach to maximize reading development. Each lesson has at least one activity related to each of the five dimensions to improve reading fluency and comprehension (Wolf, Gottwald, et al., 2009; Wolf, Miller, et al., 2000).

Review of RAVE-O Research

RAVE-O is a recently developed intervention, and only one study has been published. The initial study worked with 279 second- and third-grade students identified as having a reading disability; 135 were African American and the remaining Caucasian. Students received 70 hours of intervention from October to March in one of the following conditions: (a) PHAB + RAVE-O, (b) PHAB + PHAST (Phonology Plus Strategy Training), (c) PHAB + study skills, or (d) classroom control. Results indicated that the RAVE-O condition significantly outperformed

the other conditions on multiple measures of vocabulary and comprehension. The RAVE-O group also significantly outperformed students in the PHAB + study skills and control conditions on measures of fluency, decoding, and word reading. Similar performance was found for students in the RAVE-O condition when compared to the PHAB + PHAST condition on word attack, word identification, fluency, and one comprehension measure. Additional studies and modifications to the intervention are currently underway, and as data are analyzed, additional insights for various learner types may be available (Wolf, Barzillai, et al., 2009). Additional studies and replication of results on other student populations are needed to more fully understand how this multidimensional intervention may impact fluency development differently than other approaches.

Conclusion and Directions for Future Research

The hallmark characteristic of students with reading disabilities is a slow, deliberate, and often inaccurate approach to reading connected text (Lyon, 1998). As such, it is not surprising that reading for these students is not the enjoyable experience that typical readers encounter. Moreover, whereas regulating reading speed can be used by good readers to assist in focusing on sophisticated aspects of a passage of text, struggling readers and those with reading disabilities often read so slowly that it impairs their comprehension (Breznitz, 2006). The most common approach to addressing dysfluency has been through a combination of continued practice in word analysis but also sufficient time for students to read and reread passages that are at an instructional level that they can read with greater pace to facilitate comprehension. The repeated reading interventions reviewed here have been around in various iterations for over 20 years and have strong research backing their efficacy at improving not only fluency but also comprehension. The more recently developed multidimensional approach to addressing fluency (e.g., RAVE-O) provides a multidimensional alternative for conceptualizing and addressing reading needs. Although initial research is promising, further investigation is needed to determine whether the effects of this new approach are similar to or perhaps exceed those associated with traditional approaches for improving reading fluency, such as repeated reading and PALS. Tables 3.1 to 3.3 provide a comparison of the reviewed interventions with regard to effective repeated reading interventions and skills taught, as well as general descriptions of intervention delivery components.

Table 3.1   Features of Effective Fluency-Building Interventions Across Reviewed Interventions

Intervention Feature	Interventions		
	RN	PALS	RAVE-O
Student reads to an adult	X	Periodically	X
Students are told the goal of intervention effort is to improve comprehension	X	Implied	Implied
Student has a specific reading goal	X	Not discussed	Not discussed
Students are provided feedback within session	By teacher	By student	By teacher
Repeated reading of materials	X	X	X

Note: RN = Read Naturally; PALS = Peer-Assisted Learning Strategies; RAVE-O = Retrieval, Automaticity, Vocabulary, Engagement with Language, and Orthography; X = explicit component of intervention.

Table 3.2   Content and Skill Coverage Across Reviewed Fluency-Building Interventions

Skill	Interventions		
	RN	PALS	RAVE-O
Word analysis/phonics	X	Varies by level	X
High-frequency words	X	Varies by level	X
Connected text	X	X	X
Comprehension	X	X	X
Orthographic patterns			X
Morphological analysis			X
Semantics and syntax			X

Note: RN = Read Naturally; PALS = Peer-Assisted Learning Strategies; RAVE-O = Retrieval, Automaticity, Vocabulary, Engagement with Language, and Orthography; X = explicit component of intervention.

Table 3.3   Recommended Delivery Features of the Reviewed Fluency-Building Interventions

Delivery Feature	Interventions		
	RN	PALS	RAVE-O
Group size	Flexible up to 15	Whole class	1:4
Time (minutes)	15–30	20–30	30 for Phonics Component + 30 for RAVE-O
Frequency	3 times per week	2–3 times per week	Daily
Daily role of teacher	Direct and facilitating	Facilitating	Direct teaching
Grade level	1–8	K–12	1–4

Note: RN = Read Naturally; PALS = Peer-Assisted Learning Strategies; RAVE-O = Retrieval, Automaticity, Vocabulary, Engagement with Language, and Orthography.

CHAPTER 4

Using Collaborative Strategic Reading to Improve Reading Comprehension

Alison Gould Boardman | *University of Colorado at Boulder*

Elizabeth Swanson | *University of Texas at Austin*

Janette K. Klingner | *University of Colorado at Boulder*

Sharon Vaughn | *University of Texas at Austin*

"I think [Collaborative Strategic Reading] has been an incredible innovation in my teaching. . . . I hadn't done cooperative groups in middle school Language Arts, and it's incredible."

From *Now We Get It!: Boosting comprehension with collaborative strategic reading* (Jossey-Bass/John Wiley & Sons, Inc.).

Overview of Reading Comprehension

The goal of reading instruction is to develop skills students will need to understand and learn from text. While this goal is easily attainable for typical readers, for many students with disabilities, especially the 1.7 million adolescents with a learning disability (LD; U.S. Department of Education, 2009), this task is difficult, at best. Reading comprehension combines the basic components of reading, discussed in Chapters 3 and 5 and in upcoming chapters (e.g., decoding, fluency, vocabulary knowledge), with cognition (e.g., processing, memory), motivation (e.g., interest, perseverance), and the demands of different text types within which reading takes place (e.g., reading a textbook, a sports magazine). It involves extracting meaning from the words on the page as well as interacting with a written language to bring those words

to life (RAND, 2002). This composite set of skills that is reading comprehension is a prerequisite for the *prose literacy* needed in the workplace of the 21st century (Kaestle, Campbell, Finn, Johnson, & Mikulecky, 2001) and, of equal importance, is needed to manage the multiple daily encounters with text that can range from text messages to technical manuals and canonical literature. Although many students with disabilities struggle with reading comprehension (Snow, Burns, & Griffin, 1998), we focus much of our discussion on students with LDs because problems with reading and reading comprehension are primary characteristics of this population (Kavale & Reese, 1992). The majority of students with LD initially struggle to read at the word level and then continue with word and comprehension difficulties as they progress through school. Thus, instruction in components of word reading such as phonological processing (understanding that words are made up of sounds), the alphabetic principle (knowing that sounds are represented by letters that make up words), decoding (applying letter sounds and chunks of letters to read words), fluency (reading words accurately, automatically, and with expression), and vocabulary is essential for students who lack skills in those areas. Reading comprehension is negatively influenced when students have difficulties with any of the components of reading. Consider the amount of attention it takes to sound out a long and unfamiliar word. For students with LD, laboring over word reading requires tremendous cognitive energy and limits the attention they can focus on understanding the text. Yet, a deficit in word-reading skills is not the sole contributor to breakdowns in comprehension. In fact, students with LD who read fluently often struggle to understand what they read (Edmonds et al., 2009; Englert & Thomas, 1987; J. P. Williams, 1998, 2000). This may be a result of many other factors contributing to comprehension including vocabulary knowledge, background knowledge, and the ability to read strategically.

Given comprehension's important role in helping individuals develop as successful readers and the difficulty struggling readers experience in text comprehension, one would expect teachers to focus a substantial amount of instructional time on practices that improve reading comprehension skills. Historically, this has not been the case. More than 30 years ago, Dolores Durkin (1978–1979) conducted a seminal classroom observation study that revealed a broad weakness in the quality of comprehension instruction. Durkin characterized classrooms that lacked in both quantity and quality of comprehension instruction. More often than not, a teacher would *mention* a skill (e.g., "after you read, write down the main idea"), offer opportunities to *practice* with skill sheets or workbooks, and then *assess* students' success or failure at applying the target skill. These traditional methods do not provide struggling readers with necessary instruction or models that teach them how to perform important reading skills and strategies. Furthermore, there was an overall lack of instructional time devoted to reading comprehension. Although much has been learned about comprehension instruction in the last 30 years, observations of classrooms indicate a continued lack of instruction in essential comprehension strategies (e.g., Pressley, 2006).

Recently, Klingner, Urbach, Golos, Brownell, and Menon (2008) observed 124 reading lessons taught by 41 special education teachers to determine the extent to which and in what ways they promoted their students' reading comprehension. In approximately one third of their observations, Klingner and colleagues did not observe any comprehension instruction. When teachers did provide comprehension instruction, it consisted of prompting students to use a strategy more often than providing explicit instruction. The researchers concluded that special education teachers missed many opportunities to promote their students' reading comprehension and still seemed unsure how to teach reading comprehension strategies.

Perhaps more promising is a recent review of the five most common elementary core reading programs (Dewitz, Jones, & Leahy, 2009). Although the review of curriculum does not include observations of classroom practice, the authors conclude that more time is devoted to reading comprehension instruction than has been previously reported, including higher emphasis on modeling and guided practice. Still, these programs tend to teach skills in isolation, lack the research-supported focus on the metacognitive processes associated with each strategy (e.g., knowing why the strategy is used and when to use it), and none of the programs contain the opportunities for dialogue and higher-order thinking skills that support active engagement with text (National Institute of Child Health and Human Development [NICHD], 2000). Although quality comprehension strategy instruction has rarely been documented in classes that serve students with LD and other disabilities, the growing research base can inform teacher practice. In this chapter, we will present a summary of the literature on components of effective strategy interventions, followed by a literature review and description of Collaborative Strategic Reading (CSR)—a set of comprehension strategies that are effective for students with LD and other children at risk for problems with reading comprehension.

Summary of Literature on Strategy Instruction

Support and rationale for reading comprehension strategy instruction for students with disabilities has originated primarily from two lines of research: how successful readers understand text and effects from reading comprehension intervention studies.

Researchers have identified strategies successful readers use with the goal of teaching students with disabilities how to mimic these strategies during their own reading. These studies were often conducted by asking successful and poor readers to "think aloud" while reading. Researchers also question readers' actions before, during, and after reading text (e.g., Dole, Duffy, Roehler, & Pearson, 1991; Jimenez, Garcia, & Pearson, 1995; Klingner, 2004; Rudell & Unrau, 2004). Additional studies have investigated neuropsychological processes such as the study of eye movement to determine how individuals process text as they read (e.g., Starr, Kambe, Miller, & Keith, 2002). Overall, successful readers appear to be more strategic as they read than poor readers. These readers integrate a complex set of skills that they employ before, during, and after reading as necessary, to support text comprehension (Paris, Wasik, & Turner, 1991):

Successful readers:

- Read words fluently and accurately.
- Set goals for reading.
- Understand text structure and the organization of text.
- Make predictions, and modify predictions as needed while reading.
- Monitor understanding while reading.
- Generate main ideas as they read, connect what was read previously, and infer about what will come next.
- Connect ideas from what they are reading with prior knowledge.
- Make inferences.
- Use visualizations or other mental images to help them understand and remember.

When compared with successful readers, poor readers are less strategic in their selection and application of reading strategies (Paris, Lipson, & Wixson, 1983). Furthermore, struggling readers do not deduce comprehension strategies without specific instruction in what strategy to use, how to use it, when to use it, and why (Pressley, 2002). Students with LD most often approach reading tasks as inactive learners (Torgesen & Licht, 1983). They may lack motivation, content knowledge, vocabulary knowledge, necessary basic reading skills, and they often do not monitor their understanding as they read.

Several reviews of intervention research have reported positive outcomes for students with LD and struggling readers who are taught to use comprehension strategies (e.g., Edmonds et al., 2009; Gajria, Jitendra, Sood, & Sacks, 2007; Gersten, Fuchs, Williams, & Baker, 2001; Mastropieri, Scruggs, Bakken, & Whedon, 1996; Mastropieri, Scruggs, & Graetz, 2003; NICHD, 2000; H. L. Swanson & Hoskyn, 2001a; Talbott, Lloyd, & Tankersley, 1995; Vaughn, Gersten, & Chard, 2000). Other reviews analyze the effectiveness of unique components of comprehension instruction (see Maccini, Gagnon, & Hughes, 2002 for review of technology approaches; Kim, Vaughn, Wanzek, & Wei, 2004 for review of graphic organizers; and De La Paz & MacArthur, 2003 and Gajria et al., 2007 for reviews of strategy instruction for expository text type). Taken together, the following practices are associated with improved reading comprehension outcomes for students:

1. Facilitating students' familiarity and understanding of narrative and expository text structures, using

strategies to figure out the meaning of unknown words, accessing prior knowledge, monitoring understanding during reading, using or creating graphic organizers, generating questions about what is read, and using cooperative learning to increase engagement are associated with improvements in reading comprehension.

2. Using explicit strategy instruction benefits both elementary- and secondary-age students with LD, struggling readers, and typically achieving students.

3. Providing explicit instruction in several strategies that can be used together (e.g., preview text, monitor comprehension, and formulate main ideas) is particularly effective at improving reading comprehension outcomes.

4. Whereas interventions in decoding and fluency may contribute to increased outcomes in reading comprehension for those with deficits in basic reading skills, explicit instruction in reading comprehension strategies is essential to growth in reading comprehension.

Teaching Reading Comprehension Strategies

The growing body of research on reading comprehension has given us information about what works with students with disabilities. Good readers combine a complex set of reading processes in order to understand and remember what they read. Thus, teaching students to be more strategic readers involves not only teaching strategies that good readers use, but also how to integrate the strategies together into a reading routine. Traditionally, reading comprehension instruction includes a session after reading in which the teacher asks questions about passage content to which students respond. When students struggle to come up with a correct response, teachers might provide additional support in the form of hints from the story, by paraphrasing key ideas, offering suggestions for where to find the answer, and so on. Students with LD are the least likely to raise their hand to respond or to be called on during such whole-class question-and-answer sessions, putting them at a great disadvantage (Alves & Gottlieb, 1986; McIntosh, Vaughn, Schumm, Haager, & Lee, 1993). Although this type of questioning may be effective at helping some students understand the content of what they have just read, it does not provide students with information that will increase their comprehension when they read the next time.

Strategy instruction presents a different focus, creating students who are more actively engaged throughout the reading process. Students are taught specific comprehension strategies that activate cognitive processes before, during, and after reading. For example, when students are taught to find the main idea, they learn methods for identifying the most important information in a section of text and how to synthesize that information into a succinct main idea sentence. Instruction includes teacher modeling with think alouds, scaffolding, and opportunities to practice with feedback. In strategy instruction, the teacher focuses both on comprehension strategies and the content to be learned.

Several multicomponent reading approaches, including reciprocal teaching (Palincsar, 1986), transactional strategies instruction (Pressley, El-Dinary, et al., 1992) and Collaborative Strategic Reading (CSR; Klingner & Vaughn, 1999; Klingner, Vaughn, Dimino, Schumm, & Bryant, 2001), incorporate similar strategies such as predicting, monitoring understanding, summarizing, and generating questions. In addition, all these strategies include peer discussion as a critical component to developing understanding about how to use reading strategies and about the content that was read.

Collaborative Strategic Reading

Collaborative Strategic Reading (CSR) was designed to promote content learning, language acquisition, and reading comprehension in diverse classrooms (Klingner, Vaughn, et al., 2001) and has been effective at increasing reading comprehension outcomes for students with LD, students at risk for reading difficulties, average- and high-achieving students (e.g., Bryant et al., 2000; Klingner, Vaughn, & Schumm, 1998; Vaughn, Chard, et al., 2000), and students who are English Language Learners (ELLs)

(Klingner & Vaughn, 1996). CSR consists of a series of before, during, and after reading strategies that allows students at varying levels to engage with grade-level text more independently than in traditional teacher-led discussions (Klingner, Vaughn, & Boardman, 2007). Before reading, students preview the text, brainstorm what they know about the topic, and predict what they will learn. During reading, students identify breakdowns in understanding and follow a series of steps to "fix up" the breakdowns. Students also write several "gist," or main idea, statements. After reading, students generate questions and write a short summary statement containing the most important information from the passage.

What distinguishes CSR from other comprehension approaches is the deliberate and well-specified manner in which cooperative learning (e.g., D. W. Johnson & Johnson, 1989) and reading comprehension strategy instruction (e.g., Palincsar & Brown, 1984) are integrated. In CSR, students use assigned cooperative learning expert roles in which each person has a unique job that contributes to the group. Students engage in a recursive process of working individually and then sharing with their group. For each strategy, students first record their own ideas and then discuss them with their group members before moving on. Figure 4.1 presents CSRs *before, during,* and *after* reading strategies. Although CSR has been used primarily in content area classrooms with expository text, teachers have succeeded in using CSR with narrative texts as well (Klingner et al., 2012).

Theoretical Foundation

Based on cognitive psychology (Flavell, 1979) and Lev Vygotsky's (1978) sociocultural theory, CSR includes three important instructional features: explicit instruction, scaffolding, and peer-mediated learning.

Figure 4.1 Collaborative Strategic Reading plan for strategic reading.

Source: Adapted with permission from Klingner, J. K., Vaughn, S., Dimino, J., Schumm, J. S., & Bryant, D. (2001). *Collaborative Strategic Reading: Strategies for improving comprehension* (p. 106). Longmont, CO: Sopris West. Cambium Learning Group-Sopris.

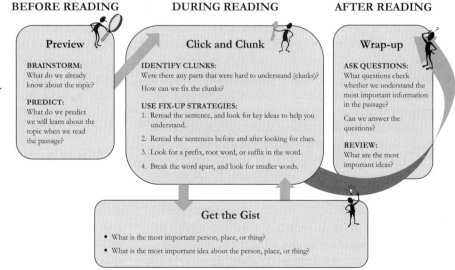

BEFORE READING

Preview

BRAINSTORM:
What do we already know about the topic?

PREDICT:
What do we predict we will learn about the topic when we read the passage?

DURING READING

Click and Clunk

IDENTIFY CLUNKS:
Were there any parts that were hard to understand (clunks)?
How can we fix the clunks?

USE FIX-UP STRATEGIES:
1. Reread the sentence, and look for key ideas to help you understand.
2. Reread the sentences before and after looking for clues.
3. Look for a prefix, root word, or suffix in the word.
4. Break the word apart, and look for smaller words.

AFTER READING

Wrap-up

ASK QUESTIONS:
What questions check whether we understand the most important information in the passage?

Can we answer the questions?

REVIEW:
What are the most important ideas?

Get the Gist

• What is the most important person, place, or thing?
• What is the most important idea about the person, place, or thing?

Explicit Instruction

A focus on explicit instruction in reading is grounded in a line of research in which teachers were taught to provide instruction in reading skills using defined teaching procedures. Results from these studies identified common practices that were associated with positive student outcomes (Carnine, 2000; Rosenshine & Stevens, 1986). These include teacher practices such as explicit teaching of skills in small steps and providing guided practice with feedback until students have a high rate of successful responses. Throughout the learning process, explicit instruction provides students with the metacognitive knowledge and self-regulation skills they need to read independently and successfully. Thus, when students learn a strategy, explicit instruction enables them to understand both its intent and its application, which, over time, translates into students' applying strategies effectively (e.g., a student learns to use fix-up strategies to find the meaning of unknown words or ideas while reading) and efficiently (e.g., the student knows how to identify the types of words or ideas that lend themselves to using fix-up strategies and knows to apply these strategies after reading a short section of text). Especially pertinent to students with disabilities, CSR does not require students to deduce or to discover the strategy or how it is used on their own. Teachers provide instruction that is clear and focused. Students learn to answer and internalize the following questions about each strategy they learn (Klingner, Vaughn, et al., 2001): What is the strategy? When is the strategy used? Why is the strategy important? and How do I carry out the strategy?

Scaffolding

In sociocultural theory, learning occurs in a student's zone of proximal development, the target area of instruction. The zone of proximal development is thought of as the difference between what students can do with help from the teacher and what they can do on their own (Vygotsky, 1978). The task for teachers is to provide just the right support to their students and then to gradually release responsibility as students become more proficient at a reading comprehension strategy. This enables students to reach their maximum learning potential.

During CSR lessons, teachers scaffold student learning. First, the teacher thinks aloud as she performs a new strategy. During this phase, you might hear a teacher say, "Watch me while I write a gist statement. Listen to the way I think about writing a gist. First, I identify the most important who or what. . . ." Slowly, the teacher turns more of the task over to students, resulting finally in students' independent application of the strategy. In sum, teachers have a plan for strategic reading, they include students in the plan, and they carefully scaffold learning through extensive modeling, guided practice, and independent practice with teacher feedback and support.

Peer-mediated Learning

Peer-mediated learning is another important component of CSR. In sociocultural theory, interaction between peers is a critical aspect of learning and cognitive development (Gallimore & Tharp, 1990). Students can assist each others' performance by providing immediate feedback at a level and in a manner that is appropriate for the group. Consider this interaction regarding a main idea, or gist statement, during CSR. Two students have just written their own gists and are sharing what they wrote:

Student A: I put that, "Scientists are making fabrics out of chicken feathers."

Student B: Okay, but I think that's a detail. And you are missing the part about the bad stuff. That fabrics use too much petroleum and that's why scientists need to make new fabrics.

Student A: Oh . . . [pause while student reworks gist]. How about "Scientists are making new fabrics that don't hurt the environment."?

Student B: Okay, I think that gets both the environmental part and that they don't use the bad stuff. And it's 10 words, right?

Student A: Good, are we ready to go on to the next section?

The influence of student–student feedback is notable. The teachers we work with are often impressed by students' ability to explain and encourage each other in cooperative learning groups. One of the strengths of CSR is the focus on strong teacher instruction and feedback in conjunction with teaching students to support each other during engaging conversations about what they are reading. Teachers encourage active learning through a cooperative learning structure (D. W. Johnson & Johnson, 1989) that includes the use of group roles, clear expectations for group work, teaching group-work skills to students, and lots of modeling and practice about how to make cooperative learning successful.

Research Support for CSR

Collaborative Strategic Reading was designed to improve the reading comprehension of struggling readers, including students with LD (Klingner, Vaughn, et al., 2001) and is supported by a corpus of promising research findings resulting from several experimental and quasi-experimental studies focused on effectiveness of

CSR among students with LD and descriptive studies of teacher implementation.

Effectiveness Studies

Early studies of CSR focused on evaluating its effectiveness within science and social studies content area instruction. In one such study (Klingner, Vaughn, & Schumm, 1998), one researcher taught CSR to intact, heterogeneous fourth-grade classes for 45 minutes per day during an 11-day Florida state history unit. The comparison group of intact classes received instruction reflective of the school's typical practice. Students in the CSR group made greater gains in reading comprehension and equal gains in content knowledge. In a separate study (Klingner & Vaughn, 2000), fifth graders who were ELLs were provided with CSR instruction for 30–40 minutes per day, 2 to 3 days per week, over a 4-week period during science instruction. Students frequently engaged in verbal discourse that supported vocabulary and content knowledge development. Students who were ELLs as well as low-, average-, and high-achieving students who were non-ELLs made gains in target vocabulary over time using CSR.

In another series of studies, researchers provided teachers with extensive professional development and coaching in CSR. Bryant and colleagues (2000) provided 10 sixth-grade teachers with three full-day workshops where they learned the Word Identification Strategy (Lenz, Schumaker, Deshler, & Beals, 1984), Partner Reading (Delquadri, Greenwood, Whorton, Carta, & Hall, 1986), and CSR. Following training, all teachers received coaching from workshop leaders and participated in teacher–researcher meetings twice per month to discuss ideas and solve implementation problems. Teachers implemented all three strategies over a 4-month period. On a measure of word identification, students with LD made statistically significant gains from pre- to post-test on measures of word identification (effect size [ES] = 0.64) and fluency (ES = 0.67). However, they did not exhibit statistically significant gains on a curriculum-based measure of reading comprehension (ES = 0.22).

In a similar study, Vaughn, Chard, and colleagues (2000) studied the differential effects of partner reading and CSR instruction on reading outcomes for students with LD and low- to average-achieving third graders. In this study, eight third-grade teachers received either CSR or partner reading training that consisted of 5 hours in professional development sessions, co-teaching and modeling by researchers, and support group meetings twice during the semester. Each strategy was implemented two to three times per week over a 12-week period. Each CSR session lasted approximately 45 minutes, and partner-reading sessions lasted approximately 25 minutes. Authors reported that CSR and partner reading groups performed equally well on tests of oral reading rate and accuracy as well as reading comprehension. Although small sample sizes precluded comparing outcomes of students with reading disabilities to students in other achievement groups, pre- to post-test gains for students with reading disabilities who participated in either CSR or partner reading varied, with effect sizes ranging from 0.14 on comprehension to 0.83 on oral reading rate.

In a third study, Klingner, Vaughn, Arguelles, Hughes, and Leftwich (2004) provided a group of five fourth-grade teachers with CSR training and in-class demonstrations. Teachers implemented CSR twice per week over an unspecified period of time. A comparison group of teachers provided instruction as usual. On a norm-referenced, distal measure of reading comprehension (a measure of the skill that was not directly taught in the program), students in the CSR group outperformed students in the typical practice comparison group (ES = 0.19). Whereas only gains made by high/average-achieving students were statistically significant (ES = 0.25), pre- to post-test effect sizes for students with LD and low-achieving students were medium in size (ES = 0.38 for students with LD; ES = 0.51 for low-achieving students).

Finally, a computer-adapted version of CSR was investigated in Kim and colleagues' (2006) experimental study of sixth- through eighth-grade students with LD who were randomly assigned to either a computer-based CSR intervention or typical school practice comparison groups. Students in the treatment group were provided with 20 to 24 sessions, 50 minutes in duration, of computer-based CSR. On a norm-referenced measure of passage comprehension, students in the CSR group outperformed students in the comparison group (ES = 0.50). Effects were larger in magnitude for students in the CSR group on more proximal measures of main idea (ES = 0.95) and question generation (ES = 1.18).

Implementation Studies

The final set of studies (Klingner, Arguelles, Hughes, & Vaughn, 2001; Klingner, Vaughn, Hughes, & Arguelles, 1999; Vaughn, Hughes, Schumm, & Klingner, 1998) used descriptive research designs to report teachers' perceptions of CSR before, during, and after implementation. Vaughn, Hughes, and colleagues (1998) worked with seven general education teachers who taught in a school recently restructured to include students with LD in the general education classroom full-time. CSR was one of four reading and writing practices implemented over the course of a 1-year period of professional development and coaching. Researchers documented the level of implementation and teachers' perceptions of effectiveness of the four practices. Findings indicated that only one teacher was familiar with CSR before professional development, and initial reactions to CSR were not positive, though teachers' enthusiasm increased after implementation. Of the four instructional practices, CSR had the lowest implementation, with only two teachers implementing it on a "consistent" basis. Facilitators to implementation of the strategies included the ability to adapt and modify the strategy and students' acceptance of the strategy. Barriers included the time it took to cover material using the approach and the perceived need to prepare students adequately for standardized tests.

Three years later, researchers (Klingner et al., 1999) returned to these teachers' classrooms to ascertain the level to which the four strategies continued to be implemented. Through focus group interviews, classroom observations, a facilitators and barriers checklist, and individual interviews, researchers found that five teachers reduced their level of CSR implementation over the 3-year period, while one increased implementation, and one maintained a high level of implementation. Two reasons were cited for the decrease in CSR implementation: the need for ongoing professional development, and CSR being viewed as appropriate only for content-area learning. Conversely, two teachers cited several facilitators to sustained use, including a support network that incorporated coaching from an experienced teacher, administrative backing, and student benefits.

In the third in this series of studies, Klingner, Arguelles, et al. (2001) conducted a follow-up study to the series of implementation studies previously described (Klingner, Arguelles, et al., 2001; Klingner, Vaughn, et al., 1999; Vaughn, Hughes, et al., 1998) to determine the extent to which the instructional practices they had taught had spread to other teachers' classrooms. They found that 57 of the 98 teachers in two schools had tried CSR, and 31 continued to use it regularly. Understandably, intermediate-level teachers were much more likely to use it than primary-grade teachers. Special education and ELL teachers also learned it. Teachers gave many reasons for choosing to learn CSR, but the primary reason was that they expected that CSR would benefit their students. Although only two of the seven teachers who had participated in the original professional development program had sustained their usage of CSR, they were influential teachers who were able to convince their colleagues to try CSR and were willing to help them learn it.

These findings support the claim that CSR is a complex set of strategies that are difficult to implement without high-quality support and modeling from expert teachers. Based on these findings, we note several trends for effectively implementing CSR. First, teachers should commit to implementing CSR over an extended period of time. It seems that far more than 30 sessions are needed to produce gains among students with LD. Second, it takes time for teachers to become facile at teaching the CSR strategies. One should seek out experts (i.e., master teachers) to provide support and guidance in mastering the strategy and cooperative grouping components of CSR.

How to Teach CSR

CSR includes four reading strategies for use before, during, and after reading (Klingner, Vaughn, et al., 2001). Before each CSR lesson, the teacher identifies an appropriate selection of text (e.g., a section of a textbook chapter, a short article, a chapter from a novel), divides the text into sections (usually three to four), identifies key vocabulary or concepts for preteaching, and formulates model gist statements. In this way, the teacher can support content learning and prepare to provide meaningful feedback to students. For instance, with preparation, a teacher can easily identify if a student's gist statement is a detail from the section or if it encompasses the most important information.

Before Reading Strategies

Preview

The purpose of previewing is to help students identify what the text will be about, to make connections to their prior knowledge about the topic, and to generate interest in reading the text. Teachers and students engage in a four-step procedure to complete the before-reading, preview strategy. First, the teacher introduces the topic in a whole-class setting. If students lack background knowledge about the topic presented in the passage, this is an ideal time for teachers to provide some base knowledge. For example, if prerequisite knowledge about the coral life cycle is necessary to understand an article about the development of coral reefs, then before reading, the teacher can provide a description or graphic that describes the structure of coral and its life cycle. Teachers may also introduce key terms such as important proper nouns or vocabulary words that can't be figured out using the "clunk" fix-up strategies (described following). Second, students activate their background knowledge by brainstorming what they already know about the topic. Third, students briefly preview the passage, looking at headings, subheadings, pictures or tables and their captions, as well as bold words and other features that stand out. The goal during this step is for students to learn as much as possible in a very short period of time. Finally, based on the knowledge gained during the text preview, students predict what they might learn. Students first record both brainstorming and predictions individually in the learning log and then share them within small groups for feedback and discussion. Figure 4.2 presents a short passage and a student's completed learning log on bison.

Figure 4.2 Sample reading passage and corresponding Collaborative Strategic Reading student learning log.

Bison

The largest mammal

The bison is the largest land mammal in North America. Males, called bulls, weigh up to 2,000 pounds. That is about as heavy as a car. Despite their large size, bison are herbivores, feeding mostly on grass varieties. Bison live on large grassy ranges in the Western Plains.

On the go

Bison are migratory animals. The time and route for migration varies depending on the weather and where food is most plentiful. It is common for bison to move towards winter migration ranges when snowfall increases. Many of these routes, carved into the earth from thousands of hoofs year after year, passing by water sources and fertile ground, were followed by Native Americans, explorers, and pioneers.

CSR Learning Log for Informational Text

Name _____ Date_____
Today's Topic *Bison* _____

BEFORE READING: Preview

Brainstorm: Connections to prior knowledge
I saw a bison when I was on a vacation in Yellowstone National Park.

Predict: What I might learn about the topic
I will learn how big a bison is. Also I'll read about where it lives.

DURING READING: Section 1

Clunks		Fix-up Strategies
herbivore = *animal that eats grass*		① 2 3 4

Gist:
Bison are very large but they only eat grasses.

DURING READING: Section 2

Clunks		Fix-up Strategies
Plentiful = *lots; there is plenty*		① 2 3 ④
Migratory Range = *area to live in winter*		1 ② ③ 4

Gist:
Bison's migration routes were also used by people.

AFTER READING: Wrap-Up

Questions: Write questions and answers.
What is a male bison called?
A male bison is called a bull.
Why did explorers and Native Americans follow the bison's migratory routes?
They probably followed the routes because they were already made into paths and went near food and water.
How are bison similar to and different from horses?
Horses also are herbivores. Horses used to live on open ranges but now they mostly live on ranches. You can ride a horse but I bet you can't ride a buffalo.

Review: Write one or two of the most important ideas in this passage.
          Be prepared to justify your ideas.
Bison live on ranges. They are herbivores and they have to migrate to avoid snow and find food when it is cold.

Source: Information from Klingner, J. K., Vaughn, S., Dimino, J., Schumm, J. S., & Bryant, D. (2001). *Collaborative Strategic Reading: Strategies for improving* comprehension (p. 105). Longmont, CO: Sopris West. Cambium Learning Group-Sopris.

During Reading Strategies

Click and Clunk

Students use the click and clunk strategy to monitor understanding during reading. When students understand what they read, everything "clicks." When something doesn't make sense, or "clunks," students must stop to figure out what went wrong. The click and clunk component of CSR involves the following steps. After reading a short section of text (e.g., one or two paragraphs), students record their clunks individually on the learning logs. Next, the clunk expert guides students to use fix-up strategies to figure out the meaning of the difficult words or concepts. In this way, students learn to monitor their comprehension and to actively work to repair misunderstandings. CSR uses four fix-up strategies:

1. Reread the sentence without the word. Think about what would make sense.

2. Reread the sentence with the clunk and the sentences before or after the clunk, looking for clues.

3. Look for a prefix, suffix, or root in the word.

4. Break the word apart, and look for smaller words you know.

Fix-up strategies are also provided to students on cue cards that can be referred to easily during reading. In their learning logs, each student writes a brief definition next to their clunk. Teachers can review clunks to see which words or ideas the students are struggling with as they read. After reviewing the clunks, teachers may decide to provide additional instruction to support vocabulary learning.

Get the Gist

Teaching students to identify and restate the main idea of passages they read is associated with improved understanding of text (Klingner et al., 2007). During "get the gist," students write the central ideas of a paragraph or short section of text. Students are taught a three-step procedure for writing a gist statement. First, students name the most important "who or what" in the paragraph. Second, they identify the most important information about the "who or what," leaving out details. Third, they write a sentence using approximately 10 words. "Get the gist" helps students distinguish between important information and details, use key concepts and vocabulary, use their own words, and write only what is needed to present the main idea. Students record their gist statements on their learning logs after reading each section of text (see Figure 4.2).

After Reading Strategies

Wrap-Up

Students learn to "wrap-up" their reading by generating questions and answers about what they have read and by reviewing key ideas. The purpose of "wrap-up" is to increase knowledge and memory for what was read, to further engage with text, and to monitor understanding. Students are taught to use question starters (i.e., who, what, when, where, why, and how) to write questions that capture key information from the text. Questions should be related to the text and should be answered either by reading the passage or by combining background knowledge with information from the reading. In most classrooms, students write individual questions and answers on their learning logs first and then share their questions with their group. Finally, students review what they have learned by writing one or two of the most important ideas from the passage and justifying why their ideas are important when they share with their group (see Figure 4.2). As with the other strategies, students first write their ideas on their own and then discuss and revise when they share with their group members. Many teachers also conduct a quick whole-class wrap-up where students can ask and answer each others' questions and present their most important ideas. At this time the teacher can also call students' attention to key ideas from the text and connect to what has been learned previously or what will be learned in future lessons.

Introducing CSR

Multicomponent reading comprehension strategies require teachers to invest planning and instructional time in order for students to achieve proficiency and to benefit from strategy use. Introducing CSR generally requires about 12 to 14 lessons (about 4 to 5 weeks) before students can work through all the strategies together in their cooperative groups. Many teachers implement CSR two to three times each week. When teachers initially introduce CSR, they model the entire process of CSR with a short passage, demonstrating how to use learning logs and discussing the benefits of CSR. Teachers may choose to show a video of students engaged in a CSR lesson or to bring in a small group of experienced student CSR users to demonstrate in front of the class. CSR includes the following explicit instructional cycle to introduce and to practice each strategy individually until all strategies are integrated into the reading routine.

During the *modeling phase,* teachers begin by providing explicit instruction in the strategy, telling students what the strategy is, why it is used, when to use it, and finally, how to use the strategy. Teachers show students how the strategy works by thinking out loud as they record their ideas on their learning log. For example, you might hear the following from a fourth-grade teacher conducting a think aloud of writing a gist after reading a passage about the Caddo Indians:

> Listen as I get the gist of this paragraph [teacher reads paragraph aloud]. There is a lot of information in this paragraph, but let's see whether we can figure out what it is mostly about. First, I'm going to identify the most important "who" or "what." This paragraph is mostly about The Caddo Indians [teacher writes "the Caddo" on blackboard]. Now, I need to decide on the most important information provided about the Caddo. The Caddo were farmers. There is also information about helping their neighbors with planting and making pottery. This seems to mostly be about the Caddo culture and some of the things the Caddo people did. So, I think the most important thing about the Caddo is that they were farmers and made pottery to trade [teacher models how to write a gist, a short sentence containing the most important information].

In the *teacher-assisted phase,* students join the teacher in using the strategy and may begin to practice in pairs or small groups. The teacher-assisted phase is a key scaffolding component as teachers monitor how well students grasp the strategy and adjust practice opportunities to meet their needs. For instance, while teaching the "get the gist" strategy, teachers may first determine the most important "who or what" with the class, and then have students create a class list of the most important ideas. Students then work in pairs to combine those important ideas into a gist statement. The teacher can then evaluate student gists as a group, pointing out examples and nonexamples of gists and highlighting key features. For example, for our sample passage on bison (see Figure 4.2), the following gists were shared with the class for the reading section titled, "On the Go": (a) *Bison migrate in winter* (too general, not all important information is included); (b) *Migration and depending on weather and to find food* (too detail focused; not a complete sentence; missing connection to people who used routes); and (c) *Bison's migration routes were also used by people* (contains the most important "who or what" and the most important ideas about the "who or what"). The teacher can lead the class in evaluating the gists and discussing features of a high-quality gist.

Another key feedback component occurs when students provide support and feedback to each other in their cooperative learning groups. Teachers gauge how long students work in the teacher-assisted phase according to student proficiency at using a strategy. The goal is that students can perform the strategy successfully on their own.

During the *independent phase* of CSR, students combine the strategies they have learned so far in their cooperative groups. Teachers are very engaged in student learning during group work, spending time with each group (about 2 to 5 minutes each) to provide substantive feedback and guidance. A benefit of strategy instruction is that it can support the feedback process for teachers. Consider the student who has written a detail for her main idea. The entry point for feedback is to draw attention to the strategy. The teacher might ask questions such as, "What is the most important 'who or what?'" "Is that 'who or what' included in your gist?" "This is a detail that is included but does not capture the most important information in the section." Teachers also address issues or problems that they observe across multiple groups by discussing them with the entire class. The teacher's role during group work also includes spending extended time with each group at least once every 2 weeks, monitoring the performance of each group, monitoring the performance of each group member, highlighting the performance of students and groups who are implementing CSR well, and supporting low-achieving students.

Cooperative Learning Group Roles

CSR uses cooperative group roles to facilitate peer-mediated discussion and learning. Groups of three to five students use the following group roles:

- *Leader:* Leads the group in the implementation of CSR by saying what to read or which strategy to do next.

- *Clunk expert:* Leads the group in trying to figure out difficult words or concepts.

- *Gist expert:* Guides the group toward the development of a gist and determines that the gist contains the most important ideas but no unnecessary details.

- *Question expert:* Guides the group to generate and answer questions.

- *Encourager:* Watches the group and gives feedback. Looks for behaviors to praise. Encourages all group members to participate and assist one another.

- *Time-keeper:* Sets the timer for each portion of CSR and lets the group know when it is time to move on. Helps keep the group on task.

Grouping is an important component of cooperative learning and CSR. Teachers assign students to heterogeneous groups, taking into consideration student characteristics such as leadership qualities, reading level, and ability to work well in groups. Because teachers vary group size according to the needs of their classrooms, roles may also vary. Essential roles are the "leader," the "clunk expert," the "gist expert," and the "question expert." When groups are smaller than four students, teachers can assign two roles to one student. For instance, one student could be the gist expert during reading and the question expert after reading. In some cases, the teacher may take on a role such as the timekeeper or the encourager. High-quality cooperative learning has several features (D. W. Johnson & Johnson, 1989) that are incorporated into the structure of CSR. These are presented in Figure 4.3. For an extensive discussion of how to implement cooperative learning, please see D. W. Johnson, Johnson, and Holubec (2008). Introducing cooperative learning can be challenging, especially in classrooms where students are not used to working together (D. W. Johnson & Johnson, 2009). CSR roles (leader, clunk expert, gist expert, question expert, timekeeper, and encourager) are taught to students so that each student becomes a valued and contributing member of the group. There are two ways that teachers introduce cooperative learning with CSR, and both have strengths. The first is to teach the CSR strategies to students in a whole-class format and to provide opportunities for pairs or triads of students to practice together and to begin providing feedback and support to each other regarding their strategy use and content learning. Once students gain proficiency at using the strategies, teachers then introduce the CSR roles and cooperative learning procedures. The strength in this method is that students become strong CSR users before learning to work together in groups. A drawback is that once students are comfortable working on their own, they may not readily see the benefit of discussing with and supporting peers during group learning. If this occurs, teachers should show students how learning is advanced with cooperative learning and demonstrate how discussion and engagement are increased when students work together in groups.

An alternative method for introducing cooperative groups within CSR is to integrate the learning of roles and group-work skills with instruction of comprehension strategies. For example, a teacher might model how to use preview in one lesson and then provide guided practice in the next lesson. On the third lesson, the teacher introduces group roles and teaches students to conduct preview in cooperative groups, using group roles. The strength in this method is that students learn group work skills as part of CSR and thus see reading comprehension strategies and cooperative group learning as interconnected parts of CSR from the beginning (Klingner et al., 2012).

Whether students first become proficient at CSR strategies or learn cooperative group roles along with the CSR strategies, it is imperative that teachers provide students with skills to function effectively in groups. Structuring cooperative group activities is not enough to help students learn to work together effectively in groups. Teachers should take time to explicitly teach the responsibilities of each group role. Just as teachers scaffold learning when teaching clunks or gist, so do teachers scaffold learning cooperative group roles. For example, teachers may provide a model of students who are experienced at CSR either with a small-group demonstration or a video. Students can then come together in role-alike groups (i.e., all "leaders" meet in one group, all "clunk experts" meet in another, etc.) and discuss how to perform their roles and why they are important. In addition, students need to be taught the rules and procedures of group work and may need explicit instruction in group-work skills such as how to support ideas with evidence and how to provide feedback to group members. Finally, students need support to process how well their group work is going. The role of the encourager guides students to debrief the quality of their group work. Teachers can also build on the encourager's role to help students recognize what worked and what they can do better the next time they do CSR. In sum, do not expect students to perform their roles, provide effective feedback to one

Figure 4.3 Features of cooperative learning (D. W. Johnson & Johnson, 1989) incorporated into Collaborative Strategic Reading.

Positive interdependence: Unique and important roles support positive interdependence because students feel that their work benefits others in group.

Face-to-face interaction among students: Group members encourage, support, and assist each other in small groups through structured sharing of responses and discussion led by expert roles.

Individual accountability: Students complete individual learning logs and understand that their individual performance is assessed regularly.

Positive social skills: Teachers provide instruction in group work skills so that students can be successful working together.

Evaluation and reflection: The encourager role leads students in reflecting how well the group worked together and in identifying strengths and shortcomings of their group work.

Figure 4.4 Sample Collaborative Strategic Reading cue cards.

Leader	Clunk Expert	Gist Expert	Question Expert
Before Reading Preview *What topic?* Prompt group to brainstorm about topic Review titles, headers, pictures Predict			
During Reading Prompt group to Read Click and Clunk Get the Gist	**During Reading** Help group identify clunks and figure out word meanings *Does someone in the group understand?* Yes! Explain No? Use fix up strategies	**During Reading** Help group identify most important who or what and the most important information about the who or what in 10 words or less	
After Reading Wrap up Prompt questions, review, share			**After Reading** Help group think of questions that check for understanding Ask and answer questions

Source: Based on Klingner, J. K., Vaughn, S., Dimino, J., Schumm, J. S., & Bryant, D. (2001). *Collaborative Strategic Reading: Strategies for improving comprehension.* Longmont, CO: Sopris West.

another, and support their ideas with evidence from the text without explicit instruction in these skills. Allow planning time to prepare for these lessons and decide before CSR implementation how the introduction of cooperative learning will be worked into the initial lessons used to get CSR up and running in the classroom.

CSR Materials

Several materials aid students and teachers in implementing CSR. Learning logs are used by students to record before, during, and after reading activities (see Figure 4.2). Learning logs are important because they provide a vehicle for individual processing and accountability and become a tool for follow-up activities, as well as a way for teachers to monitor student progress and provide feedback. Learning logs are easily adapted for younger students by providing additional space for students to write and picture cues for each strategy or for older students by decreasing the font size and including additional sections as needed. Teachers can also create a scoring rubric that includes the components of each CSR strategy and aids evaluation of student learning logs.

Another set of materials that supports CSR implementation is the CSR cue cards (see Figures 4.4 and 4.5) (Klingner, Vaughn, et al., 2001). Cue cards provide prompts about how to perform a given cooperative group role. For example, the question expert role card cues the student in this role to guide her group through the question-generation strategy and to lead students in asking and answering questions in the group (see Figure 4.5).

Figure 4.5   Sample CSR cue card: Question expert card.

Question Expert

Job Description

The question expert guides the group in coming up with questions that address important information from the reading. The question expert makes sure that students ask different levels of questions. The question expert checks to see that all students write questions and answers.

AFTER READING

Wrap-Up

- Let's think of some questions to check whether we really understood what we read. Write your questions and the answers in your learning log.

  Remember to write different types of questions:

  a. "Right there"

  b. "Think and search"

  c. "Author and you"

  [After everyone is finished writing questions, ask:]

- Who would like to share his or her best question?

  [Check that the question begins with "who," "what," "when," "where," "why," or "how."]

- Who would like to answer that question?

- Where did you find the information to answer that question?

Question Types

LEVEL ONE: "RIGHT THERE"

- Question can be answered in one sentence.

- Answers can be found word-for-word in the story.

Example: *The answer to "What is the capital of Texas?" is found in one of the sentences of the text: "The capital of Texas is Austin."*

LEVEL TWO: "THINK AND SEARCH"

- Questions can be answered by looking in the text.

- Answers require one sentence or more.

- Information is found in more than one place and put together.

Example: *To answer "How did ranchers get their cattle to the markets?" several sentences are needed to describe the steps that are presented on different pages of the text.*

LEVEL THREE: "AUTHOR AND YOU"

- Questions cannot be answered by using the text alone.

- Answers require thinking about what the reader just read, what the reader already knows, and how it fits together.

Examples: *How is the vampire bat different from other bats we have read about? Why did Jackie Robinson need to prove he could win at baseball?*

Source: Reprinted with permission from Klingner, J. K., Vaughn, S., Boardman, A. G., & Swanson, E. (2012). *Now We Get It!: Boosting comprehension with collaborative strategic reading.* John Wiley & Sons, Inc.

Students appreciate the support of the cue cards as they build confidence and become experts at their given roles. Our observations and reports from teachers indicate that many students who were previously quiet and inactive during reading activities increase on-task behavior and engagement in reading when they participate in CSR cooperative groups.

Text Selection

Selecting Text to Use with CSR

CSR can be used with a variety of reading passages. We recommend using text that contains important information for students to learn and that is relevant to their curriculum. For teachers who find themselves avoiding having students read in content classrooms or replacing student reading with teacher read alouds, CSR is an excellent way to help students gain access to text. In social studies or science, teachers may select sections of the textbook or identify additional readings that focus on the content to be learned. Students at a variety of levels can work together to tackle the dense, content-heavy text that is often found in textbooks (Mastropieri et al., 2003). In language arts, reading, and special education classrooms, teachers often choose expository text that supports a novel or unit of study. For example, when reading the *Diary of Anne Frank,* teachers may choose selections on the holocaust, diary writing, and Germany. During a unit on poetry, teachers may select text that provides background readings on poetry genres and the poets that are being studied.

Teachers introduce CSR with passages that are relatively short (one to two pages or less) and convey clear information that lends itself to the target reading strategies. Many teachers choose to begin with short sections from content-area textbooks or weekly news magazine-type articles. When focusing on a specific strategy, such as clunks or gist, short paragraphs may provide enough text to practice the strategy.

Using Narrative Text

Teachers have also used CSR with novels and narrative selections. Small adaptations to the learning log facilitate using CSR with narrative text. For example, on the learning log, brainstorm might be changed from, "what I already know about the topic" to, "what we read about yesterday." In addition, because narrative text is not usually as information laden as expository text, students may

be able to read longer sections before stopping to generate a gist statement. With longer sections, the number of words used to write the gist might also be increased. Comprehension strategies support reading in a variety of contexts. As with any reading materials, when using narrative text, teachers should be sure that the strategies in CSR support their goals for reading and provide students with strategies that will help them actively engage in reading, monitor their understanding, and improve comprehension.

Conclusion

Collaborative Strategic Reading provides both teachers and students with a systematic approach to reading comprehension. With explicit teaching that includes scaffolding instruction, students with LD and struggling readers gain the deep understanding they need to apply their newly learned strategies when they read. Still, the teaching of reading comprehension strategies does not simplify the complex decisions teachers make as they approach the profundity of content that is to be learned in their classrooms (M. W. Conley, 2008). Furthermore, the implementation of CSR and other multicomponent reading comprehension strategies is not easily accomplished. Each strategy on its own is complex and requires a unique knowledge base. Teachers who are successful at teaching CSR tend to implement CSR regularly (two to three times each week) and are responsive to student needs and adjust instruction to ensure student mastery. These teachers focus on helping students internalize and apply the cognitive strategies they are learning in CSR and provide the tools students need to do so. For example, when teaching fix-up strategies, students who have limited knowledge of prefixes and suffixes will need instruction in how to use the third fix-up strategy ("Look for a prefix, suffix, or root in the word"), but will also need to learn the affixes required to apply the strategies.

Teachers can use CSR in general education classrooms where students with special needs are included for instruction (Klingner et al., 2004) as well as in special education settings (Klingner & Vaughn, 1996). CSR takes time to learn, both for teachers and for students. Teachers who integrate the instruction of reading comprehension strategies into their curriculum, taking time for students to gain mastery in the strategies and in the skills needed to work effectively in groups, are rewarded by increased reading comprehension outcomes for students.

CHAPTER 5

Vocabulary Instruction for Students at Risk for Reading Disabilities:
Promising Approaches for Learning Words from Texts

Joanne F. Carlisle, Christine K. Kenney, and **Anita Vereb** | *University of Michigan*

From birth, children learn words that are used by others in their homes and at school. Differences in the depth and breadth of their vocabulary begin early. Once they start school, better language learners and readers might learn as many as 5,000 to 7,000 words a year, while the students at risk for reading problems might learn as few as 1,000 words a year (e.g., Beck & McKeown, 1991). For some, challenges acquiring word knowledge stem from language impairment, hearing impairment, or reading disability. Others are learning English as a second language. Vocabulary knowledge is important in its own right but particularly for school-aged students because of the strong relationship of vocabulary and achievement in reading comprehension (Cunningham & Stanovich, 1997; Wagner, Muse, & Tannenbaum, 2007). In this chapter, we examine approaches for teaching students ways to learn words and habits to engage in word learning that have the potential to improve their word knowledge and to prevent the onset of pervasive difficulties with reading comprehension.

About 90% of the approximately 3,000 words students learn each year are learned through exposure to words in their classrooms and home environments—through a process referred to as *incidental word learning* (Carlisle, Fleming, & Gudbrandsen, 2000). Students typically learn only a small number of words through teachers' instruction or activities related to the educational programs in school. Incidental word learning may sound like an aspect of language development outside the influence of the teacher, but this is a misconception. Using strategies that we describe in this chapter, teachers can assist students to become more adept at learning words from context, and these techniques have the potential advantage of providing students with life-long habits of thinking about and reflecting on the meanings of words they hear and read. Because of the demonstrated benefits to students' word learning, this chapter focuses on methods to help students learn words from texts, whether with adult or technical support or on their own.

To date, no major reviews of vocabulary instruction report on methods of instruction in word learning through reading for students with or at risk for learning and other disabilities. In fact, the National Reading Panel (NRP) (2000) reported on the limited number of high-quality studies of instruction in vocabulary of any kind and recommended that research on vocabulary instruction be regarded as a high priority. The need to determine methods of vocabulary instruction that foster improvements in students' word learning is underscored by research that shows powerful and lasting effects of vocabulary knowledge on students' reading comprehension through the school-aged years (Cunningham & Stanovich, 1997). As Roberts, Torgesen, Boardman, and Scammacca (2008) pointed out, for older students in particular, accurate and fluent word identification receives considerable attention from researchers, but fluent reading gets you nowhere if you don't know the meanings of the words you are reading. Comprehension is contingent on students' vocabulary knowledge and their ability to infer the meanings of unfamiliar words that they encounter as they read.

Even students who do not have particular challenges in acquiring vocabulary benefit from support in learning how to learn words, as vocabulary affects comprehension in content areas, whether through oral or written language. Unfortunately, recent analysis of classroom observations and surveys has indicated that little time is devoted to vocabulary instruction (E. A. Swanson, Wexler, & Vaughn, 2009). Because students with reading difficulties also spend less time reading than their peers, E. A. Swanson et al. (2009) emphasized the critical role of teachers in providing guidance for students' learning of strategies to support their word and text comprehension.

If we accept that the goal of vocabulary development is to improve students' language and reading comprehension, what methods might be most promising? Two reviews of instruction in vocabulary for students with or at risk for learning disabilities have reported research on effective vocabulary interventions (Bryant, Goodwin, Bryant, & Higgins, 2003; Jitendra, Edwards, Sacks, & Jacobson, 2004). In these reviews, most interventions focused on techniques to assist memory of taught words. Jitendra et al. (2004) found 27 studies that provided instruction in the key-word method, cognitive strategy instruction, direct instruction, constant time delay, activity-based instruction, and computer-aided instruction. Bryant et al. (2003) reported that the major emphasis of the interventions in their review was also memorization and practice of specific words out of context. The various techniques for memorizing individual words used in these studies have one important limitation: students learn a limited number of words. If they learn 10 words each week, they would work on about 400 words during a school year, perhaps 300 of which they will remember. Direct instruction can account for only a small portion of the 3,000 words that, on average, students learn in a year. Students therefore need more fluid approaches that aid in problem solving when they encounter unfamiliar words as they read.

Our focus is on methods of instruction that help students learn words while reading. Even in the preschool years, children can become accustomed to thinking about how words are used in specific contexts, to developing ways of anticipating what these words might mean, and to sharing ideas and experiences related to these words. In addition, these reflective techniques engage students in the critical process of monitoring their understanding of words and texts. As Nagy (2007) pointed out, word-learning strategies can also serve as comprehension-repair strategies.

Of course, teaching students strategies to infer word meanings as they read (or listen to) a text is not the only approach to vocabulary instruction teachers might consider using. Indeed, researchers have recommended a broad-based approach to building students' vocabulary, including direct instruction, teaching students to use resources such as dictionaries, and creating a classroom environment that stimulates word consciousness (Beck & McKeown, 1991; M. F. Graves, 2006; Jenkins, Matlock, & Slocum, 1989; Nagy, 2007). However, because our goal was to synthesize research on vocabulary instruction that might benefit not only word learning but also reading comprehension, we searched the research literature for methods teachers might use to foster students' understanding of unfamiliar words while reading. In the next three sections, we discuss studies we found in three very different areas, drawing as often as possible on methods that have been used to improve the vocabulary of students at risk for reading disabilities. The areas we focus on are (a) word learning during storybook reading, (b) word- and context-analysis strategies during reading, and (c) technological supports for word learning during reading.

We provide information about research-based instruction that might benefit students' vocabulary development in each of these three areas. Each section provides a rationale, a description of the theoretical framework, an overview of research in that area, a description of practices that have been explored, and discussion. We then discuss the extent to which the studies we reviewed have identified research-based practices, and we provide recommendations for further research.

Approaches for Learning Words During Storybook Reading

Rationale

Shared storybook reading has an established reputation as an approach to improving both the language and reading skills of young children that has lasting effects (Anderson, Hiebert, Scott, & Wilkinson, 1985).

In a review of literature on this approach, Scarborough and Dobrich (1994) identified storybook reading as an activity that particularly influences children's language development. Yet others view shared storybook reading as an opportunity to support children's vocabulary development, in particular (e.g., Senechal, 1997). The following section highlights the teaching procedures and learning activities that, when coupled with storybook reading, have been found to positively influence the vocabulary learning of young children at risk for reading disabilities.

Theoretical Framework

Within the shared storybook reading context, natural social learning takes place when adults and children work together to construct meaning (e.g., Crain-Thoreson & Dale, 1999; Sulzby, 1985). The book-reading context allows more capable readers (often parents or teachers) to facilitate the language and vocabulary growth of children who either are unable to read independently or are just beginning the reading process. While reading a story aloud, more capable readers model the mechanics of reading written texts. Regular engagement in story reading creates a predictable and safe learning environment where children can feel comfortable asking questions and making comments, including taking on the role of storyteller (Crain-Thoreson & Dale, 1999; Crowe, Norris, & Hoffman, 2000). In effective storybook read alouds, adults adjust their reading strategies to enable children to expand their thoughts and to explore use of the language of the text. With experience, children gradually show awareness of story structure and book vocabulary and improved story comprehension; regular involvement in storybook reading is likely to support development of their reading and language (Bus, van Ijzendoorn, & Pellegrini, 1995; Scarborough & Dobrich, 1994).

Storybook reading has been found to be particularly useful for the development of vocabulary. Beck and McKeown (2007) explained that when children participate in storybook readings, they are often exposed to words and language structures they would not otherwise come across in their independent reading or conversations with others. These researchers recommended that the books chosen for storybook readings contain challenging concepts and some unfamiliar words—characteristics that make them a valuable vocabulary-teaching tool. Through the adult–child partnership necessary for successful storybook reading, children can hear, discuss, and practice vocabulary they may not encounter on their own.

Unfortunately, children with limited word knowledge often do not benefit from storybook readings in the same manner as peers with higher vocabulary proficiency (Marvin & Mirenda, 1993; L. Wood & Hood,

2004). Children with smaller vocabularies are less likely to learn new words incidentally, simply through hearing a story read aloud (Coyne, Simmons, Kame'enui, & Stoolmiller, 2004; Robbins & Ehri, 1994). In addition, it is possible that adults have different levels of expectation for children with lower vocabulary skills than for children who are developing typically. Marvin and Mirenda (1993) surveyed parents and found that the expectations of parents when reading to their children with disabilities focused mainly on very basic tasks, such as pointing to pictures, turning pages, or listening. This is in contrast to the seemingly more lofty academic goals for their children without disabilities, including understanding more advanced concepts of print and story comprehension.

All in all, storybook reading has been shown to influence vocabulary development in young children; however, because children with disabilities might not reap the same benefits from storybook reading as their peers, we need to look closely at those studies focusing specifically on storybook reading and vocabulary development in children with or at risk for reading failure in order to ascertain if and how book reading impacts their overall vocabulary knowledge.

Overview of Studies on Word Learning Through Story Reading

A large number of studies have focused on the benefits of shared book reading for children who are typically developing (e.g., DeBaryshe, 1993; Elley, 1989; Senechal, 1997). A review of the research literature, however, yielded few studies that focused on vocabulary learning through storybook reading for children with or at risk for reading disabilities. One reason for this gap in the research literature might be the age at which children are typically identified as having a reading disability. The research associated with storybook reading characteristically focuses on the early childhood (often preschool) years, before children have learned to read and also before they are likely to have been identified as having a reading disability. We therefore focus on the potential benefits of storybook reading for students at risk for reading disabilities. The "at-risk" label covers a variety of conditions, including speech and language or attention difficulties. For purposes of examining approaches to vocabulary instruction through storybook reading, we are less interested in the reasons children were referred to as at risk than the features of studies that contribute to the effectiveness of the instructional approaches.

In our review of the literature, two oral word-learning approaches surfaced, both of which have been found to result in improvements in vocabulary of children at risk for reading disabilities. One of these approaches focused on training adults to use questioning and commenting styles to expand the language of children during storybook reading (e.g., Crain-Thoreson & Dale, 1999; Hargrave & Senechal, 2000; Whitehurst et al., 1994). Appropriately training the adults who participate in storybook reading in particular techniques such as the dialogic reading approach (described in the next section) greatly increases the effectiveness of the overall storybook-reading experience. The second vocabulary approach involved studies that found explicit, direct, and extended instruction of targeted vocabulary words during storybook reading to be an effective word learning approach for at-risk children (e.g., Beck & McKeown, 2007; Beck, McKeown, & Kucan, 2002; Coyne, McCoach, & Kapp, 2007; Coyne, McCoach, Loftus, Zipoli, & Kapp, 2009; Wasik, Bond, & Hindman, 2006). As discussed earlier, directly teaching specific words often involves memorization of the meanings of individual words. Through such instruction during storybook reading, children are also exposed to the use of decoding strategies, context clue strategies, and the use of prior knowledge to interpret illustrations that help convey the meaning of the passage and perhaps some words included in the story. These strategies, when internalized, may assist children in future word learning while reading independently.

In the following section we provide a brief summary of the dialogic reading approach as well as a more in-depth discussion of explicit and extended word instruction. We also outline studies that exhibit clear examples of each approach.

Description of Practices

The first approach found to improve the language skills of children at risk for reading disabilities involves questioning and commenting while reading a story. Whitehurst and colleagues (1994) studied a storybook reading method called *dialogic reading;* a goal was to equip adults with the skills necessary to read aloud to children in order to advance their vocabulary knowledge. In this study, 3-year-old children attending subsidized preschools participated in storybook reading with adults. The adults were taught to follow the lead of the child and to allow the child to take on the role of storyteller. For example, while reading a story using dialogic strategies, an adult might incorporate questions such as, "What is happening on this page?" or, "Tell me what you think might happen next," to encourage children to use longer and more elaborate language and vocabulary. Whitehurst and colleagues (1994) found that both parents and teachers used dialogic reading effectively. In addition, increased student vocabulary was demonstrated for children exposed to the dialogic reading principles.

The second vocabulary approach looked at explicit and extended word instruction. Teachers can learn a great deal about vocabulary instruction through storybook reading by studying *Bringing Words to Life: Robust Vocabulary Instruction* by Beck et al. (2002). In this book and in subsequent articles, these researchers explained how to explicitly teach children at risk for reading difficulties "rich words" through storybook readings. They also have provided guidelines about how to prepare teachers to deliver vocabulary instruction during reading with their students in the classroom environment. Their work examined the effects of a program called Text Talk, in which teachers used trade books to promote word knowledge and meaning construction among kindergarten and first-grade students. A main focus of the approach was the importance of selecting words from trade books that were "sophisticated words of high utility for mature language users and that [were] characteristic of written language" (Beck & McKeown, 2007, p. 253). These "tier-2" words were thought to be especially important for at risk learners who would be less likely to learn them independently (Curtis, 1987). Examples of tier-2 words selected by Beck and McKeown (2007) from the trade book *Mrs. Potter's Pig* (Root, 1996) were *clinged, clutched,* and *shrieked.*

Within the Text Talk program, instruction in word meanings typically took place following the storybook reading, thus allowing teachers to capitalize on the story by teaching words in a recognizable context. In addition, teachers in the treatment conditions of studies received scripted lessons for each book and were trained to deliver word instruction following the same steps for each target word. Beck and McKeown (2007) delineated the steps used in delivering the word instruction. The following section explains the steps in this instructional routine, using the word *shrieked* as an example:

Each word is discussed using the story context as a reference. For example, the teacher might say,

"In the story we read, the woman shrieked when she saw the pig in the stroller."

1. The teacher gives the definition of the word and discusses it with the children. The teacher might say, "When people shriek, they make a loud, high-pitched sound; like a scream."

2. The teacher asks children to say the word aloud with an emphasis on the phonological pronunciation of the word, "Now, everyone try saying the word aloud, *shrieked.*"

3. The children and the teacher discuss the target word using examples other than the story itself. The teacher might say, "Sometimes people shriek when they are surprised by another person, or when they see a bug crawling on the floor."

4. The teacher asks students to decide what does and does not constitute an example of the target word. For example, the teacher might ask, "If someone bumped into you and you said 'ouch' in a quiet voice, is that a shriek?"

5. Children receive opportunities to share their own examples and ideas pertaining to the target word, "Does anyone remember a time when they shrieked?"

Teachers enrolled in the study were also asked to extend students' experience with the target words by using them in other parts of the school day. For example, a teacher might insert a discussion of the word *shrieked* into the morning circle time when talking about the previous night's occurrences, "Last night I shrieked. Do you want to know why?"

Teachers who used Text Talk were fully trained in word selection and in the process of discussing these words, whereas teachers in the comparison group read aloud daily to their students using age-appropriate trade books but without specific discussion of vocabulary. Beck and McKeown's (2007) results revealed that both kindergarten and first-grade children who were enrolled in an experimental study and received direct, explicit, and extended word instruction during storybook reading showed greater gains in target word knowledge than those children in the control group who did not receive this instruction.

Other studies have used methods similar to those used by Beck and McKeown (2007); these focused on learning new words either through extended instruction or through incidental exposure during storybook reading (Coyne, McCoach, et al., 2007; Coyne et al., 2009). Coyne and his colleagues used a smaller number of words, and the researchers themselves taught the children. The following is a summary of the steps the authors used to teach targeted words (Coyne, McCoach, et al., 2007):

1. Introduce the targeted words before reading the story. Ask the children to say each of the target words aloud.

2. While reading the story, prompt children to listen carefully for the "magic words." Whenever a targeted word is identified, reread the sentence containing the word.

3. Provide a definition for the target word, for example, "Oh here is the word *scrumptious*; that means the food tastes very good."

4. Encourage children to again say the target word aloud in order to practice the phonological pronunciation.

The reader repeats the same process whenever encountering a target word within the story. Following the reading, children receive opportunities to interact with the target words outside the story context. For example, the children may be asked to describe food they find scrumptious. In contrast to this explicit word instruction, other selected words were taught incidentally; that is, students heard these words within the story but were given no additional instruction or discussion. The authors found greater gains in word knowledge when words were taught explicitly while reading a story aloud, rather than when words were encountered incidentally in the story (Coyne, McCoach, et al., 2007).

Discussion

Clearly, both dialogic reading (Whitehurst et al., 1994) and Text Talk (Beck & McKeown, 2007) assist young children in their vocabulary development. However, for either approach to influence a child's word learning substantially, adults must be able to scaffold a child's knowledge and language. Scaffolding during storybook reading is not easy; adults must know which words to focus on, what questions to ask, when to ask them, when to relinquish control, and much more. As the research discussed in the preceding section shows, some work focuses on training teachers or parents to deliver word-learning interventions during storybook reading. Beck and McKeown's (2007) work stressed the importance of training teachers to implement Text Talk. Whitehurst and colleagues (1994) trained both teachers and parents in their dialogic reading approach. The process of training teachers and parents to deliver a successful word-learning intervention may be complicated and time-consuming, but the impact on word learning is greatly increased as children participate in greater numbers of effective storybook readings where vocabulary development is a goal. The more research focuses on training teachers and parents to incorporate word-learning instruction into storybook reading (especially when working with at-risk children), the better off children will be in their vocabulary development.

Strategies for Understanding and Learning Unfamiliar Words While Reading

Rationale

The RAND report (2002) stressed the importance of providing students with strategies for working out the meanings of unfamiliar words in texts, given the impact these strategies are likely to have on reading comprehension. Earlier, the NRP (2000) report noted that relatively few studies focused on methods to teach strategic word analysis during reading; this is a neglected area of research on vocabulary instruction. In this section, we review practices that hold promise for assisting students at risk for reading disabilities in their analysis and understanding of words while reading. These methods have been studied in contexts that apply to all students (i.e., general education classrooms) as well as in clinical settings with a focus on methods appropriate for students with or at risk for reading or learning disabilities.

Theoretical Framework

Students at risk for reading disabilities commonly have limitations in their knowledge (e.g., background knowledge, vocabulary) and tend not to initiate actions to address problems they encounter during reading, as compared to same-age, skilled readers (Gersten, Fuchs, Williams, & Baker, 2001; Roberts et al., 2008). They give up easily when asked to read texts with unfamiliar words and concepts and sometimes develop an aversion to reading altogether. In theory, this problem can be addressed by equipping students with strategies for figuring out the likely meanings of the unfamiliar words that impede their comprehension during reading (e.g., Nunes & Bryant, 2006). The two word-analysis strategies that are most useful for this purpose are context analysis and morphological analysis. As Nagy and Scott (2000) stated, "context and morphology (word parts) are the two major sources of information immediately available to a reader who comes across a new word" (p. 275). As with other methods of strategy instruction, students need to understand how to apply these strategies and how the strategies can help them understand the texts they read for school and pleasure. However, they also need ample practice and guided opportunities to use the strategies on their own. What are at first deliberately applied strategies need to become habitual reading behaviors.

Word-analysis strategies provide assistance with word recognition (linked to decoding strategies, perhaps) and initial understanding of the meanings of unfamiliar words. *Morphological analysis* refers to analysis of the morphemes or units of meaning within words. This strategy is particularly useful because, from the late elementary years on, about 60% of unfamiliar words in texts are morphologically complex (e.g., base words with prefixes and/or suffixes), and most of these words are sufficiently transparent so that meaning can be inferred from the word parts (Nagy & Anderson, 1984). Through morphological analysis, students can identify the separate morphemes. These help students pronounce the word, recognize known parts, and infer the meaning of the whole. For example, students with reading problems can work out the meaning of *misplacement,* once they recognize the three parts (*mis-place-ment*).

When a student uses morphological analysis to infer the meaning of a word, analysis of the context in which the word is read also provides clues to its meaning. Context clues come from information found in text (e.g., synonyms and definitions, antonyms, examples) that help readers infer the meaning of a word. Analysis of context is useful, even when a word is not morphologically complex. In the following example (from Baumann et al., 2002, p. 161), the clue for the unfamiliar word (*befuddled*) is a synonym (*confused*): "Erica was confused about how to subtract fractions. She was usually excellent in math, but this topic had her *befuddled.*"

Overview of Studies of Word and Context Analysis Strategies

Studies of instruction in context analysis have had mixed results (see Fukkink & deGlopper, 1998, and Kuhn & Stahl, 1998, for reviews of this research). Some have shown that students taught context analysis made greater gains in vocabulary than students in a no-treatment control group (e.g., Buikema & Graves, 1993). Others did not find significant improvements in word knowledge for students trained to use context analysis (Patberg, Graves, & Stibbe, 1984). A limitation of this strategy, when used alone, is that most passage contexts provide few cues to the meaning of specific words. Nonetheless, researchers have reported that, with sufficient support, context analysis can be an effective strategy for students with poor vocabulary or language/learning disabilities (Cain, Oakhill, & Elbro, 2003; Goerss, Beck, & McKeown, 1999; Nash & Snowling, 2006; Tomesen & Aarnoutse, 1998). For example, Nash and Snowling (2006) found that students with poor vocabularies who were taught context analysis performed better than those taught definitions on tests of taught words, transfer words, and reading comprehension.

Researchers have developed methods to teach morphological analysis to students with reading disabilities as well as students who achieve at normal levels (e.g., Elbro & Arnbak, 1996). Morphological analysis has been taught both as a decoding strategy and as a strategy for inferring the meanings of morphologically complex words in texts. Results of a number of studies suggest that teaching students to use morphological and context analysis helps them decode, spell, and understand unfamiliar words in texts (e.g., Berninger et al., 2008; Henry, 1993; Lovett, Lacerenza, & Borden, 2000).

Morphological and context analysis, taught together, are likely to be more effective than either one taught alone. Students taught these strategies might perform better not just because of their knowledge of specific clues or prefixes but rather because of heightened sensitivity to analytic methods to make sense of words in texts. In two recent studies, the two strategies were taught together (Baumann et al., 2002; Baumann, Edwards, Boland, Olejnik, & Kame'enui, 2003). The results of the first of these studies showed that fifth graders taught either the context or morphological strategy performed better on inferring meanings of new words than the no-treatment control group. Furthermore, students taught both strategies performed better on new words than students taught either one of these strategies (Baumann et al., 2002). However, no significant improvements occurred on transfer passages. Baumann et al. observed that fifth graders taught the combined strategies were significantly more likely to infer the meanings of unfamiliar complex words in new passages after training than students who were taught words from their social studies texts (Baumann et al., 2003). Here, too, results were significant for new words (including delayed posttests) but not for transfer passages.

Combined context and morphological analysis has also been effectively taught to small groups made up of both normally achieving and underachieving fourth-grade readers (Tomesen & Aarnoutse, 1998). These researchers used explicit instruction combined with a dialogic method to engage small, mixed-ability groups of students in discussion of unfamiliar words in passages. The less-skilled readers benefited at least as much as the skilled readers on a measure of application of strategies to analyze unfamiliar words when reading new texts.

The positive results from studies carried out in classroom settings (Baumann et al., 2002; Baumann et al., 2003) and by teaching small groups of students with diverse learning abilities (Tomesen & Aarnoutse, 1998) suggest that the word-analysis strategies methods might be useful to practitioners in inclusive general education classrooms in various content areas. Still, further research is needed to determine methods to ensure that students transfer strategies to texts they read in content area courses.

Description of Practices

What are the characteristics of effective practices in context and morphological analysis strategies? First, an effective intervention program should have the goal of helping students become analytic and engaged readers. An important goal is to help them overcome habits of skipping hard words when reading and overrelying on prior knowledge in interpreting the text (L. Baker & Brown, 1984). To achieve this goal, students need to be invested in learning and using the strategies. Only then are they likely to become better at comprehension monitoring and learning new words. Based on this framework, we should not be surprised to find that researchers make motivating learning activities a key feature of their

programs. They want students to perceive the strategies they are learning as do-able and engaging. Sometimes researchers achieve this by presenting problems that engage students' reasoning and imagination. For example, in Nunes and Bryant's program (2006), they might pose problems such as the following: "What is the important difference between a bicycle and a tricycle? What is it about the word that gives you a clue to this difference?" (p. 91). Other researchers have given students the role of "word detectives," a clever technique to motivate older, struggling readers (e.g., Tomesen & Aarnoutse, 1998).

Second, effective programs have provided explicit instruction in the purpose and use of the strategies, accompanied by guided practice. Most use a "release of responsibility model," wherein the teacher begins by modeling and explaining the strategies but gradually encourages students to take over the role of identifying and analyzing unfamiliar words themselves. Quite often, this involves explicit instruction. This might involve studying the meanings of prefixes and suffixes, such as the ending *-ian* in *musician* and *electrician* (Nunes & Bryant, 2006). Baumann et al. (2002) covered one prefix "family" in each session (e.g., the "not" family including *un-*, *in-*, and *im-*, as in *unfriendly* and *impossible*); each context strategy session covered a different context cue (e.g., synonyms or appositives).

Third, combined strategy instruction has been studied with varied amounts and kinds of support for students' practice and application. For example, Ebbers and Denton (2008) adapted the "vocabulary rule" of Baumann et al. (2003) to guide students when they encounter an unfamiliar word in text:

1. First, look outside the word, at context clues in the neighboring words and sentences.

2. Then, look inside the word, at the word parts (prefix, root, suffix).

3. Next, reread the section, keeping the meaningful word parts in mind. Make an inference: What do you think the word might mean? (Ebbers & Denton, 2008, p. 98)

Ebbers and Denton suggested that students benefit from numerous opportunities to apply the vocabulary rule during guided reading (2008). For example, engaging students in think-aloud procedures helps by making cognitive processes more transparent, which in turn should support students' efforts to understand how to use the two strategies and the vocabulary rule.

Somewhat similarly, emphasis on guided application characterizes a program called "close reading," designed by L. A. Katz and Carlisle (2009), which placed high priority on instructional time devoted to practice using strategies while reading. In an initial study using the program with three fourth-grade struggling readers, half of each training session was devoted to shared reading of a book of African tales. During shared reading, the teacher initially took the lead, modeling his identification and analysis of unfamiliar words that stood in the way of understanding the text. Over time, the teacher guided the students to take increasing responsibility for identifying and analyzing unfamiliar words. The teacher and students then discussed the meaning of the word and passage. Other researchers have also used a dialogic process to ensure that students learn to apply the strategies they have been taught. For example, Goerss et al. (1999) taught fifth- and sixth-grade less-skilled readers to use a five-step process to infer meanings of words from context: read/reread, discuss, make initial hypothesis, place constraints or develop hypothesis, and summarize. Each student met individually with the researcher/teacher so that instruction could be designed to meet the student's needs.

Discussion

Nash and Snowling (2006) refer to teaching children to derive meanings of words from context as a self-teaching device. This characterization is true of morphological analysis as well. This term highlights a critical goal of strategy instruction—that is, to ensure that students are better able to infer independently the meanings of words in passages that were not used for training purposes. Ideally, we should also find that application of the strategies leads to improved comprehension. However, few studies have reported significant transfer effects.

An important consideration in designing instruction in strategies for learning words during reading is the amount and kind of practice provided (Kuhn & Stahl, 1998). In particular, Nash and Snowling (2006) pointed out that students with low vocabulary (and other language and reading difficulties) need substantial support for their learning and, with sufficient guidance and practice, can learn to derive meanings of unfamiliar words in passage contexts. This is promising, given previous findings that students with low vocabulary lack the semantic knowledge and linguistic flexibility so critical to success in inferring the meanings of words from context (e.g., McKeown, 1986).

An additional finding that might be important for classroom teachers is that word-analysis strategies have been successfully taught in both small-group and classroom settings (e.g., Nunes & Bryant, 2006). Furthermore, Baumann and co-workers' (2003) study suggested that word-analysis strategies can be successfully taught in content-area courses (i.e., social studies). Carlo, August, Snow, Lively, and White (2004) taught a set of vocabulary strategies, including morphological

analysis, to fifth-grade classes made up of both students who were English Language Learners (ELLs) and students who spoke only English. The authors reported significant effects of the instruction on a measure of text comprehension. The finding that instruction in word analysis for struggling readers can be delivered effectively in general education classrooms enhances its value for many teachers.

Technological Aids for Learning Vocabulary During Reading

Rationale

Interest is growing in the use of technology to support literacy learning not only for students who are typical learners but also for students who are ELLs and students with disabilities. As the capabilities of technology continue to develop rapidly, and the number of classrooms with access to technology and the World Wide Web increases, the ways in which technology can extend and support students' literacy learning are constantly expanding. This potential for enhancing students' literacy learning was acknowledged in the NRP Report (2000), which identified the use of technology as a promising avenue for providing effective reading instruction. In this section, we review technology-incorporating practices that hold promise in improving word learning through reading for students with reading disabilities.

Theoretical Framework

As noted earlier, students with reading disabilities often have limited vocabulary knowledge compared to their peers, which affects their reading comprehension and their motivation to work at understanding difficult texts. Technology offers ways to address these challenges; in effect, it serves as a viable instructional tool because of its flexibility, its ability to scaffold students' learning, and its ability to enhance students' motivation and engagement.

The adaptability and multimodality of technology open the door for improved word-learning opportunities, especially for children with reading disabilities. Beck and McKeown (1991) argued that the most effective way to improve students' vocabulary knowledge is to provide them with an assortment of techniques, including multiple exposures to unfamiliar word meanings in context. An immediate problem is that struggling readers don't engage in much reading because their basic skills aren't sufficiently developed and/or they find written texts very difficult to understand. Such features of technology as speech production, hypertext, graphics, word processing, and streaming videos are particularly valuable because they provide accommodations for basic difficulties and in doing so make it more likely that students will engage in more reading. As a result, students with reading disabilities have greater opportunities to learn word meanings through reading—including texts presented through a variety of modalities.

Another important factor is that technological features can be customized to meet individual students' needs and preferences (e.g., different fonts and font sizes, volume and rate of speech production, number of repetitions). The fact that technology can be customized to provide appropriate instruction for individual learners is a key component to what Meyer and Rose (1998) have termed a Universal Design for Learning (UDL). UDL is not a "universal" system in the sense that one program fits all, but rather a system that is flexible enough to support differentiated instruction to meet the needs of individual students. Integrating the features of technology (e.g., large print, speech production) into practice enables students with disabilities greater access to otherwise inaccessible or challenging text. This is of critical importance considering the current movement to educate students with mild disabilities in general education classrooms (Fitzgerald, Koury, & Mitchem, 2008).

As the capabilities and features of technology have advanced, the way in which practitioners and researchers use technology to support students' word learning has shifted to focus on the integration of technology into classroom instruction. In a review of the literature, Fitzgerald and co-workers (2008) addressed how the use of technology for students with high-incidence disabilities has evolved from what researchers referred to as computer-assisted instruction (CAI) to computer-mediated instruction (CMI). CAI mainly focused on software-guided, drill-and-practice activities, with the aim of learning words in isolation; it was primarily used and studied in resource room settings. Because CAI provided students with opportunities to learn and practice on their own, special education teachers had more time to focus on higher-level literacy tasks with students. In this sense, the use of technology was viewed more as a practice tool. In recent years, the focus has shifted to CMI, where the emphasis is on how to effectively integrate computers into practice maximizing students' learning and enabling students with disabilities greater opportunities for learning in a mainstreamed setting. With CMI, technology is not viewed as a separate component of instruction but an integrated one, designed to help students build on prior knowledge, to encourage the use of problem solving skills, and to scaffold students' learning of higher level strategies (e.g., predicting, monitoring),

in turn, supporting word learning and comprehension (Fitzgerald et al., 2008). CMI moves beyond drill and practice and focuses on the use of technology to scaffold students' literacy learning.

In addition to technology's capabilities to scaffold students' learning, the use of technology provides students with an opportunity to participate actively in their learning in ways that can positively influence their reading achievement (Guthrie & Wigfield, 2000). Student motivation and engagement have been shown to increase with the use of technology, as students are often provided greater autonomy over their learning (Dalton & Proctor, 2008; Strangman & Dalton, 2005). Students can choose the words they want to highlight, Web sites to explore, or graphics to display, thereby creating an interactive learning experience that can lead to greater exposure to content and new vocabulary, as well as improved motivation to read. Relevant to vocabulary learning, the use of the Internet gives students with limited background knowledge opportunities to engage in real-world experiences. Viewing a video from www.youtube .com about tornados, the subway, or farming provides life-like vibrancy and contextual depth in a way that picture books alone cannot.

The use of technology holds promise in improving word learning through reading for students with reading disabilities because of its flexibility, its ability to scaffold students' learning, and its ability to enhance students' motivation and engagement. The following section provides a review of the literature on research-based practices related to supporting word learning through reading for students with or at risk of reading disabilities.

Overview of Studies on Word Learning with the Aid of Technology

Research demonstrating the effectiveness of technology to support students' word learning includes students who are typical learners (Kolich, 1991), students who are ELLs (Proctor, Dalton, & Grisham, 2007; Proctor, Uccelli, Dalton, & Snow, 2009), children with hearing loss (Barker, 2003), children with autism (Bosseler & Massaro, 2003; Moore & Calvert, 2000), and children with learning disabilities (Hebert & Murdock, 1994; J. Xin & Rieth, 2001). Despite the increased attention on the use of technology to improve students' literacy, systematic research identifying research-based instructional practices in this area remains sparse (Fitzgerald et al., 2008; Strangman & Dalton, 2005). The majority of studies on the use of technology to support reading instruction focus on decoding skills, fluency, and reading comprehension as primary outcomes measures and address vocabulary development only indirectly. Although research in this area is limited, results imply the potential of multimedia technology as an effective tool to support students' word learning. As the integration of multimedia technology becomes more commonplace in the classroom, we expect that teachers will gradually become familiar with methods that hold promise for improving students' word learning through reading, including the use of speech feedback (otherwise referred to as text-to-speech [TTS]), hypertext, and instructional practices that combine these various features of technology. In turn, additional research will likely be conducted to better establish these technological supports and their effectiveness in improving students' literacy outcomes. For a detailed overview of the present research in this area, refer to Strangman and Dalton (2005).

One area of research on technology examines the use of video to anchor students' learning in a real-world context to support word learning and reading comprehension. J. Xin and Rieth (2001) studied the effects of video technology as a means for enhancing word learning for elementary students with learning disabilities. Instruction occurred over a 6-week period, and teachers used a videodisc about the 1989 San Francisco earthquake to anchor students' word learning in a real-world context. Results showed that students who received video-anchored instruction had significantly higher gains on a word-definition test, compared to students who received traditional instruction with a dictionary and printed texts. Although performance on a delayed post-test was not significant, J. Xin and Rieth (2001) concluded that the use of videodiscs holds promise as an effective tool in motivating and engaging students in understanding word meanings in an interactive context.

Another area that has received some attention in the literature examines the use of speech feedback, or what is often referred to as the text-to-speech (TTS) capabilities of technology. Several studies have been conducted to investigate the use of technology and speech feedback in remediating struggling readers' deficits in word recognition and phonological decoding while engaging in computer-assisted storybook reading (Olson & Wise, 1992; Wise et al., 1989; Wise, Ring, & Olson, 2000). In these studies children were instructed to click the computer's mouse on unfamiliar words they encountered when reading. Depending on their assigned study condition (i.e., whole word, syllable, or onset/rime), when students clicked on the word, they saw and heard different segments of the word to provide word-decoding support. Wise and co-workers (2000) found that children made significant gains in phonological decoding and word-reading measures, compared to classroom controls, regardless of the size of segmentation support they received.

Besides using TTS as a remediation tool to support children's word-reading skills, other researchers have examined the use of TTS as a compensatory tool to provide students with reading disabilities greater exposure to the kinds of cognitive challenge in higher-level texts that might lead to improved reading comprehension (Dalton & Proctor, 2008; Elkind, Cohen, & Murray, 1993; Montali & Lewandowski, 1996). As a compensatory tool, TTS allows struggling readers to bypass the challenges of word recognition and fluency in order to focus greater attention on constructing meaning from the text—thus, also enhancing their opportunities for learning words through reading. Hebert and Murdock (1994) examined students' gains in word learning following computer instruction with and without TTS support. They provided sixth-grade students with learning disabilities access to TTS, either synthesized or digitized speech, when reading vocabulary words, definitions, and sentences from digital text. The vocabulary words, definitions, and sentences were taken directly from the glossaries and context of the students' sixth-grade reading, science, math, and social studies textbooks. Study findings revealed that students made significant gains in vocabulary when reading digital text paired with TTS, as compared to reading digital text without TTS support. The results demonstrated the benefits of this feature of technology as a viable tool to support students' language and literacy learning.

Other researchers (e.g., Boone & Higgins, 1993; Higgins & Raskind, 2005; Proctor et al., 2007, 2009) further examined the benefits of TTS but in the context of combining TTS with additional enhancements of technology, such as hypertext, hypermedia, and access to an online glossary. These scholars examined how various features or capabilities of technology can be integrated into practice to improve the word learning and reading comprehension of students with reading difficulties. Combining these various capabilities of technology increases students' opportunities to learn word meanings through multiple modalities and sources of information.

Higgins and Raskind (2005) conducted a study to explicitly examine reading comprehension of students with learning disabilities using the Quicktionary Reading Pen II. The Reading Pen is a hand-held device that allows students to scan printed text either one word or one line at a time; the text is then displayed on the LCD screen and read aloud using the pen's TTS feature. Single words can be segmented by syllables and displayed on the screen. In addition the speech rate, volume, font size, background colors, and various enhancements of the Reading Pen can be customized to meet an individual student's needs. One enhancement of the Reading Pen is a definition function, which students can activate to provide them with primary and secondary definitions of words during reading. Even though students' vocabulary gains were not formally assessed, the study demonstrated the potential of improved word learning with use of the Reading Pen.

After using the Reading Pen for 2 weeks, students were assessed using a formal reading inventory, with and without the Reading Pen. Results revealed significant differences between the two conditions with higher passage comprehension with use of the Reading Pen. In addition, study field notes revealed that several students were motivated to examine novel vocabulary encountered by accessing the glossary while using the Reading Pen. Researchers noted that students engaged in word play, breaking words into various parts by using their knowledge of phonology and morphology to analyze unfamiliar words. This study demonstrates the promise of the Reading Pen and its multiple capabilities as a tool to support students' reading disabilities with word learning during reading.

In the next section, we discuss in greater depth promising research on an instructional practice that incorporates multiple features of technology including TTS via a scaffolded digital reading environment to support word learning and comprehension in students with or at risk for reading disabilities.

Description of Practices

Current practices in the use of technology to support word learning from texts primarily take the form of indirect, compensatory systems that increase the likelihood that students will engage in reading challenging texts. These systems may increase students' opportunities to learn strategies to address unfamiliar vocabulary and monitor comprehension. Because technological practices are becoming increasingly prevalent, teachers interested in research-based practices would benefit from becoming familiar with the affordances of technology—qualities that allow technology to offer opportunities to teach and learn or to provide supports for teaching and learning. We have selected a study examining the use of a scaffolded digital reading (SDR) environment to illustrate practices shown to be effective.

Proctor and his colleagues (2007) investigated the affordances of working in an SDR environment to support learning vocabulary and reading comprehension strategies for students with reading difficulties, including students who are ELLs, and students with learning disabilities. The SDR environment provides a variety of embedded supports (e.g., TTS functionality, hyperlinks for vocabulary, Spanish–English translations, a digital word wall, coaching of comprehension strategies) for students to access during their reading of digital text. Proctor et al. (2007) conducted a 4-week intervention study with 30 fourth-grade struggling readers, including students who were Spanish-speaking ELLs. Students engaged in an SDR environment for 45 minutes, three times per week, for 4 weeks, in a computer lab where they read and interacted with narrative and informational digital texts. The researchers purposefully chose challenging texts in order to examine how struggling readers accessed and used the various digital supports (e.g., TTS, hyperlinks, the glossary, strategy instruction prompts) to decode unfamiliar words, understand the vocabulary, and comprehend the text. In the initial step, the prereading phase of the SDR environment, students in the study were introduced to five "power words" important to the text. Students were given access to a number of embedded learning supports in the digital reading environment, including an audio pronunciation of the word, a brief definition, a contextual sentence, and graphics illustrating the word. After reviewing these, students were asked to begin reading the digital texts. While engaged in reading, students had access to a virtual coach who could model various comprehension strategies, additional hyperlinks to obtain a definition, or audio pronunciation of an unfamiliar word. Students were also required to add three unfamiliar words to their personal glossary. At the end of each page of the digital text, the system automatically prompted students to think about the story and apply a particular comprehension strategy (i.e., summarization, prediction, or questioning) to provide a written response. On completion of reading the digital texts, students engaged in a postreading retelling computer-based activity to assess their progress of reading comprehension and vocabulary knowledge.

To monitor students' progress, researchers tracked which supports readers were accessing via a remote server that maintained a usage log for each text for each individual student. Results showed that lower-performing students accessed these supports more often than their higher-functioning counterparts. In addition, increased use of the various supports (e.g., hyperlinked glossary terms or coaching avatars) was positively associated with gains at posttest in vocabulary and reading comprehension (Proctor et al., 2007). One reason for the success of the SDR environment might be that it provided students with multiple representations of new words in context, thus promoting language and literacy learning in students with reading difficulties. Furthermore, the intentional use of a meaningful purpose for accessing the supports (e.g., requirement that students add three words to their personal glossary) could have contributed to its success. In this study, the SDR environment provided a balance between student choice of using embedded supports and explicit instruction on when to use them. More information on this research and other literacy projects incorporating the UDL framework can be found at the Center for Applied Special Technology (CAST) Web site (www.cast.org).

Discussion

Research in the area of technology to aid literacy learning has largely focused on software or computer features to support the reading of text. The traditional concept of literacy—the assumption that print is the primary source of information in our culture—is changing rapidly. Digital technology, including the Internet, is quickly becoming a primary carrier of information, and this has significant implications for education (Leu, Kinzer, Coiro, & Cammack, 2004). Increasingly, students are surfing the Web for information, instead of going to the library to gather information from an encyclopedia. They are participating in social networks, such as Facebook, MySpace, and Twitter, which have their own rules of sharing information through reading and writing. We have provided an overview of current research in the area of technology that supports students' vocabulary and comprehension development. While research-based practices are limited at this time, evidence indicates that technology can help struggling readers compensate for word reading and fluency problems as well as facilitate their use of content-rich learning environments likely to foster vocabulary growth (e.g., Hebert & Murdock, 1994; Higgins & Raskind, 2005; Proctor et al., 2007). With an increased reliance on technology both in and out of school, future research will undoubtedly identify various ways in which technology can foster word learning during reading and exploring multimedia resources.

Analysis of Research Quality

The studies on research-based approaches for learning words from texts vary widely in the quality of research design and method. Some meet standards for high-quality research, including random assignment to condition, evaluation of fidelity of treatment, and efforts to determine whether effects of the treatment are lasting. However, many of the studies we reviewed fall short of current standards for high-quality research (e.g., Gersten et al., 2005).

It is important to appreciate the preliminary efforts made by a number of researchers in developing and studying a program of instruction; one goal was to determine whether the instructional techniques were sufficiently promising to warrant further study (e.g., Nunes & Bryant, 2006). We have referred to various exploratory studies in our overview of studies. These include short-term studies in clinical settings with no comparison group (e.g., Goerss et al., 1999), as well as truly novel treatments, such as the Quicktionary

Reading Pen (e.g., Higgins & Raskind, 2005). Exploratory research serves an important purpose. When results show learning gains, such studies provide evidence of the promise of innovative methods for improving vocabulary through reading and exploring words in texts—and in the long run, reading comprehension as well. The next step is to carry out larger and more rigorously designed studies, and these represent the research-based practices in the preceding review (e.g., Baumann et al., 2003; Beck & McKeown, 2007; Coyne et al., 2009).

In the area of storybook reading, results suggest that enhancing the word learning of young students might engender a habit of thinking about words as they read, possibly preventing later reading difficulties. Studies in this area were based on pretest/post-test control group designs, where the researchers thoughtfully identified the sample and teacher characteristics and measured for equivalency of groups in the area of vocabulary knowledge at pretest (e.g., Beck & McKeown, 2007; Whitehurst et al., 1994). Researchers carefully outlined the intervention materials and procedures (including examples of scripted lessons), monitored for fidelity of implementation, and used assessments that showed the extent to which children had learned the target words.

In studies of instruction in word-analysis strategies, Baumann and his colleagues (2002, 2003) and Carlo et al. (2004) designed studies that meet current criteria for high-quality research reports. Most of the remaining studies were exploratory, often employing a convenience sample and sometimes without a control group (e.g., Goerss et al., 1999; L. A. Katz & Carlisle, 2009). Overall, instruction in word-analysis strategies has been shown to foster students' understanding and use of word-analysis strategies; however, to date, the effects on vocabulary development and reading comprehension have been modest.

Similarly, many studies of the use of technology to improve literacy learning in students with reading difficulties have been exploratory. The majority used experimenter-designed dependent variables, had short intervention time frames, provided little information on transfer or long-term benefits of the intervention, and rarely addressed issues of fidelity. The studies that were more rigorous in design show the benefits of text-to-speech support for struggling readers (e.g., Wise et al., 1989) and positive influences of various supports for reading digital texts (Proctor et al., 2007, 2009). Technological supports for word learning while reading are changing at a rapid rate, and this situation makes it hard for researchers and teachers to stay abreast of current practice. Still, both theory and the evidence suggest the value of various technological supports for struggling readers.

Discussion and Directions for Future Research

We selected three areas of research for which research-based evidence shows that instructional practices can help students learn words from texts. Our choice of approaches was based on current views that students with or at risk for reading disabilities, even preschoolers, can benefit from engaging in analysis of meanings of unfamiliar words in texts and that doing so will lead to positive engagement and a can-do attitude toward reading challenging texts. These are important goals, as all too often students lack persistence and interest in reading (Gersten et al., 2001). Teachers need established practices to guide them in teaching students how to read texts, and they need to provide more guided practice for their students than is currently the case (E. H. Hiebert, 2009). However, our review of the literature has shown us that research in the three areas we investigated is still limited with regard to the impact of interventions on the vocabulary development of students with reading disabilities. Nonetheless, much can be learned from these studies, both for practitioners and researchers. We start by summarizing what we see as promising practices in the three areas we investigated. Then we provide suggestions for further research.

Research results show that the preschool years are not too early to begin to teach children to analyze and reflect on word meanings when adults are reading with them. In storybook reading, methods used with children before they are themselves readers lay a foundation of word knowledge that is critical for development of their vocabularies. Enhancing the word learning of young students might engender a habit of thinking about words as they read, possibly preventing later reading difficulties. We found two approaches that were effective in teaching young children to engage in analysis of word meanings. One involved teachers' selection of several high-utility words from a storybook and their guidance of the discussion of these words after reading (e.g., Beck & McKeown, 2007). The other involved dialogic reading, in which parents or teachers provided children opportunities to talk about and even tell stories about the text that they were reading together (Whitehurst et al., 1994). Both have been shown to lead to gains in students' word learning.

Researchers have also studied explicit instruction in two word-analysis strategies that can help students learn words and improve their understanding of texts. Results have shown that together context analysis and morphological analysis strategies support students' learning of unfamiliar words through deriving meaning from word parts and context. The two strategies work better together than either one alone (Baumann et al., 2002).

It is possible that students are not just learning specific analytic techniques, such as looking for synonyms of unfamiliar words, but rather are acquiring habits of monitoring their comprehension as they read, making an effort when necessary to figure out the meaning of words, sentences, and longer passages.

Research on these two strategies has shown that all students can benefit, whether they have reading difficulties or not, and some research indicates that students benefit whether they are in general education classrooms or working with a tutor in a "pull-out" or clinical setting. One critical factor is that students with low vocabulary knowledge need more structured learning and more extended support (Nash & Snowling, 2006). With sufficient guidance, students with reading problems have been found to make as much progress as their peers (Tomesen & Aarnoutse, 1998).

Our review showed benefits for reading and understanding words in texts that are made possible by various kinds of technology. The affordances that can come with electronic technologies are such that it might seem that students don't need teachers to guide their learning, but this turns out not to be the case (Wise et al., 2000). Hypermedia and Internet links certainly can provide very rich learning opportunities for students—opportunities that offer experiential and visual support, not just linguistic cues to meaning. However, students need help learning when and how to use such features as speech or pictorial representations of words. Still, in the area of technological advances, we found more theory than empirical support for practices that teachers might want to employ—a sign that this is still an emerging area of research. Preliminary results show the promise of technological supports for acquisition of vocabulary, word knowledge, and reading comprehension.

Our review of current research has suggested several specific areas where further research is needed. One area is the benefits of continuing to use read-aloud techniques beyond the first years of formal schooling, coupled with discussion of words in the texts, to foster students' vocabulary development. This practice is used in preschool and kindergarten, but it is likely that older students and students with (or at risk for) reading disabilities would benefit from guided discussion of text vocabulary as well.

A second area concerns technological, compensatory supports that are increasingly available and potentially helpful in improving students' understanding of words and texts. Studies have shown the value of speech-to-text options, but additional technological supports, such as those studied by Proctor et al. (2007) (e.g., text-to-speech, hyperlinks for vocabulary, Spanish–English translations), offer additional ways to make it possible for students with reading difficulties to read challenging texts. Most important, more research is needed to determine the extent to which such supports, when properly used, lead to improvements in word knowledge and comprehension.

A third area in which we see the need for further research is the effectiveness of instruction in word-analysis skills in content-area courses, particularly to arrive at a better understanding of the extent to which students with reading difficulties benefit from such instruction. In this area, as in the other two areas included in this review, studies that have included students with disabilities have generally focused on students with reading disabilities (or at risk for such disabilities); however, students with various disabilities (e.g., those with hearing impairment or autism) often experience problems understanding vocabulary while reading texts. Research should be expanded to more fully investigate the impact of interventions on these students' vocabulary development. For all students, we see particular promise in vocabulary instruction focused on learning words through reading in content area courses. Learning how to make sense of the many new words and concepts introduced in, for example, science and history textbooks offers the possibility of building students' word and topical knowledge—both of which matter for their performance in school. Support in content area vocabulary development should help students become more invested in their reading and learning in school.

CHAPTER 6

Instructional Practices for Improving Student Outcomes in Solving Arithmetic Combinations

Diane Pedrotty Bryant, Brian R. Bryant, and **Jacob L. Williams** | *The University of Texas at Austin*

Sun A. Kim | *Queens College, The City University of New York*

Mikyung Shin | *The University of Texas at Austin*

Success in mathematics achievement is a critical component for competitive advancement to post-secondary education and to enhance opportunities for careers and employment (National Mathematics Advisory Panel [NMAP], 2008). However, national indicators of mathematical achievement have shown that although overall average scores have improved for fourth and eighth graders since 1990, scores in the most recent few years do not indicate significant changes. In fact, between 2007 and 2009, scores remained unchanged for fourth graders and only slightly improved for eighth graders (National Assessment of Educational Progress [NAEP], 2009). Additionally, NAEP findings indicate a problem of underachievement that is particularly severe for students with disabilities. This lack of significant improvement in mathematics achievement for students with disabilities is of grave concern for their future educational and career opportunities. Given that

math performance remains low, one can only conclude that a need exists for educators to provide high-quality instruction to teach important mathematical ideas that lead to improved performance for all students, including students with all disabilities.

The issue of poor mathematics performance of students with disabilities underscores the need for focused attention on critical foundation skills that are prerequisites for success with higher levels of math at the secondary level, such as algebra (NMAP, 2008). For example, the NMAP recommended proficient performance with addition and subtraction of whole numbers by the end of third grade and proficiency with multiplication and division by the end of fifth grade. Specifically, students should possess "the automatic recall of addition and related subtraction facts, and of multiplication and related division facts" (p. 17). Unfortunately, all too often students with disabilities reach the secondary level

The work on this article was supported in part by a grant # R324B070164 from the U.S. Department of Education, Institute of Education Sciences. No official endorsement should be inferred.

ill-equipped on basic critical foundation skills. Yet, these students are often required to tackle curriculum that proves overwhelming to them because of the lack of mastery of concepts and skills on which more advanced mathematics (e.g., algebra) is based. Thus, high-quality instruction in solving arithmetic combinations must begin in earnest at the elementary level.

Arithmetic Combinations

In 2006, the National Council of Teachers of Mathematics published the *Curriculum Focal Points (CFPs) for Prekindergarten through Grade 8 Mathematics: A Quest for Coherence*, herein called the Focal Points, to provide guidance to school districts as they organize their curriculum standards. According to recommendations in the Focal Points, in the early grades, students should develop an understanding of the *meaning* of addition, subtraction, multiplication, and division. For example, students should be able to visually depict multiplication combinations by using area models, arrays, and number lines to construct multiplication situations before engaging in procedural activities that focus only on building fluency.

The Focal Points also include standards that focus on students learning effective strategies for solving arithmetic combinations to help develop fluent or automatic retrieval (i.e., quick recall) of the answers. Automaticity with arithmetic combinations is important because of the role it plays with more advanced mathematics, such as finding common multiples or solving algebraic equations that require factoring (Woodward, 2006). Also, quick retrieval of facts facilitates everyday living skills that involve making change, measuring for cooking purposes, computing distance and time, and so forth.

Difficulties with Arithmetic Combinations Related to Instruction

According to Siegler (2007), students with mathematics disabilities are "not only worse at retrieval of arithmetic facts, but also at understanding mathematical concepts, executing relevant procedures, choosing among alternative strategies, . . . and so forth" (pp. xix–xx). Difficulties with arithmetic combinations may stem from a variety of sources, including causes that are inherent to the individual (e.g., working memory, processing speed deficits). Empirical evidence supports the view that child-level variables can explain at least part of student performance in arithmetic combinations (Passolunghi & Siegel, 2001; H. L. Swanson & Beebe-Frankenberger, 2004). Instruction in math also plays an important role in determining students' mathematical achievement. For the purposes

of this chapter, because instruction is a more malleable factor, we chose to examine difficulties from an instructional perspective.

For many students with learning disabilities (LD) in mathematics, difficulties with fluent or automatic retrieval of arithmetic combinations may be linked to a variety of instructional issues. One issue is the insufficient development of fundamental understandings of whole numbers, the relationships among the four operations, and whole-number properties. For example, students may not understand the relationship between addition and subtraction (e.g., addition and subtraction as inverse operations, addition facts and related subtraction facts), and multiplication and division (e.g., multiplication and division as inverse operations, multiplication and related division facts). Lack of understanding of these inverse relationships limits the ability to recognize fact families (e.g., $3 + 7 = 10, 7 + 3 = 10, 10 - 7 = 3, 10 - 3 = 7$) as a strategy for solving arithmetic combinations.

Another issue that may hamper fluency or automatic retrieval is lack of understanding of the meaning of arithmetic properties. Students may have a limited understanding of the commutative (i.e., $A + B = B + A$; $A \times B = B \times A$) and associative (i.e., $[A + B] + C = A + [B + C]$; $[A \times B] \times C = A \times [B \times C]$) properties of addition and multiplication, and the distributive property (i.e., $A \times [B + C] = [A \times B] + [A \times C]$). Knowledge about these properties can help students solve more facts accurately (e.g., $5 \times 3 = 3 \times 5$) and derive answers more effectively for difficult problems (e.g., $4 \times 12 = 4 \times 10 + 4 \times 2 = 40 + 8 = 48$) (NRC, 2009). Lack of an understanding of whole-number properties hinders the ability to tackle harder arithmetic combinations strategically by using the properties to reason about how to efficiently and effectively solve problems (NRC, 2009).

Opportunities to learn, practice, and master effective and efficient fact strategies may be yet another instructional issue for students with mathematics disabilities. Students with mathematics disabilities do not master and become fluent in using efficient fact strategies such as more advanced counting strategies (e.g., Count-On strategy, described later in this chapter) and derived strategies (e.g., $9 + 6 = 9 + [1 + 5] = [9 + 1] + 5 = 10 + 5 = 15$) to solve addition, subtraction, multiplication, and division problems without focused practice and review to learn how to use the strategy correctly (Woodward & Rieth, 1997). For example, Geary (1990) found that students with mathematics difficulties did not differ significantly from typically achieving students in the *types* of strategies (e.g., counting on, use of fingers, verbal counting, retrieval) used to solve problems. Rather, students with mathematics difficulties made more errors in the *use* of these strategies than the typically achieving peer group. In sum, students with mathematics disabilities exhibit problems solving arithmetic combinations that may stem primarily from inadequate instruction. Thus, educators need to identify practices that are research based to improve student outcomes in solving arithmetic combinations.

The purpose of this chapter is to describe research-based instructional practices that are intended to promote accurate and fluent or automatic retrieval of arithmetic combinations when teaching students with LD. The studies we identified focus on intervention research that was conducted with students with LD. We think it is important to examine this body of literature to identify evidence-based intervention practices because students with LD typically exhibit difficulties learning arithmetic combinations. Thus, their teachers should employ practices that are grounded in the research. Also, although we just examined literature specific to students with LD, many other children with disabilities at the elementary and secondary level experience similar problems with mathematics; it is quite possible that the practices described in this chapter will benefit them as well.

Instructional Practices for Arithmetic Combinations

Overview, Rationale, and Supporting Theory

In this section, we briefly describe three empirically supported instructional practices—explicit practices, strategic practices, and the use of visual representations—to teach arithmetic combinations to students with LD, as well as discuss the underlying rationale and supporting theory for each approach.

Explicit Instructional Practices

Explicit instructional practices focus on a series of behavioral practices that are systematically implemented to teach mathematical ideas and procedures. A substantial body of research shows the effectiveness of systematic, explicit instruction for teaching computation to students with mathematical difficulties (S. Baker, Gersten, & Lee, 2002; NMAP, 2008; M. Stein, Kinder, Silbert, & Carnine, 2006). Explicit instructional practices are based on the behavioral theory of learning, which is linked to the early work of notable researchers such as Ivan Pavlov, B. F. Skinner, Edward Lee Thorndike, and John B. Watson. Early behavioral psychology studies focused on how behavioral changes were influenced by the arrangement of antecedents (i.e., classical conditioning) or how behavioral changes were effected by the arrangement of consequent events (i.e., operant conditioning) (Tawney & Gast, 1984). Applying the behavioral theory

of learning to education focuses on improving instructional behavior (e.g., increasing the number of facts computed correctly in a minute) by manipulating consequent events (e.g., providing reinforcement for improved academic or social performance). The influences of the behavioral theory of learning are found in educational research (e.g., H. L. Swanson, Hoskyn, & Lee, 1999) that has identified practices associated with explicit (direct) instruction that foster improved instructional performance. Additionally, the NMAP (2008) stressed that struggling students need explicit mathematics instruction on a consistent basis, particularly on foundation skills and conceptual knowledge. Thus, a teacher might use explicit instruction to teach an addition algorithm with regrouping by:

- Preteaching addition facts

- Preteaching place value concepts such as regrouping

- Modeling how to perform the algorithm by verbalizing the steps and providing an explanation of when and why it is necessary to regroup

- Providing examples illustrating when it is necessary to regroup and when it is not

- Carefully sequencing examples to show easier to more difficult problems with regrouping

- Providing multiple opportunities for students to practice

- Correcting errors immediately so students do not practice errors

- Monitoring student progress

An explicit approach to instruction includes important practices (e.g., modeling, high rates of responding and practice, repetition, error correction, review and distributed practice, frequent monitoring of performance) that help students with mathematics disabilities learn mathematical ideas. Consistent application of these practices is well supported in the research as necessary for struggling students (H. L. Swanson et al., 1999).

Strategic Instructional Practices

Strategic instructional practices focus on the rules and process of learning, including cognitive and meta-cognitive (e.g., self-regulatory) cues and the use of mnemonics for memory retention and retrieval (H. L. Swanson & Beebe-Frankenberger, 2004). Strategic instructional practices include a rationale for learning the strategy and specific steps to activate cognitive and meta-cognitive processes. Some evidence suggests that students with mathematics disabilities can benefit from learning strategies for solving arithmetic combinations with fluency (Woodward, 2006).

Strategic instructional practices are based on information processing theory, which focuses on how individuals perceive, encode, represent, store, and retrieve information (e.g., Sternberg, 1985). Regarding arithmetic combinations, individuals must possess efficient and effective strategies in order to retrieve the solutions to arithmetic combinations directly or automatically. By doing so, theoretically, this automaticity reduces the cognitive load (Sweller, 2005, p. 1) for learning higher-order mathematics skills. Moreover, the use of strategies promotes flexibility with numbers (Cumming & Elkins, 1999) and a knowledge base (Isaacs & Carroll, 1999) that can facilitate retention and retrieval (Woodward, 2006).

Use of Visual Representations

Visual representations are concrete or physical models and pictorial depictions that are intended to promote understanding of mathematical ideas. Examples include manipulatives, tallies, pictures, and number lines. Cramer, Post, and del Mas (2002) noted the importance of using multiple representations to help students develop mathematical understanding. Gersten, Beckmann, et al. (2009) explained that students' understanding of the relationships between visual representations and abstract symbols can strengthen their understanding of mathematical concepts. In their meta-analysis, Gersten, Chard, et al. (2009) found positive, moderate effects for the use of visual representations in mathematics instruction and positive effects on mathematics performance when the use of visual representations was paired with other instructional elements (e.g., systematic instruction) in computation. Thus, students should be taught how to visually represent mathematical ideas and to translate their representations into symbolic representations.

In the next section, we report on research studies investigating the application of explicit practices, strategic practices, and the use of visual representations to teach arithmetic combinations to students with LD. The discussion of research is organized into two sections: (a) studies on practices that promote the acquisition or learning of arithmetic combinations, and (b) studies on practices that promote the fluent or automatic responding of answers. In reviewing the literature, we found that researchers often combined practices in a study. So, for example, a study might include explicit instructional practices and visual representations to teach arithmetic combinations. We grouped the studies accordingly (e.g., explicit instructional practices and visual representations) and present findings from the studies in each section of this chapter. We also provide discussions of the specific instructional steps used in selected studies.

Research-Based Practices for the Acquisition of Arithmetic Combinations

Despite the importance of teaching arithmetic combinations (NCTM, 2006; NMAP, 2008) at the elementary level, we identified only nine studies that examined research-based instructional practices to help students with LD acquire or learn arithmetic combinations. We used a variety of strategies and criteria to identify studies. For example, we conducted a systematic search of psychological and educational databases (PsycINFO, Educational Resources Information Center [ERIC], and Academic Search Complete) published from 1990 to June, 2009. We examined peer-reviewed special education journals (e.g., *Exceptional Children, Journal of Learning Disabilities*) that frequently include articles of the type we were seeking. We were interested in studies that involved students with identified LDs and that focused on an intervention to teach arithmetic combinations to elementary-level students. Finally, the intervention had to include explicit instruction, strategic instruction, and/or visual representations as a major component of the intervention.

Across the nine studies, a total of 82 students with identified LD participated. The amount of time devoted to instructional practices to teach arithmetic combinations varied, with a low of eight sessions (Tournaki, 2003) to a high of 111 sessions (Mattingly & Bott, 1990). Not surprisingly, researchers designed studies that typically included a combination of instructional practices. Of the nine studies, most of the research included pairing the instructional practices. Explicit and strategic practices were paired (Beirne-Smith, 1991; Tournaki, 2003), as were explicit practices with visual representations (D. M. Williams & Collins, 1994). Studies with a combination of explicit and strategic practices with visual representations (C. A. Harris, Miller, & Mercer, 1995; D. Wood, Frank, & Wacker, 1998; Woodward, 2006) were also identified. Finally, the use of explicit practices only was found in two of the studies (Mattingly & Bott, 1990; Stading, Williams, & McLaughlin, 1996).

When examining the types of arithmetic combinations that were the focus of the studies, only Beirne-Smith (1991) and Tournaki (2003) taught addition combinations with sums 0 to 18; the remaining studies taught multiplication combinations, and one study included multiplication and division (Miller & Mercer, 1993). Missing from this group of studies was research on subtraction and more research on division combinations, which tend to be more difficult for students to master. Moreover, although teaching students the connections between the operations (addition and subtraction; multiplication and division) is a recommended practice (NCTM, 2009), none of the studies that we reviewed examined the practice of teaching combinations as fact families to help students with LD learn about the relationship between addition and related subtraction combinations, and multiplication and related division combinations. Although research is limited in the area of instructional practices that focus on explicit practices, strategic practices, and using visualizations, research findings overall hold promise for teaching students with LD arithmetic combinations (specifically, addition and multiplication).

Explicit Practices

We located two studies that focused solely on the use of explicit practices (not in combination with strategic practices or visual representation) to teach arithmetic combinations. Both studies focused on the teaching of multiplication. In the first study, Mattingly and Bott (1990) taught four students (two fifth graders, two sixth graders) in a resource room program. They examined the effects of a Constant Time Delay procedure as a means for teaching multiplication combinations 0 to 9 written on 3 × 5 index cards. Constant Time Delay involves the teacher presenting a task (reading a fact and saying the answer in this case) to the student and systematically increasing the time interval between the teacher's directions ("Read the problem. Say the answer.") and the prompt (reading the fact and saying the answer). The teacher provided the prompt systematically within a certain time frame. For example, given 3 × 4 and the teacher's directions, the student's answer should be "three times four equals twelve." The time interval for students to respond started with 0 seconds and was increased to 5 seconds between the teacher's directions and the prompt. In the 0-seconds condition, the teacher read the problem and said the answer. The goal was for the student to read the problem and state the answer within 5 seconds without a teacher prompt. Explicit practices that were used as part of the Constant Time Delay intervention included near-errorless learning, multiple opportunities to respond, and systematic prompting.

At the beginning of this multiple-probe, single-subject research study, 25 trials at 0-seconds delay were used with a continuous reinforcement system that involved giving a token for each correct answer. The criterion for mastery was 100% correct for three consecutive days. As part of the review process, mastered combinations were interspersed within the set of combinations to be learned to promote discrimination among learned arithmetic combinations. Under this condition, the criterion for mastery was 100% for two consecutive days. Results showed a high percentage of accuracy that continued in both the follow-up maintenance and generalization phases.

In another study that focused on multiplication, Stading and co-workers (1996) studied the effects of a Copy-Cover-Compare (CCC) technique for teaching ×2, ×3, ×4, and ×5 multiplication combinations with one third-grade girl with LD as part of home instruction using a single-subject multiple baseline across problem sets research design. During 15- to 20-minute sessions for 20 days, the student completed four new problems from one set (e.g., ×3) and reviewed previously taught combinations (e.g., ×2). A mixed probe (new and previously taught combinations presented together) was administered daily following the CCC technique. Explicit practices included a limited amount of instructional content taught at any one time, high rates of correct responding, immediate corrective feedback, and mixed review on the probe.

After the intervention, the student took a test (sheet of problems) with 16 multiplication combinations including the four most recently practiced and previously mastered combinations. Results from this test were part of the procedures for monitoring the student's progress with mastering sets of targeted combinations. Overall, results showed significant improvement at the conclusion of the acquisition phase of instruction from a mean of 35% correct during baseline to a mean of 100% correct after 20 days of instruction. No maintenance or generalization phases were identified.

Instructional steps for CCC.   The CCC technique followed a systematic, explicitly taught step-by-step procedure, which included having the student provide a written response to match to the model and a written response from memory. An error-correction system was also built into the technique (Stading et al., 1996). The student received four new multiplication combinations on flash cards to study before the implementation of the CCC technique. The following steps were used for the student to learn the combinations:

Step 1: Copy. The student was taught to look at the written multiplication combination, read the problem aloud, and provide the answer while copying the problem and answer.

Step 2: Cover. The student covered the problem and answer and then wrote the problem and answer again from memory.

Step 3: Compare. The student compared her written problem and answer to the original problem and answer.

Step 4: If the student was correct, she proceeded to the next problem and repeated the same steps. If the student was incorrect, she repeated the steps with the same problem (error correction).

Explicit and Strategic Practices

We identified two studies that examined the potential benefits of combining explicit and strategic practices for instructional purposes. In an experimental study, Beirne-Smith (1991) examined two methods in separate instructional groups along with a control, or no-treatment, group. The study took place in four schools (two urban and two rural) in self-contained classes. Twenty students with LD who were identified through a pretest (i.e., scored 60% or less on addition facts) were randomly assigned to the treatment condition; 10 students to Method A and 10 students to Method B. Also, an additional 10 students who scored below 60% on the pretest were randomly assigned to the no-treatment control group. The treatment group included students with a mean age of 8.7 and the control group had a mean chronological age of 8.5.

Method A, which included explicit practices and a Count-On strategy, was compared to Method B, which emphasized explicit practices combined with a rote memorization strategy. Sets of related combinations (e.g., first digit held constant and second digit increased by 1; e.g., $2 + 1, 2 + 2, 2 + 3$) were the instructional skill set for both methods. In Method A, combinations were systematically taught and the interrelationship of combinations was stated. That is, students were told that each combination started with a number (2, in our example) and the next quantity was added on. These procedures have been found successful when teaching students the Count-On strategy (Carnine & Stein, 1981). In Method B, the arithmetic combinations in the sets were presented randomly and no interrelationship was noted (i.e., the Count-On strategy was not demonstrated).

A cross-age peer-tutoring arrangement was used for instructional purposes. The pairs were matched based on scores on an arithmetic combinations test, so a stronger student without LD was paired with a student with LD who did not score as well on the test. Cross-age tutors were chosen to serve as "teachers" based on their scores of 80% or above on a pretest. Tutors were taught in two 45-minute sessions how to provide explicit instruction and either Method A (Count-On strategy) or Method B (rote memorization). Instruction occurred in 30-minute sessions. Students needed to earn five consecutive correct responses on all steps and tasks (different sets of related arithmetic combinations) for acceptable performance and advancement to the next task set. Then, the arithmetic combinations were mixed with previously learned arithmetic combinations for a review session.

Beirne-Smith (1991) found that students in the tutoring conditions (Method A and Method B) significantly outperformed students in the control group; yet no differences resulted between the two tutoring conditions.

Beirne-Smith suggested that the explicit practices, controlled materials, multiple opportunities to respond, high rates of repetition, error-correction procedures, reinforcement, and cumulative review (which were included in both methods) explained the lack of significant differences between the methods and the overall gains that exceeded the control condition.

Using a true experimental design with random assignment of participants to conditions, Tournaki (2003) also examined procedures that included explicit practices in a drill-and-practice group and strategic plus explicit practices in a Count-On group. These practices were very similar to those used by Beirne-Smith (1991) with the exception of the instructor. Eighty-four second-grade students participated in the study, 42 students with LD who had a mean age of 8.9 and 42 general education students with a mean age of 7.53. The ethnic groups represented in the school district included 75% European American, 13% African American, 10% Hispanic, and 2% Asian. One quarter of the students qualified for free/reduced lunch. The study was conducted in a classroom separate from the general education class.

Graduate research assistants (GRAs) demonstrated and verbalized (think aloud) the Count-On strategy; and the students also verbalized the strategy. The GRAs provided error correction immediately when mistakes were made. In the drill-and-practice group, neither demonstration nor verbalization was provided as part of instruction. Students were told to work as quickly as they could to complete the problems. The GRAs noted errors and asked the students to recompute the problems. The GRAs told students the answer if the correct solution was not provided. There were eight 15-minute sessions. Students moved from lesson to lesson after achieving 90% accuracy in 80 seconds. Tournaki's findings showed that students with LD in the Count-On strategy group outperformed their counterparts in the drill-and-practice (effect size of 1.5) and control (effect size of 1.35) groups when computing addition combinations. These differences were statistically significant, and the effect sizes represent meaningful differences between the treatment and control groups. These findings offer initial evidence in support of teaching students a counting strategy, such as Count-On, in combination with explicit practices to solve addition combinations.

Instructional steps for the Count-On strategy and explicit practices.   Beirne-Smith (1991), who used cross-age tutors as instructors, followed several steps in implementing the Count-On strategy with explicit instruction. In Method A, Counting On, the tutor first showed the tutee a file folder with the designated addition combinations with the answers and then turned over the file folder to show the combinations without the answers. The procedures included the following:

1. The tutor stated the Count-On rule: start with the bigger number, count on by the smaller number.

2. The tutor demonstrated how to apply the strategy to solve a combination using the Count-On strategy (e.g., for the problem 6 + 3, the teacher says "6 . . ., 7, 8, 9" while counting to 3 on her fingers).

3. The students in unison stated the rule and how to apply it.

4. The students took individual turns in using the steps.

5. Testing.

During testing, the tutor presented the flash-card sets, asking the tutee to read the problem and give the answer. Cards were shuffled and the process was repeated.

In Method B, which involved rote memorization, the tutor displayed the file folder with the combinations but without the answers. The tutor modeled how to say and answer the problems. The Count-On strategy was not taught. The file folder was removed from view, and the tutee was asked for answers to random problems within the task set. The tutee read the problems presented in random order and provided answers. Beirne-Smith's (1991) findings for the two tutoring groups, Method A and Method B, showed that they performed better than the control group but no significant differences existed in performance between the two methods. As noted, the use of the Count-On strategy was the difference between the two methods; explicit practices were used in both studies. One might conclude that using explicit practices for teaching combinations in and of itself is sufficient; however, findings from other studies (e.g., Tournaki, 2003; Woodward, 2006) show that the use of cognitive strategies (e.g., Count-On strategy) help students with LD learn arithmetic combinations.

Explicit Practices with Visual Representations

In examining the literature, one study was identified that investigated the use of explicit practices paired with visual representations for improving the acquisition of arithmetic combinations for students with LD. Using a single-subject, multiple-probe across groups of facts design, D. M. Williams and Collins (1994) compared two procedures, Constant Time Delay + Teacher-Selected Prompts and Constant Time Delay + Student-Selected Prompts, to teach $\times 6$, $\times 7$, and $\times 8$ multiplication combinations to four male students with LD. The four students were White and ranged in age from 9.6 years to 13.10 years; they received instruction in a self-contained day school.

The Constant Time Delay procedures were similar to those used by Mattingly and Bott (1990). The prompts (i.e., visual representations), which included poker chips, number lines, and fingers, were introduced to help students solve problems if they were not able to answer the problems correctly during the time-delay procedure. The two instructional conditions were teacher-selected prompt and student-selected prompt. During the teacher-prompt condition, if the student gave the wrong answer or did not provide an answer within 5 seconds, the teacher instructed the student to use a visual prompt. Instruction continued on the facts and involved the teacher's using a hierarchy of prompts from most to least intrusive across 9 days of instruction. The prompts included 3 days of chips, 3 days with the number line, and 3 days counting on fingers. In the student prompt condition, for incorrect or no responses within the designated 5-second time period, students could choose one of the three material prompts they wished to use.

The teacher taught a set of multiplication facts ($\times 6$, $\times 7$, $\times 8$) for 15-minute sessions five times per week for a total of 35 sessions. Students were not permitted to move to a new problem until giving a correct answer. Each student completed 30 trials per session.

Results showed that the time needed to reach criterion to move to another problem and the number of errors were less during the student-selected prompt condition, although no pattern was noted across the four students in choice of prompt and accuracy on probes. Three of four students performed above 90% correct on probes during the maintenance condition. Moreover, all of the students generalized knowledge of the target facts to two- and three-digit problems and to story problems. The findings demonstrated that although both conditions were effective, perhaps self-selection had some motivating appeal for students in this study.

Explicit and Strategic Practices with Visual Representations

We located two studies that focused on combining explicit practices, strategic practices, and using visual representations for acquisition of arithmetic combinations. In one study that used the combined practices, D. Wood, Frank, and Wacker (1998) used a multiple-baseline design across three 10-year-old students with LD to examine the effects of an instructional package on student performance in solving multiplication combinations $\times 0$ to $\times 9$. The school was located in a multiethnic district; two students in the study were White and one student was Black. All three students were identified as low socioeconomic status. The students were taught individually, separate from one another and the other students in the class.

Multiplication combinations were categorized as zeros, ones, doubles, fives, nines, and pegword (the remaining 18 combinations) facts. For instance, 4 × 4 was a double and belonged in the doubles group. Students were taught explicitly to say the steps for solving the arithmetic combinations in each group for facts. For example, for zeros facts, students were taught to look for a zero in the problem and then to write a 0 for the answer. For the ones facts, students were taught to look for a 1 in the problem, ignore it, and write the other number in the fact as the answer.

For doubles facts, real objects were introduced (e.g., skateboard has 2 sets of 2 wheels = 4 wheels, two toy octopi with 8 legs each = 16 legs) to illustrate the facts followed by pictures that depicted doubles. Students then practiced the double facts using flash cards with the mnemonic pictures. Participants were taught to solve five facts (e.g., 3 × 5) by counting by fives (e.g., 5, 10, 15). Students were taught to solve nine facts in three lessons. In the first lesson, they were taught to associate or link the numbers that add up to 9 (i.e., 1 and 8, 2 and 7, 3 and 6, 4 and 5). In the second lesson, they were taught to solve for the first digit of the answer by subtracting one from the number by which 9 is being multiplied. For example 9 × 6 = 5_, because 6 – 1 = 5. In the final lesson on nine facts, teachers provided instruction on solving for the second digit in the answer by adding the linked number. For example, 9 × 6 = 54 because 4 is linked with 5, which was identified in the previous step.

A pegword mnemonic strategy was used to teach the remaining 18 combinations. Pegwords are pictorial (visual) representations that are associated with key rhyming words for a particular item (see Scruggs & Mastropieri, 2013). D. Wood et al. (1998) provided the example of depicting an elf (pegword for 12) standing in a door (pegword for four) of a tree (pegword for three) to help students remember that 4 × 3 = 12. Students were first taught pegwords for numbers. For each combination, they were then presented with flash cards, then taught verbal elaborations to accompany the mnemonic (e.g., "an elf is in the door of the tree"), and finally solved the combinations by saying the verbal elaboration without the flash card.

A special education teacher administered the intervention for about two months with 20 to 40 minutes of instructional time per day in small groups. Results showed that during baseline one student scored 15% accuracy and two students scored 4% accuracy. At the end of the study, two students scored above 90% accuracy while one student scored 87% accuracy. Overall, results showed that all three students with LD made substantial gains from testing to intervention training and maintained a high percentage of accuracy. Moreover, as a result of the instructional package, "participants appeared to be more enthused about math instruction," resulting in multiplication assignments being "completed quickly and often chosen first, with few or no negative comments" (D. Wood et al., 1998, p. 336).

In another study that used combined practices, C. A. Harris and colleagues (1995) reported two simultaneously administered studies that evaluated the effectiveness of several instructional components on the math performance of students with LD when taught by their general education teachers. In one study, 12 students with LD and one student with emotional disturbance participated. All of the students were White. Nine of the 13 students were eligible for free/reduced lunch; their ages ranged from 7.11 to 9.6 years. In the other study, the 99 participants did not have disabilities; 83 were White, 15 were Black, and 1 was Hispanic. The ages ranged from 7.1 to 9.4, and of the 99 students, 42 qualified for free/reduced lunch.

Using a multiple-baseline design across three classes, multiplication combinations (×0 to ×9) were taught using a concrete-representational-abstract (CRA) instructional sequence, rule instruction (e.g., any number × 0 = 0; any number × 1 = the number), and the DRAW strategy (defined in the following section). The CRA sequence and the DRAW strategy have been previously validated (e.g., Miller & Mercer, 1993). C. A. Harris et al. (1995) were interested in knowing the effects of the intervention when taught in a larger group setting.

The CRA sequence began with concrete objects or manipulatives to develop conceptual understanding, including paper plates used to represent groups and plastic counting discs to show the objects in each group. At the visual representational level, the manipulatives were exchanged for pictures of boxes with dots or tallies to show the multiplication problems. After six lessons at the concrete and representational levels, the students moved to the abstract and symbolic level. Two mnemonic strategies were taught to help students remember how to solve the problems.

The DRAW strategy is a mnemonic intended to help students recall the steps of problem solution (DRAW). The strategy includes a mnemonic in which each letter of the word signals a procedure for students to follow (e.g., D = Discover the sign). The mnemonic features of the DRAW strategy are described in detail in the following section.

The CRA sequence used explicit practices along with concrete objects and pictures; rule instruction involved repetition; and the DRAW strategy was taught explicitly. A total of 21 lessons over 8 weeks were conducted with all participants (C. A. Harris et al., 1995). As part of each lesson, students independently completed a Learning Sheet with 10 problems; the lesson was retaught to students who did not achieve a score of at least 80% accuracy. Additional student progress-monitoring data included completion of a Multiplication Minute sheet under timed conditions throughout the study.

Instructional steps for the DRAW strategy. The lessons were teacher directed and included describing and modeling the process for solving the problems, providing guided practice and error correction, and having students complete 10 problems independently as part of monitoring their progress (C. A. Harris et al., 1995). When teaching students this strategy, the teacher (a) explained the purpose of the lesson; (b) modeled, using "think alouds," how to use the mnemonic to solve problems; and (c) taught students the mnemonic (i.e., "say the mnemonic, name the letters, and tell what action to do for each letter"). The DRAW strategy includes a semi-concrete component (i.e., draw). Teachers used the following steps to teach students the mnemonic strategy:

> **D** = Discover the sign (The student looks at the sign to figure out the operation.)
>
> **R** = Read the problem (The student says the problem aloud.)
>
> **A** = Answer or draw and check (The student thinks of the answer or draws tallies to solve the problem.)
>
> **W** = Write the answer. (The student writes the answer in the answer space.)

Once students set up the problem, they use DRAW to solve the computation. The goal is that students learn the mnemonic steps and apply them independently to successfully solve both multiplication and word problems. Findings showed that all students with LD improved their performance, ranging in improvement from 50 to 85 percentage points. When using the DRAW strategy, the students with LD performed similarly to their typically achieving peers on instructional probes.

Research-Based Practices for Building Fluent Responding with Arithmetic Combinations

In this section, we identify and describe the instructional practices—explicit practice, strategic practices, and visual representations—that researchers used to promote fluent or automatic retrieval of arithmetic combinations. Again, we found that researchers frequently combined instructional practices in their studies. Quick retrieval (i.e., fluent responding) of arithmetic combinations (i.e., addition and related subtraction combinations; multiplication and related division combinations) is a critical element of mathematics instruction and a foundation

skill for algebra success in later school years (Gersten, Beckmann, et al., 2009; NCTM, 2009; NMAP, 2008).

We located only three studies in this category. One study (McIntyre, Test, Cooke, & Beattie, 1991) focused on explicit practices and strategic practices; one study included explicit practices and visual representations (Miller & Mercer, 1993); and one study consisted of explicit practices, strategic practices, and visual representations (Woodward, 2006). A total of 21 elementary-level students participated in these three studies in three different settings (i.e., resource room, general education classroom, media center). Each of the studies included approximately 20 instructional sessions.

Explicit and Strategic Practices

Using a multiple-probe design, McIntyre et al. (1991) examined the effects of the Count-By strategy on fluency with multiplication combinations for which other strategies are not typically employed (i.e., $\times 4$, $\times 7$, $\times 8$) for one African American fourth-grade boy with LD. The Count-By technique is rooted in studies that examined effects of "attack" strategy training whereby students are taught procedures that can then be applied to the solving of multiplication problems (Lloyd, Saltzman, & Kauffman, 1981). The Count-By strategy was taught explicitly using the Model-Lead-Test procedure in which the teacher modeled the procedures, then guided or led the student through the steps, followed by the student performing the steps independently while being assessed. The student first practiced counting by one set of numbers until fluency (e.g., saying "4, 8, 12, 16, 20, 24, 28, 32, 36, 40" in 10 seconds or less). The student was then taught to turn a multiplication combination into a Count-By problem. For example, 7×4 would be solved by counting by 7 four times—7, 14, 21, 28. Practice consisted of oral and written responses. Then, a test was conducted (i.e., 1-minute timing of the combinations) to determine how many more combinations the student answered correctly during each timing. Overall, findings showed that it took the student nine sessions to learn the $\times 4$ facts, 11 sessions to learn the $\times 7$ facts, and 21 sessions to master the $\times 8$ facts. On the generalization test across time, the student improved from 6 digits per minute to 49 digits per minute on a test of all multiplication facts.

Explicit Practices and Visual Representations

Miller and Mercer (1993) examined the effect of a Concrete-Semiconcrete-Abstract (CSA) instructional sequence on the mathematics performance of addition arithmetic combinations with sums from 10 to 18 and division arithmetic combinations with quotients from 0 to 9 using a multiple-baseline across subjects design.

Six boys and three girls ranging in ages between 7.7 and 11.3 years were involved in this study; five students were identified as having LD, one student had developmental disabilities, and three students were at risk for LD. The students with disabilities received their instruction in resource rooms; the students were in first to fifth grade.

The CSA routine is the same as the CRA routine discussed earlier in this chapter (see C. A. Harris et al., 1995). The teacher taught ten 20-minute lessons. During the concrete phase, the teacher used various concrete materials (e.g., buttons, coins, popsicle sticks) as part of instruction to promote generalization of responding across objects. In the semi-concrete phase, students were taught to represent problems using drawings; the drawings were then replaced by the use of tally marks. In the abstract phase, students were instructed not to use drawings or tallies when solving problems.

One-minute timings were done each day to collect fluency data that included the number of correct and incorrect responses. Results indicated that all students demonstrated significant improvement at the abstract level (i.e., on daily 1-minute timings) as noted in increased correct rate and decreased error rate scores. Findings showed that students in this study required three to seven lessons in concrete and semi-concrete activities using manipulative devices and pictures before they could transfer their learning to a test sheet (e.g., correct responses per minute were higher than error responses per minute) that was at the abstract level.

Explicit and Strategic Practices with Visual Representations

In a true experiment, Woodward (2006) studied the effects of Integrated Strategy Instruction (i.e., strategies and timed practice drills) compared to Timed Practice Drills on student fluency with a range of multiplication combinations including common, hard, and extended (more than one digit) problems. The teacher provided instruction in the general education classroom for 25 minutes per day, 5 days per week, for 4 consecutive weeks. Fifty-eight students participated in the study; 15 students had identified LD. Participants were matched by pretest score, and one member of each pair was randomly assigned to either the integrated condition or the timed practice drills-only condition. Six boys with LD and two girls with LD, of which five were Black and three were White, were assigned to the integrated condition. In the timed practice drills-only condition, seven participants were classified as LD—four boys and three girls, three White and four Black. The average age was 9 years and 5.6 months.

The Integrated Strategy Instruction method included strategic and explicit practice with visual (pictorial) representations. Daily instruction consisted of teaching combinations using different strategies depending on the nature of the combinations. Rule-based strategies were taught for relatively simple combinations (i.e., perfect squares, 0s, 1s, 2s, 5s, 9s). More difficult problems were taught using derived and doubling approaches coupled with number lines or arrays (e.g., blocks). For example, using the derived approach, the answer for 6×7 was derived from the previously mastered problem 6×6 by breaking down 6×7 into $6 \times 6 + 6$. As represented on a number line, 6×6 was shown as a series of "hops" (i.e., hopping in increments of 6 from 6 to 12 to 18 and so on) to reach 36. Then 6×7 simply involves one additional hop of 6, showing the answer to be 42. Thus, students were taught explicitly to use their knowledge of one combination to find the answer to a more difficult combination (e.g., neighbors on the number line). The doubling and doubling again strategies also used students' knowledge of relatively basic multiplication and applied them to combinations that involve 4, 6, or 8 as a multiplier. For example, $4 \times 7 = 2 \times 7$ doubled (i.e., $14 + 14$). This can be represented on either a number line or with manipulatives during instruction. Strategies and corresponding combinations were introduced in order of difficulty.

Strategies were also included to extend students' understanding of solving single-digit multiplication combinations to combinations involving two- and three-digit numerals. Extended combination instruction consisted of linking number line knowledge of single-digit combinations to combinations with two- or three-digit multipliers. For example, knowledge of $4 \times 7 = 28$, represented by making 7 hops of 4 on the number line, was extended to the multidigit problem of $40 \times 7 = 280$ by making 7 hops of 40 on a number line in 10-digit increments. Similarly, using blocks, students' knowledge that $4 \times 2 = 8$, as represented by 2 sets of 4 blocks, was extended to $40 \times 2 = 80$ by showing two sets of four 10-block rows. More difficult multiplication combinations involving a one-digit multiplier and a two- or three-digit multiplier were taught using the partial product algorithm. This algorithm breaks down multiple-digit combinations into a series of combinations that the students can solve based on their previously learned strategies. For example, 6×387 can be broken down into $6 \times 7 + 6 \times 80 + 6 \times 300$, all of which students had been taught to solve.

In the timed practice drills-only condition, instruction focused on teaching facts using explicit practices. Daily instruction consisted of teachers eliciting choral responses to teach new combinations (e.g., "7 times 3 is 21. What is 7 times 3?") or review previously taught combinations (e.g., "3 times 4 is what?"). Combinations were taught using a hierarchical approach from easiest to hardest facts (e.g., $\times 2$ facts to $\times 8$ facts). Instruction also involved students completing computation sheets using traditional computation algorithms to solve previously taught math combinations.

Findings showed that both interventions were effective in helping students to achieve fluency with multiplication combinations. Although the study found no differences between the two groups' performance on the difficult multiplication combinations, students in the integrated strategy instruction group did better than students in the timed practice drills-only group on the extended combinations. Furthermore, students' scores in the integrated strategy instruction group remained at mastery level from post-test to maintenance, whereas students in the timed practice drills-only group did not.

Instructional steps for the integrated strategy instruction method and timed practice drills-only method. The two methods involved the following steps:

Method 1: Daily Instruction in the Integrated Strategy Condition

1. *Phase 1:* Students were introduced to a new strategy or reviewed previously taught strategies. Overheads or number lines were used as visuals. Students were encouraged to discuss the strategy and contrast it to previously taught strategies.

2. *Phase 2:* Students completed a 2-minute timed practice drill. Teacher dictated answers following the drill. Students circled any incorrect answers and wrote correct response. When 70% of students in the class achieved 90% or greater on the drill, the teacher moved to the next skill.

3. *Phase 3:* Students extended and applied their knowledge of the strategies taught in Phase 1 in different ways. On some days, students were taught the relationships between one-digit problems and extended multiplication combinations through number lines and manipulatives (e.g., blocks). On other days, the partial product algorithm was taught (e.g., $243 \times 6 = 6 \times 3 = 18, 6 \times 40 = 240, 6 \times 200 = 1,200; 18 + 240 + 1,200 = 1,458$). Approximation and rounding were taught using number lines on some days. And on other days students completed word problems as a class.

Method 2: Timed Practice Drills Only

1. Students were introduced to or reviewed previously introduced combinations (no strategy instruction took place) in teacher-directed instruction. The teacher introduced combinations and answers, followed by students repeating combinations and answers chorally.

2. Students completed 2-minute timed practice drill in the same manner as the integrated instruction.

3. Students completed worksheet practice on computational problems.

Summary and Directions for Future Research

Summary of the Instructional Practices

We located nine studies for teaching arithmetic combinations to students with LD. We identified only three studies for teaching fluency. In terms of the instructional practices, the findings reinforce extensive previous research (e.g., the importance of *explicit practices* as part of an intervention to teach arithmetic combinations to students with LD). All 10 studies included the following hallmark characteristics of explicit practices: modeling, high rates of responding and practice, repetition, error correction, review and distributed practice, and frequent monitoring of performance. These practices are well documented as effective in promoting mathematics performance in students with LD and low achievement (S. Baker et al., 2002; Bryant, Bryant, Gersten, Scammacca, & Chavez, 2008; Bryant, Bryant, Gersten, Scammacca, Funk, & Winter, 2008; Gersten, Beckmann, et al., 2009). Moreover, 6 of the 10 studies also included *strategic practices* (e.g., Count-On strategy for addition arithmetic combinations, DRAW to cue memory for multiplication procedures, Count-By strategy for multiplication arithmetic combinations) for prescribed sets of related arithmetic combinations, which were effective in promoting student performance related to acquisition and fluency.

This combined instructional focus, explicit practices and strategic practices, has been documented as most effective when teaching students with LD (H. L. Swanson et al., 1999). Yet, interestingly, findings were mixed when examining strategic practices compared to timed drills/ rote memorization. Beirne-Smith (1991) found that although students in the strategy and rote memorization conditions did better than the control group, no differences were noted between the two methods. However, in Tournaki's (2003) study, students in the strategy condition did better than students in the timed drill condition. And Woodward (2006) found that although students in the integrated strategies condition did better than students in the timed drill condition in both mastery and maintenance, no differences were found between groups for the harder combinations.

Finally, results across studies showed that *visual representations* were important for students to acquire, master, and develop fluency in arithmetic combinations. However, because the studies combined visual representations with other practices (e.g., explicit, strategic), it is not possible to determine which specific practices might be more or less beneficial. More research that involves unpacking multicomponent interventions to test the effectiveness of visual representations appears warranted.

Limitations and Directions for Future Research

First, the overall sample size across the studies was relatively small, and most of the studies occurred in special education settings. Moreover, with the exception of two studies (Tournaki, 2003; Woodward, 2006), all of the studies were conducted in the 1990s. Clearly, given that most students with LD who are struggling with mathematics now receive their instruction in general education settings, more studies are needed in the general education setting with interventions delivered by a general education teacher alone or by a pair of co-teachers.

Second, missing from this review was research on the effect of these practices when teaching subtraction and division arithmetic combinations. Research that examines the effects of teaching both subtraction and addition, as well as both division and multiplication, is needed. Students must conceptually understand inverse operations to help them see and make connections across mathematical concepts.

Third, it is widely accepted practice and expected in intervention research that sufficient information about participants is provided to demonstrate that they have the learning problems presented; thus, the procedures for how districts identified students as having LD (or other disabilities) is necessary. The participants must be described with sufficient detail to allow replication of the study. Information such as age, gender, ethnicity, primary language, and achievement is necessary to better understand the characteristics of the participants (Gersten et al., 2005; Horner et al., 2005; Rosenberg et al., 1992). Inclusion of these participant characteristics varied across the articles, and information about primary language was absent in all of the studies. Thus, the degree to which findings apply to English Language Learners is unclear and should be investigated in future research.

Conclusion

Robinson, Menchetti, and Torgesen (2002) proposed that instruction for students with poor mastery of arithmetic combinations should include providing interventions that develop conceptual knowledge of the four operations and fluent retrieval of answers to arithmetic combinations. Additionally, students must have ample time and opportunity to practice the strategies to develop meaning as well as fluency (NCTM, 2009). In sum, the overall findings from the studies in this chapter support and reconfirm the effectiveness of *explicit practices, strategic practices,* and *visual representations* when teaching arithmetic combinations (specifically addition and multiplication) to students with LD in mathematics. Not only must students master combinations, they must also be able to automatically retrieve answers to basic combinations. In closing, this chapter was not an exhaustive review of effective practices for promoting acquisition, mastery, and automatic retrieval of arithmetic combinations for students with mathematics disabilities at the elementary level. Certainly, findings from other studies (e.g., computer-based technology, early elementary "prevention" studies) can provide a more comprehensive view of effective instructional practices for students who struggle with mathematics. The findings from studies in this chapter, however, do shed important light on ways to help students with LD become more proficient in foundation skills.

CHAPTER 7

Strategies for Improving Student Outcomes in Mathematics Reasoning

Asha K. Jitendra | *University of Minnesota*

Marjorie Montague | *University of Miami*

"All young Americans must learn to think mathematically, and they must think mathematically to learn."

(National Research Council, 2001, p.1)

*T*he centrality of mathematical reasoning is clear, as indicated in the National Council of Teachers of Mathematics' (NCTM) *Principles and Standards for School Mathematics* (NCTM, 2000):

> Being able to reason is essential to understanding mathematics. By developing ideas, exploring phenomena, justifying results, and using mathematical conjectures in all content areas and—with different expectations of sophistication—at all grade levels, students should see and expect that mathematics makes sense. . . . Systematic reasoning is a defining feature of mathematics. (pp. 56–57)

Learning mathematics goes beyond recalling facts and fluency with algorithms to mathematical reasoning and critical reflection. Yet despite 20 years of research and reform in mathematics education emphasizing students' thinking and reasoning, many students continue to engage in rote thinking (J. Hiebert, 2003; Lithner, 2008; National Research Council, 2001) and are often "unprepared for complex and novel problem solving" (Nathan & Kim, 2009, p. 91). Students with disabilities, in particular, experience difficulties employing effective problem-solving

strategies in making sense of mathematical situations (Jitendra, 2008).

Traditional forms of instruction that focus on getting the correct answer to word problems using the key-word strategy, for example, exacerbate the problems these children experience in applying mathematical skills in flexible ways to solve novel problems. Consider the following problem:

> "One morning, Maya was cleaning out her bookshelves in her room and decided to give away 12 books from her collection of Babysitter's Club to her cousin, Tanya. That afternoon, she gave away 20 of her books. How many books did she **give away** that day?"

Keisha, a third-grade student, solved the problem by using the key-word method. Her answer was eight books, because she reasoned that the key word *give away* implies subtraction as the operation. In this example, rather than engaging in sophisticated mathematical reasoning, Keisha applied a simple, rote procedure that ignores the meaning and structure of the problem. In the situation above, the rule associating the key word with the operation is misleading; thus, use of the key-word approach would not result in successful problem solving.

In fact, "mathematical reasoning is no less than a basic skill" (Ball & Bass, 2003, p. 28). Students must be able to verbalize their reasoning processes and explanations as well as critically reflect on their understanding of the underlying concepts. Toward this end, teaching all students, including students with disabilities, complex mathematical reasoning and critical reflection is of great importance. At the same time, it is important to address learner characteristics and scaffold instruction for students with disabilities, who may have memory and conceptual difficulties, background knowledge deficits, linguistic and vocabulary difficulties, strategy knowledge and use difficulties, and self-regulation problems (S. K. Baker, Simmons, & Kame'enui, 1995).

In the sections that follow, we review two practices—schema-based instruction (SBI) and cognitive strategy instruction (CSI)—that research has shown to be highly effective in facilitating mathematical reasoning of higher-order problem-solving skills for students with disabilities. For the purpose of this chapter, we define reasoning as "the line of thought adopted to . . . reach conclusions in task [problem] solving" (Lithner, 2008, p. 257).

Schema-Based Instruction

Schemata are hierarchically organized, cognitive structures that are acquired and stored in long-term memory. According to schema theory, the acquisition of the problem schema, or semantic structure of the problem, is critical to successful problem solving (Sweller, Chandler, Tierney, & Cooper, 1990). Working memory load during cognitive processing is reduced when recognizing a problem's schema, because multiple elements of information are grouped into and conceptualized as a single schema (Kalyuga, 2006). Although the initial acquisition of problem schemata requires working memory resources, with practice the use of schemata becomes automated and requires minimal working memory resources (Kalyuga, 2006).

In the domain of arithmetic word problems, the most comprehensive set of schemata described in the relevant literature include Change, Group, Compare, Restate, and Vary (Marshall, 1995). These schemata are separated into two problem categories, additive and multiplicative structures. Change, Group, and Compare problems belong to the additive field in that the solution operation is either addition or subtraction; the multiplicative field involves Restate (i.e., Multiplicative Compare) and Vary (i.e., Equal Groups and Proportion) problems, because the solution operation is either multiplication or division (Christou & Philippou, 1999). Solving word problems requires mentally representing the different elements described in the problem text. Therefore, the difficulty of the problem may be a function of the difficulty in understanding the problem situation.

Our instructional model uses schema training to focus students' attention on the problem schema (e.g., Change, Compare) and helps them represent the relations between the different elements described in the text using schematic diagrams (e.g., Hegarty & Kozhevnikov, 1999; Janvier, 1987). Unlike pictorial representations of problems that include concrete but irrelevant details, which "are superfluous to solution of the math problem" (Edens & Potter, 2006, p. 186), a schematic diagram depicts the spatial relations between objects in the problem text (Hegarty & Kozhevnikov, 1999). The nature of representations in our SBI model not only facilitates recognition of the problem schema (e.g., Compare) and organization of problem schema knowledge, but also emphasizes information (nonmathematical) contained in the situation model (Van Dijk & Kintsch, 1983). The situation model "is a temporary structure stored in working memory [that] . . . corresponds to a level of representation that specifies the agents, the actions, and the relationships between the events in everyday contexts" (Thevenot, Devidal, Barrouillet, & Fayol, 2007, p. 44).

Given that many students with disabilities, especially learning disabilities (LD), lack skills to translate word problems, SBI focuses on comprehending the sentences (nonmathematical information) in word problems, especially sentences that express a relation between two quantities. For example, consider the following problem:

> Music Mania sold 56 CDs last week. It sold 29 fewer CDs last week than this week. How many CDs did it sell this week?

(Jitendra, 2007, p. 118). Instruction in SBI emphasizes that compare words such as "fewer than" in this problem can cue the learner to the schemata (e.g., Compare) and identify the key comparison or relational sentence as, "*It (Music Mania) sold 29 fewer CDs last week than this week.*" Further, SBI teaches that the comparison sentence can help the student figure out the two things compared (i.e., number of CDs sold last week and number of CDs sold this week) as well as identify the bigger quantity in the problem. Students trained in SBI would then deduce that the bigger quantity is the number of CDs sold this week, because the number of CDs sold last week is *fewer than* the number of CDs sold this week. In addition, SBI instruction would focus on the need to determine the difference between the two things being compared in the comparison sentence. Finally, information in the remaining verbal text specifies the known and unknown quantities for the two things compared necessary to solve the problem.

Successful problem solvers can translate and integrate information in the problem into a coherent mental representation that mediates problem solution (Mayer, 1999; Mayer & Hegarty, 1996). For students with LD, teaching them to represent the situation described in the problem using schematic diagrams is critical to reduce working memory resources. The use of schematic representations as a means to identify the underlying structure of problems is a key recommendation in the practitioner literature on Response to Intervention (RtI) in mathematics (Gersten, Beckman, et al., 2009). At the same time, helping students with LD collectively use language and representations to reason and solve problems is of great importance (Hegarty, Mayer, & Monk, 1995). As Ball and Bass (2003) argued, "these things [mathematical reasoning and solving problems] need to be taught and learned if they are to be known" (p. 40). In sum, SBI focuses on teaching students to comprehend the problem, represent the problem, plan to solve the problem using appropriate strategies, and reflect on the solution. Teachers therefore play an important role in scaffolding the use of problem-solving processes (e.g., representing, reasoning) via "think alouds." Following is a description of how SBI in conjunction with self-questioning to monitor the learning process can be used to help students develop mathematical reasoning in solving word problems (e.g.,Compare).

Teaching Problem Solving and Mathematical Reasoning with SBI

The SBI intervention described here is based on our work with elementary school students with learning difficulties (see Jitendra, 2007). In our word problem-solving program, we have used a four-step strategy to anchor student learning, called FOPS:

> F—Find the problem type
>
> O—Organize the information in the problem using the diagram
>
> P—Plan to solve the problem
>
> S—Solve the problem

The teacher uses a checklist based on the strategy steps to scaffold the cognitive processes as she thinks aloud to solve word problems (see Jitendra, 2007). See Figure 7.1 for a checklist for applying FOPS to a Compare problem.

Figure 7.1 A checklist for applying FOPS to a compare problem checklist.

COMPARE PROBLEM CHECKLIST

Step 1. Find the problem type

☐ Did I read and retell the problem?

☐ Did I ask if it is a compare problem? (Did I look for compare words – taller than, shorter than, more than, less than?)

Step 2. Organize information using the compare diagram

☐ Did I underline the comparison sentence or question and circle the two things compared?

☐ Did I reread the comparison sentence or question and ask, "Which is the LARGER amount and the SMALLER amount?" and write names of things compared in the diagram?

☐ Did I underline important information, circle numbers and labels, and write numbers and labels in the diagram?

☐ Did I write a "?" for what must be solved? (Did I find the question sentence?)

Step 3. Plan to solve the problem

☐ Do I add or subtract? (If the "Total" or "Whole" is given, subtract. If the "Total" or "Whole" is not given, add.)

☐ Did I write the math sentence?

Step 4. Solve the problem

☐ Did I solve the math sentence?

☐ Did I write the complete answer?

☐ Did I check if the answer makes sense?

Given the question of how many CDs Music Mania sold this week (described earlier), the teacher identifies the problem type using Step 1 of the strategy by reading, retelling, and examining information in the problem to recognize it as a Compare problem via self-instructions (e.g., Are there compare words in the problem that tell me about a comparison? Does the *comparison* statement tell what the problem is comparing?). In addition, the teacher makes the connection between previously solved problems (e.g., Change, Group) by noting that this problem differs from a Group problem solved earlier, because the problem compares two distinct, disjoint sets (i.e., last week's sale of CDs and this week's sale of CDs) that are not combined into a new, pooled set. In contrast, Group problems involve two disjoint sets (e.g., red crayons, blue crayons) that combine to make a new set (i.e., red and blue crayons). It is also unlike a Change problem, in which a permanent change occurs over time in the starting quantity when a direct or implied action causes an increase or decrease of that quantity to result in a changed quantity (e.g., Toshi had 56 CDs in her music collection. Then her brother borrowed 29 of her CDs. How many CDs does Toshi have now?).

For Step 2, the teacher demonstrates how to organize information using the schematic diagram. This step includes self-instructions to read the problem to identify critical information and represent it using the appropriate schematic diagram. For example, questions such as, "What does this problem compare?" (i.e., number of CDs sold last week and number of CDs sold this week) and "What does the comparison sentence tells us about?" (i.e., the difference between the number of CDs sold last week to number of CDs sold this week), are used to make sense of the problem schema. Specifically, the questioning makes clear the difference amount (i.e., 29), which is first represented in the diagram followed by reading the comparison sentence to find the bigger and smaller sets and writing the terms associated with those sets (i.e., this week's sales of CDs is the bigger set, and last week's sales is the smaller set). Next, the quantities for each of the two sets are identified by reading the problem text and writing the given amount(s) or a "?" for what must be solved in the diagram. The teacher then analyzes the problem situation using the completed diagram in Figure 7.2 as follows: "This week's sales of CDs is more than last week's sales of 56 CDs. The difference between this week's sales and last week's sales is 29 CDs. We need to solve for the number of CDs sold this week."

Step 3 involves translating the information in the diagram into a number sentence. During this step, students also learn to discriminate between instances when addition or subtraction is appropriate based on whether or not the whole (i.e., total) is known. In this instance, students learn that the bigger quantity is the whole, which is unknown. The teacher models using self-instructions by asking, "Do I add or subtract to solve for the '?' or the whole?" The teacher reasons that addition would be the operation, because the whole (bigger amount) is the sum of the parts (smaller amount and difference amount). Then, the teacher writes the number sentence: $56 + 29 = ?$

Finally, Step 4 has the students solve the problem using the operation identified in Step 3, justify the derived solutions using the schema features as anchors for explanations and elaborations, and check the accuracy of not only the computation but also the representation. The following provides an illustration of a teacher modeling the mathematical reasoning to make sense of the answer:

> Let's see . . . the number of CDs sold this week is 85 and the number of CDs sold last week is 56. This seems right, because the number of CDs sold this week (85) should be more than the number of CDs (56) sold last week. So, the answer 85 CDs sold this week, which is more than 56 CDs sold last week, seems right. I will also check the answer by subtracting: $85 - 56 = 29$, which is the difference amount.

In sum, SBI encourages student think alouds to monitor and direct problem-solving behavior along the following dimensions: (a) problem comprehension

Figure 7.2 Sample compare schematic diagram.

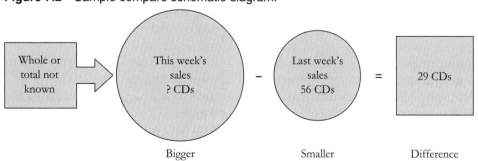

Source: From *Solving Math Word Problems: Teaching Students with Learning Disabilities Using Schema-Based Instruction* (p. 118), by A. K. Jitendra, 2007, Austin, TX: PRO-ED. Copyright 2007 by PRO-ED, Inc. Reprinted with permission.

(e.g., "Did I read and retell the problem to understand what is given and what must be solved?" "Why is this a Compare problem?" "How is this problem similar to or different from ones I already solved?"), (b) problem representation (e.g., "What diagram can help me adequately represent information in the problem to show the relation between quantities?"), (c) planning (e.g., "How can I set up the number sentence? What operation can I use to solve this problem?"), and (d) problem solution (e.g., "Does the answer make sense?" "How can I verify the solution?") (see Jitendra et al., 2007, 2009).

Research Evidence in Support of SBI

Since the 1990s, researchers have investigated the effectiveness of SBI to help students struggling in mathematics solve arithmetic and algebra word problems. These investigations have typically involved schema-based instruction or external modeling emphasizing the semantic structure of problem types (L. S. Fuchs, Seethaler, et al., 2008; Hutchinson, 1993; Jaspers & Van Lieshout, 1994; Jitendra et al., 1998, 2007, 2009; Jitendra, DiPipi, & Perron-Jones, 2002; Jitendra & Hoff, 1996; Jitendra, Hoff, & Beck, 1999; Y. P. Xin, 2008; Y. P. Xin, Jitendra, & Deatline-Buchman, 2005; Y. P. Xin, Wiles, & Lin, 2008; Zawaiza & Gerber, 1993) and schema-broadening instruction focusing on transfer (SBI-T) (L. S. Fuchs, Fuchs, et al., 2008; L. S. Fuchs, Fuchs, Finelli, Courey, & Hamlett, 2004; L. S. Fuchs, Fuchs, Hamlett, & Appleton, 2002; Owen & Fuchs, 2002). Although SBI-T, not unlike SBI, teaches students to recognize problems as belonging to specific problem types (e.g., Shopping List, Half, Buying Bags, Pictograph), the problem types are not based on the common set of schemata for arithmetic word problems (e.g., Change, Group, Compare, Multiplicative Compare, Equal Groups) described in the literature (Marshall, 1995). In addition, SBI-T focuses on transfer by teaching students to search novel problems for familiar problem types that may seem different based on different format, different key vocabulary, additional or different question, and irrelevant information. A total of 758 students participated in these studies, including students with LD and students with mild intellectual disabilities, as well as students who were English Language Learners (ELLs) and students without disabilities struggling in mathematics. Students ranged in age from 8-10 to 26-7 years. SBI research focused on elementary, middle, and high school students; SBI-T research focused primarily on elementary school students.

Schema-Based Instruction

The early work on schema training focused on modeling the semantic structure of arithmetic word problems using a number line (Zawaiza & Gerber, 1993) or concrete materials (Jaspers & Van Lieshout, 1994) and emphasized schema development by embedding metacognitive strategy instruction to represent and solve algebra word problems (Hutchinson, 1993). SBI that emphasized modeling the semantic structure of word problems using schematic diagrams was studied extensively by Jitendra and colleagues in a series of single-subject and randomized controlled group design studies examining mathematical problem solving for elementary and middle school students. For example, in two single-subject studies (Jitendra & Hoff, 1996; Jitendra et al., 1999), students with LD who were provided SBI intervention in solving addition and subtraction problems involving Change, Group, and Compare not only demonstrated improved word problem-solving performance (mean increase ranged from 47% to 69%), but also maintained their problem-solving performance 2 to 4 weeks following the intervention. Further, transfer effects from one-step to two-step problems were seen for three of the four middle school students in the Jitendra et al. (1999) study. Interestingly, the mean gains on one-step problems for all four students were comparable to those for a normative sample of third graders. However, the mean performance on two-step word problems was substantially higher for students with LD trained in SBI (71% correct) compared to the normative sample (28% correct).

While these two studies suggested that SBI is a potentially promising approach for improving the word problem solving of students with LD, other studies by Jitendra et al. (1998, 2007) used randomized controlled trials to validate its effectiveness for elementary school students with disabilities (e.g., LD, intellectual disabilities, emotional and behaviorial disorders [EBDs]) and students at risk for poor problem-solving outcomes. Results of the Jitendra et al. (1998) study showed that students in the SBI group not only scored significantly higher than the control group, but also performed at the same level as average-achieving students on math problem-solving post-tests. Further, results revealed transfer effects to novel problems for students in the SBI group. Effects sizes comparing SBI with the control condition were $d = 0.65$ at post-test, $d = 0.81$ at delayed post-test, and $d = 0.74$ for generalization, all medium-to-large effect sizes.

Jitendra et al. (2007) improved on the SBI approach by embedding metacognitive strategy instruction, described earlier, in a study conducted in five third-grade classrooms ($N = 88$ students) in a high-poverty elementary school with a sample of mostly low-achieving students, including students with LD, students who were ELLs, and Title I math students. General education teachers provided all instruction during their regularly scheduled mathematics class. Results suggested that SBI was more effective than typical classroom instruction in improving students' mathematical problem-solving skills (post-test: $d = 0.52$; 6-week delayed post-test: $d = 0.69$). Moreover, students in the SBI group outperformed the comparison group on the state assessment of mathematics performance ($d = 0.65$).

The next set of studies by Jitendra and colleagues extended this work on SBI to the domain of multiplication and division word problem solving involving Multiplicative Compare and Proportion problems. In a single-subject research study, Jitendra et al. (2002) found that four middle school students with LD who received SBI not only improved their word problem-solving performance on both problem types (mean improvement ranged from 50% to 71%), but also maintained their performance 2 to 10 weeks following the end of the intervention and generalized to more complex problems, including multistep problems. Y. P. Xin et al. (2005) and Jitendra et al. (2009) further validated the effects of SBI using randomized controlled trials. Y. P. Xin et al. (2005) worked with 22 students with LD, behavior disorders, and students at risk for poor problem-solving outcomes. Results showed that students receiving SBI significantly outperformed a comparison group on an immediate post-test ($d = 1.69$), delayed post-tests ($d > 2.50$), and a transfer test ($d = 0.89$) that included items from standardized mathematics achievement tests.

Jitendra et al. (2009) provided professional development on SBI to seventh-grade general education teachers in preparation for using SBI as part of the curriculum on ratios and proportions. Students were taught the concepts of ratio and rate and also how to solve proportion word problems using multiple solution methods (e.g., unit rate, equivalent fractions, cross multiplication). Seventh graders from eight classrooms in one middle school ($n = 148$) in a large, urban school district participated in a 10-day intervention. The students who received SBI instruction outperformed students in the comparison classrooms on the problem-solving post-test ($d = 0.45$) and on a 4-month delayed post-test ($d = 0.56$). Thus, the research conducted by Jitendra and colleagues suggests that SBI is effective for solving various types of math problems (2009).

Other research teams have also investigated the impact of SBI on students' problem-solving performance. For example, Xin and colleagues (Y. P. Xin, 2008; Xin et al., 2008; Xin & Zhang, 2009) modified SBI by using schematic diagrams and word-problem story grammar instruction to test what they term "conceptual model-based problem solving" to improve student learning. This series of single-subject design studies showed promising results for studies of Equal Groups, Multiplicative Compare, and Part-Part-Whole (e.g., Group) problems. L. S. Fuchs, Seethaler, et al. (2008) and L. S. Fuchs et al.

(2009) tested the efficacy of schema training on the math problem-solving performance of third-grade students with math and reading difficulties. In these studies, the intervention not only focused on recognizing addition/subtraction word problem types, but also emphasized "transfer solution methods to problems that include irrelevant information, 2-digit operands, missing information in the first or second position in the algebraic equation, or relevant information in charts, graphs, and pictures" (p. 155). Results of the study by L. S. Fuchs, Seethaler, et al. (2008) conducted with 35 participants indicated that the schema-training group made significantly greater gains when compared to the control group at post-test ($d = 1.80$), although transfer to a standardized math word problem was not evident.

L. S. Fuchs et al. (2009) extended their research on SBI to evaluate whether difficulties in mathematics only or a combination of reading and math difficulties differentially impact word problem-solving learning. Across two sites, the authors stratified the 133 participants by mathematics disability status and randomly assigned them to three conditions: number combinations tutoring, word problem-solving tutoring (i.e., SBI), and control (no tutoring). Both tutoring groups outperformed the control group on number combinations ($d = 0.55$) and word problem-solving skills ($d = 0.62$); differences between tutoring groups were not significant.

Schema-Broadening Instruction Focusing on Transfer

L. S. Fuchs and colleagues validated the effectiveness of SBI-T for elementary students with LD, intellectual disabilities, or at risk for poor problem-solving outcomes in four randomized controlled studies. In all four studies, the control-condition group received instruction from a district-adopted mathematics textbook. Results of the study by L. S. Fuchs et al. (2002) conducted with 40 students with mathematics disabilities indicated that both the problem-solving tutoring group and problem-solving tutoring plus computer-assisted practice group showed significantly greater math problem-solving scores on the post-test as well as on transfer tests than students in the computer-assisted practice only and control groups (d ranged from 0.83 to 2.10).

Owen and Fuchs (2002) worked with 24 students with LD, intellectual disabilities, speech and language disorders (SLDs), or attention deficit hyperactivity disorder (ADHD) to examine the differential effects of problem-solving treatments compared to a control condition on solving one-step word problems involving "half" problems (e.g., "Every day Tony spends 8 hours at school. Yesterday he got sick and had to go home after 1/2 of the school day. How many hours was he at school?"). Students in the acquisition treatment condition received a six-step method that included drawing circles to represent the given number and distributing circles evenly into each half of a rectangle over 4 days. Students in the low-dose acquisition + transfer condition received both acquisition instruction (an abbreviated dose of instruction over 2 days) and instruction on how to transfer skills to solve novel problems. The full-dose acquisition + transfer condition was the same as the low-dose acquisition condition, except for the duration of the acquisition instruction (which occurred over 4 days, as in the acquisition condition). Effect sizes comparing the treatment groups with the control condition showed that the full-dose acquisition + transfer condition outperformed the other groups (d ranged from 0.93 to 1.63). This study showed that a combination of problem-solving instruction and transfer instruction was more effective than either component alone.

Similarly, L. S. Fuchs et al. (2004) compared the differential effects of SBI-T, expanded SBI-T, and a control condition with 30 students with disabilities. SBI-T involved teaching solution rules for solving similar problem types and emphasized transfer skills (identifying similar problem structure by searching for superficial changes such as cover story, quantities); expanded SBI-T focused additionally on challenging problem features (e.g., irrelevant information, combining problem types, combining superficial problem features). Results indicated significant improvement in math problem solving for students in the treatment groups compared to the control group on all four transfer problem-solving measures (d ranged from 1.28 to 1.76 for expanded SBI-T and from 1.03 to 2.02 for SBI-T).

A recent study by L. S. Fuchs, Fuchs, and colleagues (2008) with 243 at-risk students for poor problem-solving outcomes supported the added value of supplemental SBI-T instruction (d ranged from 1.34 to 1.52) to either classroom SBI-T or conventional classroom instruction on a range of proximal (d ranged from 0.23 to 1.52) and distal (d ranged from 0.23 to 0.49) measures of word problem solving. In addition, on proximal measures of word problem solving, students at risk who received only supplemental tutoring in SBI outperformed or performed as well as students not at risk.

Findings from these 20 studies indicate that schema training is effective for many different groups of students, including students with LD, ADHD, EBD, and SLD as well as students who are ELLs and students who are not disabled and are struggling in mathematics. Schema training appears to be effective whether the focus is on SBI, external modeling to emphasize the semantic structure of problem types, or teaching for transfer as in schema-broadening instruction. The positive outcomes of SBI were found for students instructed in general education

classrooms, special education classrooms, and outside the students' classrooms by either researchers or classroom teachers. Further, instruction was effective whether implemented individually, in small groups, or class-wide. Our review of the 20 studies indicated that the supports provided in studies with positive effects included explicit instruction via modeling and/or elaborative explanations of the strategy using visuals (e.g., a number line, schematic diagrams), prompt cards containing critical information, and posters or checklists of strategy steps. In some studies, manipulatives (e.g., L. S. Fuchs, Fuchs et al., 2008) and calculators (e.g., Y. P. Xin et al., 2005) were used to further scaffold student learning. Partner learning in some studies presented additional opportunities for students to immerse themselves in problem solving and reasoning as well as to communicate orally with their peers when they shared their solutions and explanations (e.g., Jitendra et al., 2007).

In sum, SBI is a research-based, conceptual teaching approach that meets the diverse needs of students in classrooms in several ways. SBI promotes understanding and reasoning by moving away from direct translation methods to problem representation using relevant semantic cues. Also, it reduces cognitive memory load for students struggling in mathematics. Finally, it provides the kind of scaffolding (e.g., explicit explanations) that is necessary to support these students as they make sense of word problems and independently solve word problems. In the next section we describe CSI research and its application to math problem solving.

Cognitive Strategy Instruction

SBI and CSI are complementary interventions in that they are cognitively based and specifically develop students' ability to represent mathematical problems. However, SBI is more specific than CSI in its emphasis on recognizing different problem types and constructing an appropriate schema or symbolic representation to reflect the unique problem type (e.g., Compare, Change), whereas CSI provides a cognitive routine that can be applied across problem types. CSI is more generic in its emphasis on the cognitive processes that help students translate and transform the linguistic and numerical information into symbolic representations of the problem that serve to organize the information and set up the solution plan.

CSI focuses on teaching students a range of cognitive and metacognitive processes and strategies that facilitate learning. These strategies may be relatively simple or complex, depending on the difficulty of the task and the context. Strategic learners and successful problem solvers have a repertoire of strategies and use them effectively and efficiently when they understand, analyze, represent, execute, evaluate, and solve problems. They are self-regulating and motivated problem solvers who know what strategies to use and when and how to use them (Pressley, Borkowski, & Schneider, 1987). In contrast, students with learning difficulties and disabilities such as LD and ADHD usually have not acquired strategies needed for successful problem solving, have difficulty selecting and using strategies appropriate to the task, do not abandon ineffective strategies, do not adapt previously learned strategies, and do not generalize strategy use to other tasks or settings (H. L. Swanson, 1990, 1993)—and therefore typically need explicit strategy instruction. Thus, CSI—which teaches students how to think and behave like successful problem solvers—appears to meet the needs of many students with learning difficulties and disabilities.

CSI is grounded in cognitive theory and considers students' development and how they process information. The approach provides instruction in cognitive processes (e.g., visualization) and metacognitive or self-regulation strategies (e.g., self-questioning). To illustrate, Montague's (2003) model designed for students in middle school includes seven cognitive processes critical to solving mathematical word problems: (a) reading the problem for understanding, (b) paraphrasing by putting the problem into one's own words, (c) visualizing by drawing a schematic representation, (d) hypothesizing or setting up a plan, (e) estimating or predicting the answer, (f) computing, and (g) checking that the plan and answer are correct. The model also incorporates self-regulation in the form of a "SAY, ASK, CHECK" procedure whereby students give themselves instructions, ask themselves questions, and monitor their performance as they solve problems.

The instructional format for CSI is explicit instruction, which is characterized by highly structured and organized lessons that include techniques and procedures such as appropriate cues and prompts, guided and distributed practice, cognitive modeling, interaction between teachers and students, immediate and corrective feedback on performance, positive reinforcement, overlearning, and mastery (Montague, 2003). The basic CSI routine has several stages (Graham & Harris, 2003). First, teachers develop and activate students' background knowledge. Then they discuss the strategy and model its application with the targeted task. Students are required to memorize the strategy. Then teachers provide the necessary guidance and support as students learn and practice the strategy until they can apply it independently. Modeling the strategy is critical to the success of CSI. Cognitive modeling, sometimes referred to as process modeling, is simply thinking aloud while demonstrating a cognitive

activity. The teacher and then students model how successful problem solvers/strategic learners think and behave as they engage in the academic tasks (e.g., math problem solving). This technique stresses learning by imitation and provides students the opportunity to observe and hear how successful problem solvers understand and analyze a problem or task, develop a plan to complete the task, and evaluate the outcome. CSI thus teaches students both cognitive and metacognitive processes and strategies using a specific and explicit instructional routine.

Teaching Problem Solving Using CSI: Solve It! Instruction

The CSI intervention described here is Solve It!—an instructional program designed to teach students with LD how to solve math word problems. Solve It! teaches the cognitive processes that are necessary for developing and applying declarative, procedural, and strategic knowledge of arithmetic when solving math word problems. *Declarative knowledge* refers to the ability to recall math facts from memory, *procedural knowledge* is knowledge of basic algorithms, and *strategic knowledge* can be described as a storehouse of multiple strategies that enable individuals to approach math tasks and problem solving effectively and efficiently.

Math problem solving has two major phases: problem representation and problem execution (Mayer, 1985). Problems can be represented with physical objects or manipulatives, a symbolic representation written on paper, a carefully constructed arrangement of the problem information in one's mind, or a combination of these levels of representation (Janvier, 1987). Problem representation strategies are needed to comprehend and integrate problem information, maintain mental images of the problem in working memory, and develop a logical plan to solve the problem (Silver, 1985). Problem solvers must be able to translate and transform the linguistic and numerical information in math problems into verbal, graphic, symbolic, and quantitative representations that show the schemata or relationships among the information in the problem (Mayer, 1985; Montague & Applegate, 1993; van Garderen & Montague, 2003) in order to develop a plan to solve it. Then the problem solver executes the solution. Problem execution requires the problem solver to develop the plan and move between the problem information, problem representation, and the solution path. If students cannot or do not represent the problem correctly, they cannot solve it. The Solve It! intervention places particular emphasis on teaching students how to represent mathematical problems by paraphrasing problems, using visualization strategies such as diagram drawing or mental imaging, and hypothesizing or setting up a plan.

Specifically, the Solve It! intervention introduces cognitive processes and self-regulation strategies that students memorize by using verbal rehearsal. Verbal rehearsal is a memory strategy that enables students to recall automatically the math problem-solving processes and strategies. Solve It! uses the acronym RPV-HECC to help students remember and internalize the labels and definitions for the processes and strategies (R = Read for understanding, P = Paraphrase in your own words, V = Visualize—draw a picture or diagram, H = Hypothesize–make a plan, E = Estimate—predict the answer, C = Compute—do the arithmetic, C = Check— make sure everything is right). Cues and prompts are used to help students as they memorize the processes and their definitions. The ultimate goal of the program is to have students internalize the cognitive processes and metacognitive strategies and use them automatically. Figure 7.3 presents the cognitive processes and metacognitive strategies that are the foundation for the Solve It! intervention.

Solve It! is flexible because it allows teachers to adapt the teaching routine and tailor instruction to

Figure 7.3   Solve It! math problem-solving cognitive routine.

READ (for understanding)

Say: Read the problem. If I don't understand, read it again.

Ask: Have I read and understood the problem?

Check: For understanding as I solve the problem.

PARAPHRASE (your own words)

Say: Underline the important information. Put the problem in my own words.

Ask: Have I underlined the important information? What is the question? What am I looking for?

Check: That the information goes with the question.

VISUALIZE (a picture or a diagram)

Say: Make a drawing or a diagram. Show the relationships among the problem parts.

Ask: Does the picture fit the problem? Did I show the relationships?

Check: The picture against the problem information.

HYPOTHESIZE (a plan to solve the problem)

Say: Decide how many steps and operations are needed. Write the operation symbols ($+$, $-$, $\times$, and $/$).

Ask: If I ..., what will I get? If I ..., then what do I need to do next? How many steps are needed?

Check: That the plan makes sense.

ESTIMATE (predict the answer)

Say: Round the numbers, do the problem in my head, and write the estimate.

Ask: Did I round up and down? Did I write the estimate?

Check: That I used the important information.

COMPUTE (do the arithmetic)

Say: Do the operations in the right order.

Ask: How does my answer compare with my estimate? Does my answer make sense? Are the decimals or money signs in the right places?

Check: That all the operations were done in the right order.

CHECK (make sure everything is right)

Say: Check the plan to make sure it is right. Check the computation.

Ask: Have I checked every step? Have I checked the computation? Is my answer right?

Check: That everything is right. If not, go back. Ask for help if I need it.

Source: From Montague, M. (2003). *Solve It: A mathematical problem-solving instructional program.* Reston, VA: Exceptional Innovations. Copyright by Exceptional Innovations. Permission to photocopy this figure is granted for personal use only.

accommodate the strengths and weaknesses of students. It includes a detailed instructional guide, informal assessments, curriculum-based measures, scripted lessons that facilitate explicit instruction, instructional materials, and procedures for helping students apply, maintain, and generalize skills and strategies. The time frame for initial instruction can range from 3 to 15 days, which makes this program feasible and practical as a complement and supplement to the standard curriculum. Weekly practice sessions across the school year with word problems drawn directly from the school and/or district curriculum provide the application and distributed practice vital to developing not only effective but efficient problem solving. The mathematical problems used for initial instruction and practice include typical textbook problems; state assessment-type problems; and authentic, situated, real-life problems, such as the following:

- *Typical textbook problem:* A store sells shirts for $13.50 each. On Saturday, it sold 93 shirts. This was 26 more than it had sold on Friday. How much did the store charge for all the shirts sold on both days?

- *State assessment-type problem:* It costs an initial fixed cost of $2 plus an additional $1.50 per mile to rent a taxi. What is the total cost for a 5-mile trip?

- *Real-life problem:* Your group is planning to go to a matinee movie on Saturday and then to Burger King for dinner. How much money will each person need? What will be the total cost for the group?

In this way, students are engaged in a variety of problem-solving applications and have many opportunities to solve problems independently, in teams, and in cooperative groups. After students have mastered the Solve It! routine and have had sufficient independent practice, they can pair up for solving problems where one student models the routine while the other student acts as the coach. Group problem solving is most effective when students work together to solve a real-life problem, such as the movie and Burger King problem mentioned in the preceding list. Solve It! ensures that students are actively engaged during instruction, develop the ability to communicate about mathematics with their peers, become competent in demonstrating what they have learned, and learn to correct errors and reinforce themselves for accuracy and progress over time. To illustrate, Figure 7.4 presents an example of a Solve It! introductory lesson that focuses on conceptual understanding of paraphrasing as a translation and comprehension process (Montague, 2003).

Research Evidence in Support of Using Solve It! to Improve Math Problem Solving

All of the research studies that have focused on CSI for improving math problem solving used Montague's (2003) Solve It! or used a cognitive routine similar to Solve It! (Case, Harris, & Graham, 1992; Cassel & Reid, 1996; K. H. Chung & Tam, 2005; Hutchinson, 1993; Montague, 1992; Montague, Applegate, & Marquard, 1993; Montague & Bos, 1986). A total of 142 students with LD or mild intellectual disabilities ranging in age from 8-4 to 16-7 years participated in these studies. For a detailed review of these studies, see Montague and Dietz (2009). Solve It! was designed to teach students how to understand, analyze, solve, and evaluate mathematical problems by developing the processes and strategies that effective problem solvers use. Montague's research focused primarily on middle and high school students with LD and, most recently, also on middle school students in general education classes who were identified as at risk for mathematics failure (Montague, Enders, & Dietz, 2009).

The first study was a single-subject, multiple-baseline design with six secondary students with LD (Montague & Bos, 1986) who met participation criteria (e.g., minimum reading level, computation competence). Following intervention, all students improved to criterion (at least 70% correct on at least three of four consecutive tests of math problem solving) and also generalized strategy use to more difficult problems. Additional validation studies using both single-subject and group designs were then conducted as part of a federally funded grant to improve mathematical problem solving for middle school students with LD (Montague, 1992; Montague et al., 1993).

In the group study (Montague et al., 1993), 72 middle school students with LD were given the Solve It! intervention and, following intervention, they performed at the same level as average-achieving students on math problem-solving tests and maintained performance over a 4-month period. Within-group pretest/post-test analyses produced large effect sizes based on pretest performance ($d = 1.09$ post-test, $d = 1.08$ maintenance at 1 month, $d = 0.74$ maintenance at 2 months, and $d = 1.25$ following a booster session). Furthermore, participants generalized the problem-solving routine to more complex problems. This study also indicated that the combination of cognitive and metacognitive components of instruction was more effective than either component alone. Daniel (2003) used Solve It! and also found significant improvement in math problem solving for middle school students with LD compared with a control group. She reported that their knowledge and awareness of strategies improved

Figure 7.4   Example of a Solve It! introductory lesson.

Teacher: Yesterday you began to learn a routine for solving math problems. What is the name of the routine? (Call on a student.) Yes, that's right. The problem-solving routine is called *Solve It!* What was the acronym for *Solve It!?* (Call on a student and write RPV-HECC on the board.)

That's right. RPV-HECC. Together, let's review what the acronym stands for. (Point to the Master Chart and read the routine.) R … Read … P … Paraphrase … V …. Visualize …. etc.

Now, let's review the entire *Solve It!* routine. (Review the entire RPV-HECC routine. The teacher leads a group recitation of the routine.)

Teacher: Now I want to talk more about the paraphrasing process. Remember, good problem solvers put the problem into their own words and they remember the information. What does paraphrase mean?

Students in unison (S): Put the problem in your own words.

Teacher: Again. What does paraphrase mean?

Students: Put the problem in your own words.

Teacher: What does that mean … put the problem in your own words? (Elicit student responses and write them on the board.)

Teacher: Excellent ideas. Okay, you said that paraphrasing has to do with using different words to say the same thing. It also has to do with eliminating unimportant or unnecessary information to get the meaning only. Paraphrasing gets at the basic meaning of the message or, in this case, the math problem. Paraphrasing helps us to understand what we read. Sometimes we call paraphrasing "retelling," which means telling it again. Any other ideas, questions, or comments?

Let's look at this problem (on overhead projector). (Read the problem to the students. Then read in unison.)

Jose and Nancy are selling greeting cards to raise money for the school camping trip. Together they sold cards totaling $88.50. Nancy sold $67.00 worth of cards. How much money did Jose make selling cards?

(Distribute the problem.) Now I want you to underline the important information. Go ahead.

What did you underline? (Call on students and ask why that information is important and then, on the transparency, underline the important information.) Now, put the problem in your own words. Say it aloud. Okay, let's have some examples of paraphrasing. (Call on students individually and discuss each person's "paraphrase.")

Very good! So, when you paraphrase a math problem, what do you do to locate the important information? (Elicit responses, for example, use important information only, names of people are not important, the question is important, etc.)

Let's try another problem. (Use the same procedures.)

Look at the Paraphrase process in RPV-HECC. (Use Master Class Charts.) First you say to yourself (Recite as a group):

Say: Underline the important information. Put the problem in my own words.

Then you ask yourself (Recite as a group):

Ask: Have I underlined the important information? What is the question?

Finally, you check yourself (Recite as a group):

Check: That the information goes with the question.

Let's try another problem. (Use the **Say – Ask – Check** procedure for additional problems.)

---

to the level of average-achieving students following Solve It! instruction. Thus, the program was validated in four studies of students with LD, a group of students who frequently struggle with mathematics (Geary, 1994; Jitendra & Xin, 1997). These students characteristically have limited cognitive strategies, particularly problem representation strategies, poor self-regulation, and low motivation and self-efficacy.

Researchers have also established that Solve It! has the potential for addressing students with other types of disabilities. Coughlin and Montague (2011) successfully adapted Solve It! for three adolescents with spina bifida.

As a result of a pilot study, the researchers eliminated the estimation process, provided manual support for visual representation, and built in a graduated program whereby students demonstrated mastery with one-step problems before they advanced to two-step problems. All students improved to criterion on both types of problems. Whitby (2009) successfully adapted Solve It! and improved the problem-solving performance of three middle school students with high-functioning autism/ Asperger's syndrome by adding a video modeling component and gradually increasing the difficulty level of the problems.

Solve It! is the focus of a federally funded U.S. Department of Education study (Montague et al., 2009) that provided general education math teachers with professional development to incorporate Solve It! instruction into the prescribed curriculum. Results from the first year of the study indicated that students in grades 7 and 8, including average-achieving students as well as at-risk students and students with LD ($n = 185$), made significantly greater growth in math problem solving over the school year than students in the comparison group ($n = 127$) on curriculum-based measures of textbook-type problems ($d = 0.44$). They also made significantly greater growth in math problem-solving self-efficacy and math confidence over the school year than students in the comparison group ($d = 0.37$). Year 2 results, with grade-8 students ($n = 719$), indicated that students who received the Solve It! intervention demonstrated significantly greater increases across the school year on the curriculum-based measures compared with students in the control condition who received typical classroom instruction only ($d = 0.91$). By the end of the school year, students with LD in the Solve It! condition performed significantly better than the average-achieving students in the control condition.

In sum, the research conducted thus far has suggested that CSI is a promising approach not only for teaching students math problem solving but also for teaching other higher-order skills such as reading comprehension and composition. For a review, see Wong, Harris, Graham, and Butler (2003). Like SBI, it meets the diverse learning needs of students with and without disabilities who are at risk for mathematics failure.

Recommendations for Practice

Promoting effective problem-solving and reasoning skills using SBI and CSI requires adhering to several guidelines. One important consideration for students struggling with mathematics is to ensure that students understand problem representation and develop the ability to represent problems accurately using schematic representations that show the relationships among the problem parts. Students with and without disabilities who struggle with mathematics have difficulties in generating coherent problem representations that mediate problem solving (van Garderen & Montague, 2003). SBI provides them with schematic representations that illustrate the mathematical relationships between objects and facilitates translating information from the diagram into an appropriate number sentence (Hegarty & Kozhevnikov, 1999). Similarly, CSI explicitly teaches students problem-representation processes (i.e., paraphrasing and visualization) that provide the foundation for deciding on an appropriate solution path.

Another consideration in the case of SBI is that a four-step problem-solving process is used to guide problem solving. However, it is critical that students become actively engaged in the process of reasoning rather than simply applying the steps in a rote fashion to obtain the correct answer. That is, coherently representing information in the problem using a diagram requires more than following the steps. It involves identifying the problem schemata (i.e., Change, Group, Compare), understanding the various features and semantic relations that characterize the problem, and integrating the information to accurately represent it. Students struggling in mathematics may prematurely focus on the problem solution without understanding the problem situation that is essential to successful problem solving. Therefore, initial tasks could include story situations with no unknown information to inhibit direct translation methods (e.g., the word *altogether* suggesting the use of addition) that ignore mathematical reasoning.

Specifically, the focus of instruction should be on critical thinking and reasoning as students learn to represent information in the problem using the schematic diagram. For example, students should read to understand the problem situation to first find the two things compared in the Compare problem before identifying the larger and smaller quantities, which may pose difficulties for some students when there is irrelevant information and the comparison statement describes the compared quantity to be less than the referent quantity. In the following story situation, "Mahesh, a shoe salesman, works at Harry's Shoes. He sold 68 shoes last month. He sold 12 fewer shoes this month than last month. Mahesh sold 56 shoes this month." "Mahesh, a shoe salesman, works at Harry's Shoes" is irrelevant information. Although "shoes sold this month" and "shoes sold last month" are the two things compared from the comparison statement, it is important for students to understand that the order of information presented in the comparison statement does not translate to "shoes sold this month" is the bigger quantity to represent in the diagram. The same caveat is true for CSI. Students must be provided with ongoing, distributed practice with a variety of problem types to ensure that the acquired processes and strategies are "overlearned": that is, they are internalized and used automatically.

Clearly articulated explanations are critical to help students identify and eliminate irrelevant information and ensure that they understand problems conceptually, represent problems accurately, and develop a logical plan to solve them. To do this, students must understand the problem situation. Finally, checking to see whether the answer makes sense or is reasonable is another crucial component of both SBI and CSI. Checking the answer should emphasize reasoning and critical thinking, which involves going beyond checking the computation to having students check the problem-solving process. This often involves working backward and may include having students check whether their diagram accurately represents the problem.

Conclusion

Meaningful differences related to children's mathematical problem-solving skills are evident when children enter first grade (National Research Council, 2001). These differences grow wider over time and are difficult to ameliorate without "direct school-based instruction" (National Research Council, 2001, p. 19). For several reasons, the research on SBI and CSI is promising for improving mathematical reasoning by focusing on math word problems. First, the benefits of SBI and CSI for students struggling with mathematics are evident from the research base showing that students' math problem-solving skills improve significantly and substantially following systematic and explicit instruction in these approaches.

Second, many of the studies addressed maintenance and transfer aspects of word problem-solving skills that are particularly difficult for students with mathematics disabilities. These students struggle to transfer their learning to novel problems, particularly if their original exposure to word problems is superficial and is not reinforced over time. Therefore, it may be necessary to specifically teach transfer to novel situations (e.g., L. S. Fuchs, Seethaler, et al., 2008). Third, the content addressed in SBI and CSI studies ranged from arithmetic word problems involving all four operations to algebra problems, including two-variable two-step equations. While the approaches have been successful with varying types of problems, future research should also address word problems representing other mathematical content strands (e.g., fractions, measurement, geometry). For example, in recent SBI research (Jitendra et al., 2009), positive outcomes for improving student learning of ratios, proportions, and percents have been noted.

In sum, both SBI and CSI provide direction to facilitate students becoming more effective and efficient problem solvers, which in turn helps students to become more independent problem solvers. As a consequence, improved math problem solving should have a positive impact on students' overall math performance, as has been documented in the research. Theoretically, these approaches may also positively impact other student outcomes such as high-stakes test performance and graduation rate.

CHAPTER 8

Strategies for Improving Student Outcomes in Written Expression

Linda H. Mason | *The Pennsylvania State University*

Karen R. Harris and **Steve Graham** | *Vanderbilt University*

"The pages are still blank, but there is a miraculous feeling of the words being there, written in invisible ink and clamoring to become visible."

Vladimir Nabokov

Many students with disabilities likely share Nabokov's sentiment that the words remain invisible and the pages are blank, or close to blank, as they produce few ideas and little detail when they write (Graham & Harris, 2003). An important educational goal for these students is to make sure that they have the tools to improve this situation so that their thoughts and ideas take form in writing, becoming both visible and powerful. This chapter presents research-based instructional practices that provide teachers with tools for meeting this goal.

Why is it important for students with disabilities to develop as writers? Writing is critical to students' school, occupational, and social success. Poor writing directly impacts students' learning in classroom contexts (Mason & Graham, 2008). Writing is an important educational tool, as it provides students with a means for personalizing information as well as reformulating and extending it (Langer & Applebee, 1987). Over 90% of white-collar workers and 80% of blue-collar workers indicate writing is important to job success (National Commission on Writing, 2007). Writing has also become a primary means for communicating and keeping in touch with friends, colleagues, and others, as electronic forms of communication, such as e-mailing, texting, and blogging have become so prominent. Thus, students who do not learn to write well are increasingly at risk in almost all facets of life.

This presents major problems for students with disabilities, as the overwhelming majority of them have not developed the writing skills needed for success. When compared to students without disabilities, they are not as effective in using writing as a tool for communication, expression, or learning (K. R. Harris & Graham, 1999; Mason, 2010). Results from the National Assessment of Educational Progress 2007 writing test, however, make it clear that writing is a challenge for most students in our schools: approximately 74% and 95% of students without disabilities in eighth and twelfth grades did not meet the proficiency skill level in writing (Salahu-Din, Persky, & Miller, 2008).

Students with disabilities experience even greater difficulties than their normally achieving peers mastering the process of writing (K. R. Harris & Graham, 1999), as a result of multiple factors. Their knowledge about different writing genres and tasks is typically incomplete, resulting in selection of inefficient and ineffective strategies for planning, drafting, monitoring, evaluating, and revising what they write (K. R. Harris, Graham, & Mason, 2003). They experience difficulties managing or regulating these same processes (H. L. Swanson, Hoskyn, & Lee, 1999) and, just as importantly, they exhibit little goal-directed behavior, persistence, or effort when writing (Graham & Harris, 2003). Further, their writing performance is often affected negatively by conditions such as attention problems, hyperactivity, acting out, withdrawal, or other behaviors (Bos & Vaughn, 2006). Other difficulties, such as memory and poor language abilities, provide additional barriers to their writing development.

Fortunately, considerable evidence indicates that teachers can overcome each of these barriers and that children with disabilities can learn to be skillful writers (Graham & Perin, 2007; Rogers & Graham, 2008). Perhaps the most significant roadblock to achieving this goal, however, resides in the classroom. While many teachers do an excellent job of teaching writing, too often teachers simply provide too little writing instruction (Kiuhara, Graham, & Hawken, 2009), or the instruction provided in both general education and special education settings is ill-defined, providing inadequate development for students (Cutler & Graham, 2008; Graham & Harris, 2003). Such instruction is contrary to what has been shown to be effective in research: students who struggle with writing need explicit and systematic instruction that helps them master and regulate critical aspects of the writing process (Graham, 1999; Schumaker & Deshler, 2003). Effective instruction for these students should include careful progress monitoring; planning that considers flexible groupings, adaptation, and scaffolding; appropriate pacing for individual students; plenty of opportunity to be actively engaged; and positive and facilitative feedback. Fortunately, researchers have developed and validated well-designed instructional methods for teaching students writing skills, strategies, processes, and knowledge. This includes teaching the essential building blocks of composing: the processes of planning, organizing, and revising text; taking ideas and shaping them into interesting and syntactically correct sentences; and transcribing these sentences onto paper through handwriting/word processing and spelling.

In this chapter, we present research-based instructional programs for developing these basic building blocks in writing for students with disabilities. The first program, the Center on Accelerating Student Learning (CASL) Handwriting/Spelling Program, addresses basic transcription skills for young students with disabilities (Graham & Harris, 2006). The next program,

the Strategic Instruction Model (SIM), focuses on strategies instruction for adolescents with disabilities (Schumaker & Deshler, 2003). In this chapter, we highlight SIM strategies for sentence construction and paragraph writing. Finally, we present the Self-Regulated Strategy Development (SRSD) model for teaching strategies for planning, drafting, and revising text as well as self-regulation procedures for carrying out these processes. SRSD has been validated for students with disabilities from elementary through secondary grades (Graham & Harris, 2003).

Effective Practices for Teaching Writing-Transcription Skills

Students with disabilities often have difficulty with both handwriting and spelling (Graham, 1990). These difficulties can interrupt the composition processes, interfere with intended messages, constrain writing development, and impact vocabulary use in writing (Graham, Harris, et al., 2008). In addition, difficulties with handwriting and spelling may lead students to avoid writing and to believe they cannot write (Berninger, Mizokawa, & Bragg, 1991). Given the potential negative impact of poor transcription skills, students with disabilities would benefit from effective handwriting instruction that teaches efficient ways for writing letters and words legibly and fluently (Graham, Harris, et al., 2008). Furthermore, students with disabilities should be taught how to spell words they use frequently in writing, generate reasonable spellings for unknown words, check and correct spelling errors using multiple resources, and develop a desire to spell correctly (Graham, 1999).

Effective handwriting instruction for students with disabilities should include (a) individualization to meet a student's needs; (b) teaching skills through frequent and short lessons; (c) modeling how to form letters; (d) comparing and contrasting letter features; (e) providing facilitative supports such as marks for paper placement on student desks and tripod grip molds for pencils; (f) teaching students how to independently evaluate and improve their handwriting; (g) promoting handwriting fluency; and (h) teaching letter formation in isolation, quickly followed by application in context (Graham, 1999).

Based on the available empirical evidence (Graham, 1999), effective instruction for spelling difficulties includes explicitly teaching spelling words, skills, useful rules, and phonological awareness. This includes mastery of words students are likely to use when writing and individualized instruction as needed. In addition, word-study approaches, such as word sorting by spelling patterns, have proven effective for students with disabilities.

Maintenance and generalization should be supported by continual review of previously learned words and integration of spelling words with students' reading and writing. The CASL Handwriting/Spelling Program includes these recommended instructional practices in a program that addresses both handwriting and spelling.

CASL Handwriting/Spelling Program

> My spelling is Wobbly. It's good spelling but it Wobbles, and the letters get in the wrong places.
>
> A. A. Milne

The CASL Handwriting/Spelling Program was designed to improve developing spellers' skills in writing the letters of the alphabet, handwriting fluency, knowledge of sound–letter combinations, spelling patterns involving long and short vowels, and words commonly used when writing (K. R. Harris & Graham, 2009). Before starting the lesson units, a pretest of 94 of the most commonly used words in young children's writing is given (Graham, Loynachan, & Harris, 1993). Misspelled words from this list, as well as words misspelled during instruction, combined with a spelling phonics sequence, are used for the handwriting/spelling lessons. The phonics unit sequence includes: (a) Unit 1: short /a/ and /o/; (b) Unit 2: short /o/ and /e/; (c) Unit 3: short /i/ and /u/; (d) Unit 4: short and long /a/; (e) Unit 5: short and long /i/; (f) Unit 6: short and long /o/; (g) Unit 7: short and long /e/; and (h) Unit 8: long /a/. In Unit 8, three spelling patterns are contrasted: long /a/ with silent e, /ai/, and /ay/.

Lesson Activities Overview

Forty-eight 20-minute lessons, divided into the eight units previously noted (six lessons per unit), are included in the program. Each unit includes six short activity-based lessons (see Table 8.1). Five different activities are included in Lessons 1 through 5. Lesson 6 has one activity.

Activity 1. Across the 48 lessons, students work on 46 different sound–letter combinations during a 2-minute Phonics Warm-up activity. Each sound–letter combination is represented on a card with a picture on one side (e.g., in Unit 2, a picture of a bed) and corresponding letters on the other side (e.g., "b," "e," "d"). The teacher holds up a card and says, "What letter(s) make the sound you hear at the (beginning, middle, or end) of this word?" If an incorrect response is given, the teacher says the correct letter and repeats the process. The purpose of this activity is to improve students' skills in correctly identifying the letter(s) that correspond to sounds for consonants, blends, digraphs, and short vowels.

Table 8.1 CASL Program for Handwriting/Spelling

	Description	Purpose
Lessons 1–5		
Activity 1	2-minute Phonics Warm-up	Letter identification
Activity 2	5-minute Alphabet Practice	Letter formation
Activity 3	4-minute Word Building	Spelling
Activity 4	4-minute Word Study	Spelling
Activity 5	5-minute Writing	Letter formation practice
		Word selection
		Skill application
Lesson 6	Word Sorting	Rules for spelling patterns

Activity 2. In a 5-minute Alphabet Practice activity, students are taught how to form letters of the alphabet previously determined on a letter-writing pretest to be written incorrectly, inefficiently, or both. Two letters are taught in each lesson, starting with lower-case letters and moving to capital letters after the lower-case letters are mastered. During the first two lessons, the teacher models how to form each letter. Using cards with numbered arrows indicating the order and direction of strokes for each letter, the teacher models by tracing and discussing aloud letter formation. Next, the student imitates the teacher, tracing each letter while describing how to write it. This letter-writing activity is followed by a discussion about how the two target letters are similar and different. The student then practices by tracing, copying, and writing each letter. Finally, the student circles her best-formed letters.

Procedures for Alphabet Practice in the next two lessons replicate the ones used in Lessons 1 and 2, with two differences. First, teacher and students do not discuss similarities and differences in how target letters are formed. Second, practice in tracing, copying, and writing individual letters is reduced and substituted with additional practice in copying words containing the target letters (e.g., "bad" for the letters "b" and "d"). One additional modification is made for Lesson 5. In this lesson, students copy "hinky-pinkys" that contain the target letter (e.g., "muddy-buddy" for the letter "d"). Students are asked to circle their best-formed word or "hinky-pinky," respectively, in Lessons 3 to 5.

Activity 3. The third activity is a 4-minute Word Building. Word Building is based on the rime introduced in the lesson's previous Phonics Warm-up activity. For example, in the Unit 2 lesson for short /e/ and short /o/, the teacher begins by showing a card containing the rime (i.e., the part of a syllable that consists of its vowel and the consonant sounds that come after the vowel) "ed" and says the sound that the rime makes. The teacher then models building a word by placing a card containing either a consonant (e.g., "b") or blend (e.g., "sl") in front of the rime. The student then builds as many real words as he or she can by adding consonants, blends, and diagraphs to the rime. During Lesson 2 students build words on a worksheet instead of with cards. Procedures in Lessons 3 and 4 are identical to Lessons 1 and 2 except that a new rime is introduced (e.g., "en"). Students review rimes taught in the previous unit by using these rimes to build words via a worksheet activity in Lesson 5.

Activity 4.   A 4-minute Word Study is the fourth activity in Lessons 1 to 5. Students practice learning to spell correctly words previously missed on the pretest or during Activity Five: Writing (see the following section). The words are studied using the "add-a-word" method described by Graham (1999). The teacher selects five words that the student misspelled on the pretest/writing for the student to study. Each word is written on a card, which in turn is attached to a ring. Students study the misspelled word by saying it, studying its letters, writing it from memory, and then checking for spelling accuracy. The word is corrected if it is not spelled correctly. Once a word is spelled correctly six times in a row over a period of two lessons, it is removed from the ring, and a new word is added. Periodically, mastered words are reviewed and restudied as needed.

Activity 5.   The final activity is 5-minute Writing. The Writing activity serves three purposes: (a) writing provides a context in which students can apply skills taught in Alphabet Practice; (b) writing provides a source for selecting words for students to learn during Word Study; and (c) writing provides a context in which to apply skills learned in Word Building, Word Study, and Word Sorting (a Lesson 6 activity described in the following section). The prompt for the writing task asks students to write a story or personal narrative that incorporates words practiced during Word Building (e.g., students are asked to write a story during Unit 2 about "Fred wanting to buy a red sled bed" when working on the "ed" rime). The teacher and the student place a star next to any word that the child uses in the story with the target rime pattern practiced during Word Study and emphasized during Word Sorting (e.g., the short /e/ during Unit 2).

Activity for lesson 6.   During the sixth lesson of each unit, students participate in a Word Sorting activity (Graham, Harris, & Loynachan, 1996). Word Sorting is designed to help students learn the rule for each of the spelling patterns emphasized in the phonics unit. For example, in Unit 2, words are sorted into two categories: CVC-type words containing the short-vowel sounds of /e/ (e.g., bed) and /o/ (e.g., top). The teacher begins the Word Sorting by placing a master word card for each category next to each other (e.g., "bed" and "top"). The teacher pronounces each master word and then says the word again, emphasizing the target feature (e.g., short-vowel sound for /e/ in bed and /o/ in top). Students are asked to consider how the master words are similar and different. The teacher focuses students' attention on critical features, such as how the letter "e" is pronounced in the master word, and the combination of consonants and vowels in the master word.

The teacher then tells students that they are going to look at other words and decide within which category they should be placed, with the idea of figuring out the rule for why the letter "e" makes the short /e/ sound in "bed" and the "o" makes the short /o/ sound in "top." Using a pack of 12 cards (containing an equal number of words that fit each pattern), the teacher draws a card, reads and says the word (emphasizing the target sound), thinks out loud about where to place the word, and places it under the appropriate master word card. The teacher continues to do this until the students understand the process. Students are then encouraged to think out loud while categorizing and placing the remaining word cards under the appropriate master card. If an error is made in placing a word card, the teacher corrects it and models out loud thinking about where to place the word card. Once all of the words are appropriately placed, the teacher helps students state a rule for the patterns emphasized in the word sort. Students then generate words of their own, writing them on blank word cards, and placing them under the appropriate master target card. If time permits, students are encouraged to hunt for words in their writing that fit these patterns. Finally, it should be noted that the word-sorting, word-study, and word-building activities all focus on strengthening the same set of spelling patterns.

Tips for Implementation

The manual for the CASL Handwriting/Spelling program can be obtained by contacting Steve Graham (steve.graham@vanderbilt.edu). It is necessary to create or obtain some materials to implement the program (these are detailed in the manual), and it is better to obtain or develop all of these materials before putting the program into place. It is also useful to practice presenting one or two units before using the program with students.

Research Base for CASL Handwriting/Spelling Program

The full program has been validated in one study with first-grade students (Graham & Harris, 2006); the handwriting portion of the program and the spelling portion were validated in studies with grade-1 (Graham, Harris, & Fink, 2000) and grade-2 students (Graham, Harris, & Fink-Chorzempa, 2002), respectively. All three studies took place in inner-city schools, where the majority of the students were culturally and linguistically diverse. Each student scored at or below the 25th percentile on a norm-referenced story-writing measure before instruction, and a variety of children with disabilities were included in the three studies, including children with learning disabilities (LDs), attention deficit hyperactivity disorder (ADHD), and behavioral problems. Instruction was provided in sessions outside the regular classroom, and each instructor was taught to apply the instructional procedures until he or she could do so correctly and fluently. All three studies were randomized field trials, with high levels of implementation fidelity, and comparison groups that received either phonological awareness instruction (Graham & Harris, 2006; Graham et al., 2000) or math instruction (Graham et al., 2002). Across the three studies, students' spelling improved dramatically, as did their handwriting legibility and fluency. All three of these studies were randomized control trials, and effect sizes for handwriting and spelling measures ranged from 0.54 to 1.46. The studies also demonstrated positive carryover effects to the students' writing (sentence construction skills and output when writing improved) and reading skills (word-recognition and word-attack skills improved). These effect sizes were in the moderate to large range (0.76 to 1.21).

Effective Instruction for Composition Skills

Good writers spend time recursively planning, revising, monitoring, evaluating, and regulating the writing process (K. R. Harris & Graham, 1999). Students with disabilities, on the other hand, tend to spend little time involved in such processes, focusing much of their attention on lower-level transcription skills (i.e., handwriting, spelling, capitalization, and punctuation). A process approach to writing (prewriting by planning and organizing, drafting, revising, editing, and publishing) combined with strategy instruction and self-regulation procedures has been validated as a highly effective instructional approach for improving performance in higher-level skills for composition (Graham & Perin, 2007). In this chapter we describe two evidence-based approaches that use effective instruction in strategy development for teaching composition. As noted previously, the first approach, SIM, has been validated as effective in improving sentence and paragraph writing abilities among adolescents with high-incidence disabilities (Schumaker & Deshler, 2003). The second approach, SRSD, has been validated as effective in improving planning, composing, and revising for students who are normally achieving and students with high-incidence disabilities from elementary through secondary grade levels (Graham & Harris, 2003).

SIM for Sentence and Paragraph Development

> A perfectly healthy sentence, it is true, is extremely rare.
> Henry David Thoreau

Writing research focused on adolescents with LD began in the late 1970s and early 1980s, as Deshler, Schumaker, and their colleagues began to conceptualize and validate learning strategy interventions for adolescents with disabilities (e.g., Deshler & Schumaker, 2006). They developed a Learning Strategies Curriculum with three major strands: the acquisition strand, storage strand, and expression strand. The expression strand includes strategies for sentence writing, paragraph writing, error monitoring, spell checking, and organizing and writing short themes. Research has been reported and evidence established on teaching the strategies for writing sentences and paragraphs using the SIM approach (Mason & Graham, 2008; Schumaker & Deshler, 2003).

The goal of instruction using SIM is to support students in acquiring the knowledge, motivation, and practice necessary to successfully use a strategy as needed for tasks in the general education setting. All strategies included in the Learning Strategies Curriculum share common features. Each strategy consists of a set of sequenced steps leading to a specific, successful outcome. The strategy steps cue students to use specific cognitive and metacognitive activities; students learn to select and use required procedures, skills, and rules that are observable. The strategy steps are kept short and are expressed in an easily remembered mnemonic (e.g., COPS for Capitalization, Organization, Punctuation, Spelling). The learning strategies are typically seen as strategy systems, because any one step can often cue the use of multiple cognitive or metacognitive strategies for a given task (Deshler & Schumaker, 2006; Schumaker & Deshler, 2009). SIM instruction includes eight instructional stages as described later. Lessons are mastery based; that is, students are required to demonstrate the skill taught before moving to another intervention component.

SIM for Sentence Construction

The Sentence Writing Strategy program includes two parts, Fundamentals in the Sentence Writing Strategy and Proficiency in Sentence Writing Strategy (Schumaker & Sheldon, 1985). With these two SIM programs, students are taught to apply a series of formulas and steps for writing four types of sentences: simple, compound, complex, and compound-complex. The mnemonic PENS (Picks, Explores, Noted, and Subject) prompts students to remember the steps for writing a sentence. Students learn to apply 14 different sentence formulas, with each formula corresponding to a specific sentence structure. To write a sentence, a student first picks a formula and then explores words to fit the formula. Once the student decides on which words to use, these are noted or written down, and the student checks to make sure the sentence is complete (i.e., contains a subject and verb).

SIM for Paragraph Development

The Paragraph Writing Strategy program is used to teach students to write four types of paragraphs (Schumaker & Lyerla, 1991): paragraphs that list or describe, show sequence, compare/contrast, and demonstrate cause and effect. The mnemonic SLOW CaPS prompts students to remember the strategy for writing paragraphs. Each letter (with the exception of the small "a") reminds students to carry out a step or process: (S)—show the type of paragraph in the first sentence; (L)—list the type of details you plan to write about; (O)—order the details; (W)—write the details in complete sentences; and cap off the paragraph with a (C) concluding, (P) passing, or (S) summary sentence.

Instructional Overview

The teacher emphasizes mastery at each of the eight stages of SIM instruction and provides specific and individual feedback after each lesson (Schumaker & Deshler, 2009). Lessons are scaffolded so that students initially apply the strategy to a simple task, with the goal of teaching students to apply the strategy to grade-level tasks. The SIM instructional sequence includes eight stages of strategy acquisition.

Pretest and make commitments. Students' preskills are tested in the first SIM instructional stage. A purpose for using the strategy for writing sentences/paragraphs is established, and the benefits of using the strategy for the specific task are presented. The students and teacher collaboratively set goals for learning the strategy, for memorizing the mnemonics for the strategy steps, and for applying the strategy to the task (e.g., sentence and paragraph writing).

Describe. In the next stage, the teacher describes the purpose of the strategy and how each strategy step helps with the skill to be learned. The teacher explains how to use the strategy for the target skill; describes when the strategy should be used (and when it should not be used); and tells the students why the strategy is important for helping with sentence and paragraph writing skills.

Model. Modeling, the third instructional stage, is the heart of effective strategy instruction. To be an effective model, the teacher thinks out loud each step of strategy application for the targeted skill. The teacher also clearly demonstrates effective use of instructional support materials such as graphic organizers or strategy mnemonics while using the strategies to write sentences/paragraphs.

Verbal practice. In the fourth instructional stage, the teacher conducts practice activities that enable the students to memorize the strategy steps. The goal is for students to become fluent so that they can self-instruct while applying the strategy to the target skill.

Controlled practice. During the initial stages of acquisition, students practice using the strategy with easy tasks. In the fifth instructional stage, practice is scaffolded by increasing task difficulty only after easier tasks are mastered. The teacher provides specific and individual feedback after each practice attempt.

Advanced practice. By the sixth instructional stage, students practice the strategy in grade-level contexts. Writing assignments may come from the students' teachers or may be developed by the SIM instructor.

Post-test and obtain commitment for generalization. In the seventh instructional stage, students' skills are post-tested. The teacher also obtains the students' commitment to continue to use the strategy and to use the strategy in other settings.

Generalization. In the eighth and final instructional stage, students are supported in generalizing application of the strategies learned to the general education classroom and maintaining strategy use across the school years. Teachers create situations that give students chances to use the strategies learned across tasks, situations, and settings. Four phases of generalization instruction are required.

1. Orientation: awareness of the variety of opportunities for generalization is stressed.

2. Activation: students are given numerous opportunities to generalize with feedback provided.

3. Adaptation: focuses on helping students learn to modify the strategy to meet demands in different settings.

4. Maintenance: consists of periodic probes to see if the student continues to use the strategy effectively in multiple settings.

Tips for Implementation

SIM developers note that positive results are typically found when the eight-stage instructional methodology is implemented. Daily lessons with multiple opportunities for practice and teacher feedback are recommended (Schumaker & Deshler, 2003). SIM instruction highlights the importance of explicit instruction and guided practice for strategy acquisition in writing for adolescents with LD. Professional development is a critical component of SIM instruction, as is the support of administrators and general education teachers in order to achieve generalization across classrooms and writing tasks (Deshler & Schumaker, 2006). Coaching may be very helpful for teacher development, and fidelity needs to be addressed through frequent classroom observations, monitoring of student performance, and meetings with teachers. Most SIM instructional materials, including the sentence writing and paragraph writing programs, are available only in conjunction with professional development provided by certified SIM Professional Developers. Contact the University of Kansas, Center for Research on Learning (KU-CRL's) director of professional development at crl@ku.edu for information. Further information including newsletters, videotapes/DVDs, and CDs that can be ordered is found at www.kucrl.org/.

Research Base for SIM

Effects of SIM instruction for sentence writing for 64 urban, suburban, and rural school students in grades 6 to 12 have been examined in five single-subject studies (Beals, 1983; Eads, 1991; First, 1994; C. S. Johnson, 2005; Schmidt, Deshler, Schumaker, & Alley, 1988). As summarized by Rogers and Graham (2008), students with disabilities, primarily LDs, were included in the five studies. Sixty-six percent of the students in these studies were male. Race/ethnicity was reported in four studies, with a total representation of 47% Hispanic, 44% Caucasian, 7% African American, and 2% Hispanic and African American across the studies. Results of the five studies indicated that students' writing of complete sentences improved with a range of 78% to 100% for the percentage of nonoverlapping data (PND), with a mean PND of 83% (PND > 0.90 are considered very effective, PND between 0.70 and 0.90 are effective; Scruggs, Mastropieri, & Casto, 1987). These results indicate that SIM instruction for sentence writing was effective to very effective.

Four single-subject studies examined the effects of SIM instruction for paragraph writing for students who were average and low achieving in grades 8 and 9 (Dowell, Storey, & Gleason, 1994; Moran, Schumaker, & Vetter, 1981; Sonntag & McLaughlin, 1984; G. W. Wallace & Bott, 1989). Two thirds of the suburban and urban participants were male students with LD; race/ethnicity was not reported. SIM instruction for paragraph writing was effective to very effective, with results of 89% to 100% PND (for structural elements of a paragraph; Rogers & Graham, 2008).

Some caution must be applied in interpreting the effectiveness of SIM writing instruction, because experimental control was not adequately established in any of the sentence or paragraph writing studies. For the 11 quality measures (R. H. Horner et al., 2005) assessed in the studies reviewed by Rogers and Graham (2008), for example, these single-subject studies averaged addressing 61% of the quality indicators for sentence writing and 58% of quality indicators for paragraph writing. This finding places these studies slightly below the mean of quality indicators addressed across all single-subject design studies in writing. Furthermore, although researchers have noted that SIM instruction for sentence and paragraph writing have been used effectively with elementary school-aged students (Schumaker & Deshler, 2003), no study, to date, has empirically documented effects of SIM for younger students.

SRSD for Planning, Composing, and Revising

> A writer is somebody for whom writing is more difficult than it is for other people.
>
> Thomas Mann

One approach for teaching written expression to students who struggle with writing, SRSD, blends explicit instruction in self-regulation procedures with cognitive strategy instruction. SRSD was, and continues to be, developed by integrating research on learning and teaching from multiple theoretical perspectives (K. R. Harris & Graham, 2009). Six strategy-acquisition stages are typically included in SRSD regardless of the genre (e.g., persuasive writing, informative writing) and for any planning, composing, and revision strategies being taught: (a) develop background knowledge, (b) discuss the strategy, (c) model the strategy, (d) memorize the strategy, (e) guided practice, and (f) independent performance. Students' self-regulation of strategy use is supported by teaching students to use four procedures (i.e., goal setting, self-monitoring, self-instruction, and self-reinforcement) throughout the writing process. SRSD instruction is recursive and criterion-based; lessons, instructional stages, and principles are repeated and revisited based on individual student needs. Instruction continues until each student has mastered the strategy. SRSD has been used effectively for teaching planning, drafting, and revising strategies across narrative, persuasive, and expository genres to students with disabilities (Graham & Harris, 2009).

Planning and Composing Strategies

A well-constructed planning and composing strategy will guide students to organize their writing for narrative, persuasive, and expository writing. While different genres require different strategies, a general writing strategy can be paired with a genre-specific strategy (K. R. Harris, Graham, Mason, & Friedlander, 2008). The POW (*P*ick an idea, *O*rganize notes, and *W*rite and Say More) strategy, for example, guides students to: (a) think about, brainstorm, and pick ideas before writing; (b) select a genre-specific planning strategy to help with organizing notes; and (c) write from a plan and remember to add new information while writing. Researchers have validated a number of planning and drafting strategies for stories (e.g., K. R. Harris, Graham, & Mason, 2006), persuasion (e.g., Mason & Shriner, 2008), and expository text (e.g., De La Paz, 2001). Table 8.2 highlights examples of evidence-based planning and composing strategies.

Revising Strategies

Two different revising strategies (see Graham & MacArthur, 1988; MacArthur, Schwartz, & Graham, 1991) have been taught and tested within the SRSD framework. We highlight the more general revising strategy here (MacArthur et al., 1991) because it can be applied more broadly and has been tested in more than one experiment. With this peer-editing strategy, each student receives and gives feedback for revising and editing to another student. Once each student has finished a first draft, she reads it to her partner. The partner first identifies strengths and the goals met and then provides constructive feedback on specific aspects of the composition, such as places where more detail would be helpful or text that is unclear. The students then use this feedback to revise their papers. After revision, the partner provides specific editing feedback, concentrating on issues of form such as spelling, punctuation, and so forth.

SRSD Stages of Instruction

As noted, six recursive, flexible stages of instruction are typically used to introduce and develop planning and

Table 8.2   Examples of Self-Regulated Strategy Development Planning and Composing Strategies

Narrative Writing	*POW + W-W-W, What = 2, How = 2*
	Pick my idea.
	Organize my notes—Use W-W-W, What = 2, How = 2!
	Write and say more.
	+
	Who is the main character?
	Where does the story take place?
	When does the story take place?
	What does the main character do or want to do?
	What happens next?
	How does the story end?
	How do the characters feel?
Persuasive Writing	*POW + TREE*
	Pick my idea.
	Organize my notes—Use TREE!
	Write and say more.
	+
	Topic Sentence—Tell what you believe!
	Reasons—3 or more
	Why do I believe this?
	Will my readers believe this?
	Explain reasons—Say more about each reason.
	Ending—Wrap it up right!
Expository Writing	*PLAN and WRITE*
	P = Pay attention to the prompt, set goals
	L = List main ideas to develop your essay
	A = Add supporting ideas (details, examples, etc.)
	N = Number major points in the order you will use them
	and
	W = Work from your plan to develop a thesis statement
	R = Remember your goals
	I = Include transition words for each paragraph
	T = Try to use different kinds of sentences
	E = Exciting, interesting, $1,000,000 words

Note: For complete strategy lesson plans and materials see: Harris, K. R., Graham, S., Mason, L. H., & Friedlander, B. (2008). *Powerful writing strategies for all students.* Baltimore: Brookes.

composing strategies, revising strategies, and self-regulation knowledge: Develop Background Knowledge, Discuss It, Model It, Memorize It, Support It, and Independent Performance (see Figure 8.1 for an overview of the Stages of Instruction). These stages provide a general format and guidelines for teachers and students as they acquire, implement, evaluate, and modify the strategies. One or more days of instruction occurs in each stage,

Figure 8.1   Stages of self-regulated strategy development instruction.

Develop and Activate Knowledge Needed for Writing and Self-Regulation

- Read model papers in the genre being addressed (stories, persuasive essays, informative), to develop students' knowledge of genre characteristics and components.
- Develop students' appreciation of effective writing (e.g., how did the writer make the story fun to read?).
- Explore and discuss both writing and self-regulation strategies to be learned; may begin development of self-regulation by introducing goal setting and self-monitoring.
- Continue developing students' knowledge through the next two stages as needed until all key knowledge and understandings are clear.

Discuss the Strategy

- Explore students' current writing and self-regulation abilities, their attitudes and beliefs about writing, and what they are saying to themselves as they write.
- Introduce graphing (self-monitoring). Prior compositions may be used to assist with goal setting. Skip graphing prior writing if the student is likely to react negatively.
- Further discuss strategy to be learned by focusing on the purpose and benefits.
- Discuss how and when the strategy can be used appropriately (begin generalization).
- Establish the students' commitment to learn the strategy and to act as collaborative partners.
- Establish role of student effort and strategy use.

Model How to Use the Strategy

- Model and/or collaboratively model how to use the strategy and self-regulation procedures for the writing tasks, resulting in an appropriately written composition.
- Analyze and discuss strategies and the model's performance, making changes as needed.
- Model self-assessment and self-recording by graphing the components of the composition.
- Continue the students' development of strategy and self-regulation procedures across composition and other tasks and situations (continue generalization support).

Memorize Strategy Mnemonics and Steps

- Typically begun in earlier stages by providing student practice in memorization of strategy steps, mnemonic(s), and self-instructions.
- Continue to support memorization in the following stages.
- Students should have strategy steps and mnemonics memorized, as well as what each means, before Independent Performance.

Support Students' Strategy Use

- Initially, teachers and students use writing and self-regulation strategies collaboratively to achieve success in composing. Prompts such as strategy charts, self-instruction sheets, and graphic organizers are used to support students' writing.
- Collaboratively establish challenging initial goals for genre elements and characteristics of writing with individual students; criterion levels increased gradually until final goals are met.
- Prompts, guidance, and collaboration are faded individually (e.g., graphic organizer replaced with student creating mnemonic on scratch paper) until the students can compose successfully alone.
- Goal setting, self-instructions, self-monitoring, and self-reinforcement are all being used by this stage; monitor students' use of these procedures.
- Self-regulation components not yet introduced may begin (e.g., environmental control, use of imagery, and so on, may be used as desirable).
- Discuss plans for maintenance, continue support of generalization.

Independent Performance

- Students are able to use writing and self-regulation strategies independently; teachers monitor and support as necessary.
- Fading of overt self-regulation may begin (e.g., graphing may be discontinued).
- Plans for maintenance and generalization continue to be discussed and implemented.

Source: Information from Harris, K. R., & Graham, S. (2007). Marconi invented the television so people who couldn't afford radio could hear the news: The research on powerful composition strategies we have, and the research we need. In M. Pressley (Ed.), *Shaping literacy achievement: Research we have, literacy research we need.* New York: Guilford.

with some stages expected to take longer than others, depending on student needs and rate of progress. Changes to this typical framework and individualization to differing student needs should be made as needed (cf. Lane et al., 2008; Sandmel et al., 2009).

Develop and activate background knowledge.

During this initial stage of instruction, students acquire the vocabulary, knowledge, and concepts needed to use the writing and self-regulation strategies they will be learning. This stage begins with a teacher-led discussion about what good writers do when writing. The strategy parts are introduced and each step is described. For example, for the POW strategy, the teacher would explain that the first step or thing to do when planning is "Pick a good idea." Additional "tricks" used by good writers, such as writing a catchy opening, are discussed. The teacher and students then read one or more model compositions for the genre (written at the students' level) and identify how the author used each strategy part for planning and composing or revising. Self-regulation is introduced as students set a goal to learn and use the strategy, with the instructor committing to do her best in teaching the strategy. In this and each subsequent lesson, the teacher provides students time to practice memorizing the strategy steps and the corresponding mnemonic; then the teacher tells students that they will be asked to share the steps from memory in the next session. In addition, students may begin sharing opportunities and ideas for transfer of this strategy to other settings or tasks as appropriate; this continues throughout the rest of instruction. The teacher, if possible, should arrange opportunities for such transfer and scaffold student success in other settings once strategies are learned.

Discuss it.

Although a great deal of discussion obviously takes place during stage 1 and in later stages, stage 2 is called "Discuss It" because not only does the initial discussion of the strategy continue, but also discussion expands when the teacher asks students to evaluate and discuss their previous writing using what they have learned. The teacher asks students to evaluate a composition they wrote before they began learning the new strategies by: (a) counting how many of the genre elements (i.e., the required parts of a composition, such as a topic sentence for an informative essay or setting for a story) their composition contained, (b) editing for ways to revise, and (c) identifying strengths in the composition. The teacher stresses that it is not a problem if the paper is imperfect: "Of course, the story/essay does not have all the parts; you hadn't learned POW yet!" The teacher and students then discuss what could have been done to improve their papers. Students record their prior performance on a graph and learn that they will

continue to use this graph to self-monitor their writing as they plan and compose or revise new compositions. Students set a goal to include all of the genre elements next time they write, and set individualized goals to improve other elements of their writing. Students proceed to stage 3 (Model It) when the teacher determines they have developed the necessary background knowledge, vocabulary, and understanding of what they are learning and why they are learning it.

Model it.

In the third stage, the teacher models the complete writing process, using the strategies to plan, compose, and/or revise a paper. Strategy acquisition is supported by developing self-instructions and teaching students self-monitoring and self-reinforcement strategies. Following memorization practice, the teacher models, while thinking aloud, how to use the strategies. The teacher also models how and when to use instructional support materials such as mnemonic chart reminders, graphic organizers for planning and organizing, and charts for self-monitoring performance. The teacher thinks out loud while planning, composing, and revising, using six types of self-instruction (i.e., problem definition, strategy use, focusing of attention, coping, self-evaluation, and self-reinforcing self-statements). The teacher models how to monitor strategy use during and after writing and how to self-reinforce success in using the strategies. Students can participate by helping the teacher plan and make notes on a strategy step graphic organizer and write the first draft. Following the teacher's modeling, students develop and record personal self-instructions in their own words to be used while thinking of good ideas ("Relax," "Take my time, good ideas will come"), while working ("What is my first strategy step?" "I can do this"), and to check work ("Do I have all of my parts?" "Perfect!").

Memorize it.

While listed here as a separate stage, memorizing the mnemonic and the strategy step procedures has been occurring since stage 1. The goal is for students to have the strategy memorized and to be able to write the mnemonic on blank paper so they can make notes in the future using the mnemonic without a graphic organizer. Students who need it are provided more practice of the mnemonic and its meaning (including why each step is important) until it is memorized. As one student we worked with said, "You can't use what you can't remember!"

Support it.

This stage is typically the longest. Research indicates, however, that students may make the biggest jump in performance in this stage, and that support in using the strategy is necessary even after the explicit, collaborative modeling in stage 3 (K. R. Harris & Graham, 1999). At first, students work with the teacher to plan and write a first draft. For example, students may provide ideas for the paper while the teacher writes the notes. The teacher re-models and provides any assistance necessary. At first, students keep out their mnemonic chart and list of self-statements while they work, and use the graphic organizer. The student continues to set goals, self-monitor, self-instruct, and self-reinforce while applying the strategy. Over time, the teacher provides less help, and students begin writing independently; pace is individualized to students' needs.

Independent performance. At this point, students can write successfully without teacher or peer support. Students are encouraged to write the genre mnemonic and element steps on blank paper before writing; the graphic organizer is no longer used. Graphing of performance can be continued for one or two more compositions. Once students can independently apply the strategies to the writing task, the student can be asked to plan, compose, and/or revise in a different academic class with a different teacher, or to generalize strategy use in other ways (i.e., to determine when these strategies, or some subset of them, can be used for other writing tasks).

Tips for Implementation

It is critical to remember that the six stages are not intended to be implemented in a rigid or linear format. Stages should be repeated and revisited based on the needs of individual students. Instruction should continue until students demonstrate mastery in applying these strategies to their writing. SRSD instruction takes time, practice, and careful planning (K. R. Harris et al., 2008). Further, students need to be able to write a complete sentence before beginning SRSD. SRSD is meant to supplement, not supplant, the writing curriculum. Research indicates that for most struggling writers, all six instructional stages and all four self-regulation procedures (i.e., goal setting, self-monitoring, self-instruction, and self-reinforcement) are important (Graham, Harris, & Mason, 2005).

SRSD has been used successfully with whole classes, small groups, individual students, and in tutoring situations. K. R. Harris et al. (2008) do not recommend a prescribed set of strategies taught in a specific order; teachers and administrators should decide what strategies to use with whom, and at what time, based on student needs and the larger writing curriculum. Students who are already writing effectively in a given genre do not need to be taught basic genre strategies; this may actually encourage them to do less than they are capable of. These students should work with their teachers to set individualized goals and learn additional strategies for

refining their writing (K. R. Harris et al., 2008). Finally, learning validated strategies using the SRSD approach is only a beginning for all students, because learning to write is a complex, developmental process.

Detailed lesson plans and support materials for instruction are provided in K. R. Harris et al. (2008), and a detailed example of classroom implementation is provided by K. R. Harris, Graham, and Mason (2003). All of the stages of instruction can be seen in both elementary and middle school classrooms in the video *Teaching Students with Learning Disabilities: Using Learning Strategies* (Association for Supervision and Curriculum Development, 2002). Online interactive tutorials on SRSD are available at http://iris.peabody.vanderbilt.edu/pow/chalcycle.htm. Finally, lesson plans and student support materials for elementary students (grades 1 through 3) can be found online at http://hobbs.vanderbilt.edu/projectwrite/.

Research Base

Since 1985 more than 40 studies conducted by K. R. Harris, Graham, and their colleagues or independent researchers using the SRSD model of instruction have been reported in the area of writing involving students from the elementary grades through high school. These studies have included students with LDs, emotional and behavioral disorders (EBDs), at-risk for EBDs, other disabilities (e.g., ADHD), and normally achieving students (cf. Graham & Harris, 2009; Lane et al., 2008). Four recent reviews have reported the effectiveness of SRSD for students with disabilities (S. K. Baker, Chard, Ketterlin-Geller, Apichatabutra, & Doabler, 2009; Graham & Perin, 2007; K. R. Harris, Graham, Brindle, & Sandmel, 2009; Rogers & Graham, 2008; Taft & Mason, 2011). Summary of the primary findings from these reviews follows.

Results of a meta-analysis of 15 group planning studies indicated that SRSD has large positive effects, improving the quality, number of essay elements, and length of students' writing (K. R. Harris et al., 2009). The average weighted effect size (ES) for writing quality at post-test, for example, was 1.20 (Cohen, 1988, considered ES >0.80 large). These group studies involved a broad range of students in second- to eighth-grade settings.

Equally positive effects have been obtained for SRSD planning studies investigated using single-subject design methodology. A total of 108 suburban and urban second- through eighth-grade students have participated in 21 SRSD single-subject planning studies reviewed by Rogers and Graham (2008). Of these students, 55% were Caucasian, 37% African American, 5% Turkish, 2% Hispanic, and 1% Asian. Effect sizes from comparing post-instruction to baseline performance for 18 single-subject studies ranged from 67% to 100% PND at post-instruction and 25% to 100% for maintenance. The majority of students, in 18 of the 21 studies, were struggling writers or students with LD.

Fourteen single-case studies have investigated the effects of SRSD planning strategies for students with EBD, at-risk for EBD, ADHD, speech and language impairments, Asperger's syndrome, autism spectrum disorder, and mild intellectual disability (Taft & Mason, 2011). Students ranged from second to eleventh grade. Of these participants, 61% were male, 39% female; 60% were Caucasian, 32% African American, 7% Turkish, and 1% Hispanic. PND at post-test ranged from 83% to 100% for number of text parts written for these students.

Only a few studies have examined the effectiveness of SRSD with revising strategies. MacArthur et al. (1991) obtained an effect size of 1.09 for improvements in writing quality (see Graham & Perin, 2007) for the peer revising strategy described earlier. Stoddard and MacArthur (1993) obtained 100% PND for number of revisions at post-test, maintenance, and generalization in a single-subject design study (see Rogers & Graham, 2008). Both of these studies involved students with LDs in self-contained classrooms.

The overall quality of SRSD research studies was assessed in Graham and Perin (2007) and Rogers and Graham (2008). In both of these meta-analyses, study quality was high and treatments were delivered with fidelity. This was confirmed in part by an independent review by S. K. Baker et al. (2009) assessing the quality of five group experimental and quasi-experimental studies and 16 single-subject studies. All group studies met standards established for high-quality research. Of the 16 single-subject studies reviewed, 9 met all of the standards required for high-quality single-subject research.

Conclusion and Directions for Future Research

> Once a pond time. There was a boy named Sam. It happen at 11 2000. In the math and science center. Sam wanted to be a writer. Ms. Smith came to the school. Ms. Smith tried to teach Sam how to writing. Then she taught him POW. Then he became a great writer. He feel so happy that he will be a story writer went he grow up.
>
> Sam, second-grade student with a disability
> (K. R. Harris, Graham, & Mason, 2006)

Learning to write well is a challenging task for all students; it is a particularly difficult one for students with disabilities. During the last 30 years, researchers and teachers have learned much about how to effectively teach writing to students with disabilities. Although much still remains to be done, and we do not yet have research-based practices that represent a complete writing curriculum, we now have a number of well-validated practices that research shows to be effective for teaching core writing skills and processes to these students. This includes effective practices for teaching handwriting, spelling, sentence construction, paragraph development, planning, drafting, and revising. A strength of the types of instructional practices presented here is that evidence shows that they work, and the positive effects obtained were replicated in multiple studies (such replication is a central hallmark of scientific investigation). Moreover, confidence can be placed in these findings, as the research was generally of high quality.

It is important to note, however, that these practices have not been tested in all possible contexts, and in most instances (with the exception of SRSD), they have involved a small range of disabilities. Although a larger number of studies have been conducted involving the SRSD approach, numerous research issues and challenges remain, such as maintenance and generalization of strategy use (K. R. Harris et al., 2009; K. R. Harris & Graham, 2007, 2009). Further, implementing research-based treatments is a difficult and complex task. A procedure's effectiveness in the studies included in this chapter does not guarantee that it will be effective in all other situations. Consequently, the safest course of action for teachers is to carefully monitor the effects of evidence-based practices as they are implemented in their classes to gauge directly whether they are effective under these new conditions.

Because learning to write is a complex, developmental process, students' growth as writers will be enhanced only if their writing programs engage them in frequent and extended writing; broaden their knowledge about writing and writing genres; automatize basic text transcriptions skills (i.e., handwriting and spelling); facilitate the development of flexible and facile sentence and paragraph construction skills; enhance the ability to plan, draft, monitor, evaluate, and revise text; and promote a positive, "I can do this" attitude toward writing. Although research-based practices exist for some of these elements, they do not exist for all. As a result, to meet the writing needs of students with disabilities and other struggling writers, teachers must apply a judicious mixture of research-based practices and practices not yet validated, which increases the importance of teachers monitoring the effectiveness of their writing practices. Clearly, further research is needed to identify additional effective writing practices and to determine how these practices can be combined to successfully meet the needs of students with disabilities.

CHAPTER 9

Improving Academic Outcomes in the Content Areas

B. Keith Ben-Hanania Lenz | *SRI International*

Janis Bulgren | *University of Kansas*

Twenty years ago, components of the standard K–12 curriculum could be easily characterized based on grade levels. During grades K–3, the curriculum focused on teaching basic skills (e.g., phonics, word reading, basic computation). During grades 4 to 6, the curriculum focused on teaching students how to use the basic skills and strategies learned in the earlier grades to learn the foundational vocabulary, concepts, and ideas to be learned in content areas such as social studies, science, language arts, and mathematics. This focus constituted the introduction of formal content areas or "subjects." Also at this level, students were introduced to textbooks, lectures, and content area tests. In grades 7 to 12, the curriculum focused on exposure to an increasingly complex set of content elements in courses requiring a high level of independent learning by the student.

Today, the K–12 curriculum is not so easily characterized. Instead, it now reflects national efforts to improve student achievement on high-stakes tests, address the increasing role of technology in our economy, improve our nation's international performance in math and science, support higher-order reasoning and collaborative problem-solving efforts, and close the achievement gap between higher-achieving and underperforming groups of students (e.g., students from minority groups, students

with disabilities, others at risk for failure). Specifically, today's K–12 curriculum, as reflected in the Common Core Standards (www.commoncorestandards.org), introduces more complex content elements earlier in school. At the same time, direct instruction and practice of both learning strategies and thinking skills are being extended into secondary school. As a result, the lines have blurred that had once distinguished when skill instruction and content area instruction occur.

Challenges for All Students

To succeed in our increasingly complex and specialized society, it is imperative that individuals think divergently and creatively and see the relationships between and among seemingly diverse concepts (F. J. King, Goodson, & Rohani, 1998). Many adolescents have developed sufficient literacy skills in reading and writing to pass basic literacy tests. Nonetheless, these students may not be able to apply successfully the sophisticated thinking skills required to succeed in core content courses and pass content area subtests of state assessments (M. W. Conley, 2008; R. Heller & Greenleaf, 2007). As a result, too many high school graduates have difficulty with the tasks required in contemporary content area curricula, such as formulating and solving problems, evaluating and incorporating reference material appropriately, developing a logical and coherent argument or explanation, interpreting data or conflicting points of view, and completing their assignments and projects with precision and accuracy (D. T. Conley, 2008). In fact, many high school students arrive at college largely unprepared for the intellectual demands and expectations of postsecondary education.

Challenges for Students with Disabilities

The curricular shifts have had a significant impact on what students with disabilities are now expected to learn, how they are expected to learn it, and which instructional settings and personnel will be involved. Students with disabilities are now more likely to (a) be enrolled in more rigorous content area courses reflecting a move to increase success in the regular education curriculum; (b) be required to pass courses in algebra in order to graduate from high school; (c) experience use of technology to support content area learning, which can occur in the form of a major course component to support learning or as a specific accommodation provided to support learning for a student with a specific disability; and (d) be provided with direct instruction of strategies to increase content area learning as part of a class in special education.

Students with disabilities may also receive additional instruction in the same strategies in the content area classroom in order to provide additional tiers of supportive and aligned instruction with a goal of improving student performance in literacy on high-stakes measures (Deshler et al., 2001; Fore, Hagan-Burke, Burke, Boon, & Smith, 2008; M. Kennedy & Deshler, 2010). Instruction in and reinforcement of the same strategies related to acquiring, storing, retrieving, and expressing information and demonstration of competence increase the likelihood that students will learn the strategies and see how they can be applied in different content area courses. For example, the language arts teacher might instruct and model for students the use of a mnemonic device in literature using the first-letter mnemonic device to help students remember that there are four types of poetry: lyric, epic, narrative, and descriptive. The first letters of each of the types of poetry can be used to create the word "LEND." Then, the students and teacher create a reminding sentence to link the mnemonic device to the content: "Will you LEND me your poetry book?" To consolidate the learning, the special education teacher instructs and models how to use the same mnemonic,

reinforces instruction provided by the language arts teachers, provides more practice, and helps the student apply the strategy to other content area work.

Although the shifts in expectations and curriculum reflect a desire to improve student outcomes, progress in improving the outcomes of students with disabilities has been slow. According to the U.S. Department of Education (2006), students with disabilities drop out of school at a significantly higher rate than their peers without disabilities. In addition, in the 2001 to 2002 school year, only 51% of students with disabilities graduated from high school with a standard high school diploma, indicating that they are not succeeding in the general education curriculum. Many factors must be considered as teachers and educators respond to the challenges faced by students with disabilities.

A Framework of Approaches for Responding to the Challenge

Helping students learn the types of thinking required in today's world must begin with recognizing that students with diverse learning abilities, including students with disabilities, will be present in many content classes. Furthermore, given the difficulties involved in promoting content area learning for students with disabilities, it is important to begin by identifying a general framework for organizing how we might think about and respond to the challenge. Figure 9.1 presents a basic framework for considering intervention approaches for students with disabilities who are expected to successfully participate and succeed in content area classes.

IEP-Related Learning Goals

At the top of Figure 9.1, we list three primary goals associated with improving content area learning based on specific learning barriers. These goals are typically addressed on a student's individualized education program (IEP). The first goal focuses on improving how a student initially acquires content area information. Interventions designed to address this goal are developed when a disability interferes with the student's ability to understand and comprehend information presented in the typical learning activities provided in the content area classroom. The second goal focuses on improving a student's storage of information in short- and long-term memory and the appropriate retrieval of this information when required. Interventions designed to address this goal are developed from the assumption that the student may understand new content but may have difficulty storing information in notes, making important content

Figure 9.1 Approaches to ensuring content mastery.

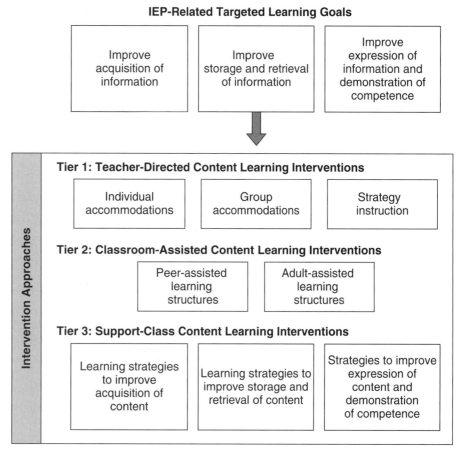

IEP-Related Targeted Learning Goals

| Improve acquisition of information | Improve storage and retrieval of information | Improve expression of information and demonstration of competence |

Intervention Approaches

Tier 1: Teacher-Directed Content Learning Interventions

| Individual accommodations | Group accommodations | Strategy instruction |

Tier 2: Classroom-Assisted Content Learning Interventions

| Peer-assisted learning structures | Adult-assisted learning structures |

Tier 3: Support-Class Content Learning Interventions

| Learning strategies to improve acquisition of content | Learning strategies to improve storage and retrieval of content | Strategies to improve expression of content and demonstration of competence |

associations that put the information into perspective, or remembering information when it is needed. The third goal focuses on improving how a student expresses what has been understood and remembered—verbally, in writing, on assignments, and on various formative and summative assessments. These three goals point to the inherent learning barriers that must be addressed to promote learning for students with different types of learning problems.

The IEP should play an important role in defining how teachers or teams of teachers should help students gain access to the general education content area curriculum by focusing on two critical efforts. One effort is to ensure mastery of critical content when specific disabilities prevent students from being able to access the content independently. For example, the teacher might plan to be more explicit in his instruction to the whole class by using more visual representations of the content in order to make the most important content more concrete. The second effort involves providing direct instruction to teach the skills and strategies necessary to learn independently without content area supports. For example, the teacher might teach the specific skills or strategies for interpreting visuals used to display content or for paraphrasing passages and summarizing sections so that students learn to monitor comprehension of text.

These efforts must be achieved within and among the different types of educational services provided. Some services are provided by the content area teacher, some by the special education teacher, and some via collaboration between the content area teacher and the special education teacher.

Tiered Intervention Approaches

Approaches to using interventions that help teachers promote content area learning for students with disabilities generally fall into three categories. The interventions in the first category are designed to improve learning outcomes through teacher-directed learning activities as part of ongoing content area instruction. In a Response-to-Intervention (RtI) or a multi-tiered system of supports (MTSS) context, these interventions are typically considered first-tier interventions. The interventions in the second category are designed to improve learning outcomes through assisted learning arrangements in which peers or adults other than the primary teacher work to enhance content area learning in an academically diverse group of learners. These interventions are typically considered second-tier interventions. The interventions in the third category are designed to improve learning outcomes by providing instruction in learning strategies provided outside the content area classroom that will enable students to learn independently once they are in content area classes. These interventions are typically considered third-tier interventions.

This chapter will build on the basic framework presented in Figure 9.1. A brief description of the intervention areas will be provided in the next section. Because of the critical role that the content area teacher plays in providing effective whole-group instruction, we will highlight intervention areas that have been found to improve the performance of students with disabilities in that context. In addition, two teacher-directed interventions (i.e., the Question Exploration Routine and the Recall Enhancement Routine) will be described more extensively in the second part of the chapter.

Content Area Intervention Approaches

As shown in Figure 9.1, we conceptualize contemporary models of content area teaching as falling into one of three tiers: Tier 1 (teacher-directed interventions), Tier 2 (classroom-assisted interventions), and Tier 3 (support-class interventions). In this section, we briefly describe the primary instructional approaches associated with each tier.

Teacher-Directed Content Area Interventions

Teacher-directed interventions consist of three approaches: individual accommodations, group accommodations, and strategy instruction.

Using Individual Accommodations to Support Content Area Learning

A central part of planning and supporting content area learning for students with disabilities is the use of specific accommodations that reduce or eliminate the impact of a disability. Nolet and McLaughlin (2000) described an instructional accommodation as "a service or support that is provided to help a student fully access the subject matter and instruction as well as to demonstrate what he or she knows" (p. 71). An accommodation does not change the content or expectations for what must be learned or the required level of competence that must be demonstrated. Because a disability may impact a student's ability to acquire, store, retrieve, or express what the student has learned in content area classes, accommodations may be needed. Accommodations are used during content area learning and evaluation activities to ensure that a student who has the intellectual ability to

master content demands has an opportunity to learn content that she would be able learn without the disability. Some examples of individual accommodations include audio books, special seating arrangements, note takers, alternate or modified assignments or assessments, text-to-speech devices and software, and talking calculators. These accommodations are compensatory supports intended to reduce the impact of a disability and to ensure access to the general education curriculum in content area classes.

Using Group Accommodations to Support Content Area Learning

Some scholars have called for equal access to content area knowledge and skills through universal design for learning (UDL) (e.g., Rose & Meyer, 2002). One approach to implementing UDL is to provide a group accommodation, defined as an instructional activity used as part of whole-group instruction to promote learning for students with specific learning needs. However, the use of the accommodation can lead to benefits in learning that may be realized for all students in the class. The study of teaching adjuncts or mediators (e.g., graphic organizers, teaching routines, guided notes, study guides) to enhance or promote content area learning of students with disabilities has been steadily growing since the 1980s (for a review of early studies, see Bulgren & Schumaker, 2006).

Based on some of the same principles as those embodied in UDL, an approach to promoting content area learning for struggling students is represented in a set of well-researched interventions called Content Enhancement Routines (CERs; Lenz & Bulgren, 1995; Schumaker, Deshler, & McKnight, 2002). CERs were designed to move explicit, direct, strategic, organized instruction found to be successful with struggling learners (H. L. Swanson & Deshler, 2003) into large-group, content area classroom instruction. When a CER is used correctly, a teacher introduces an instructional device, such as a graphic organizer, to the whole class and teaches the class how to use the device. The teacher then identifies the content and expected learning outcome that must be achieved and leads the class through a co-constructed process to complete the strategic thinking process required to learn and review the information. Once initiated, the teaching process involved in the use of the device to achieve an intended learning outcome (e.g., compare concepts) is repeated throughout the course. The goal is that it becomes routine for both the teacher and students to use the strategy to manipulate the information. We will highlight a more detailed example of the components and procedures related to the implementation of CERs later in this chapter.

Strategy Instruction in the Content Area Classroom

Use of the CERs provides a type of compensatory instruction required when students do not have good learning strategies to ensure content learning. Some students, however, may not acquire a learning strategy unless the teacher explicitly teaches the strategy. While teaching subject matter material, teachers can look for opportunities to point out to students particular strategies that would help them manipulate the information being taught. For example, a teacher may teach, model, and prompt the use of paraphrasing, prediction, or self-questioning to learn content. In this scenario, teachers not only tell students about a strategy that would be helpful for them to use, they also explain how to use the strategy, model its use, and then require students to use the strategy in relation to their content assignments.

The purpose of doing this is to teach students "how to learn" the subject matter material. By teaching students strategies that are directly relevant to the demands of their course, teachers shift from a single instructional emphasis on learning course content to simultaneously helping their students acquire the underlying cognitive processes that will enable them to independently understand and remember the content. Some students need support to recognize and use the underlying cognitive processes, and these students can be guided by instruction in strategies associated with different cognitive demands. Embedding explicit instruction in learning strategies—especially strategies tied to literacy (e.g., reading comprehension strategies) as part of instruction provided in content area courses in middle and high school—reflects a departure from traditional approaches to teaching content. However, the national trend toward adoption of the Common Core Standards by states indicates that secondary general educators teaching the core courses required for graduation will be required to provide a variety of instructional supports that help students engage in a continuum of content area learning and strategic thinking and reasoning (Porter, McMaken, Hwang, & Yang, 2011).

Several approaches are effective for embedding strategy instruction in content area learning. One approach is to link strategy instruction to a group accommodation. For example, almost all content supports are provided because one or more students lack a good strategy for doing a task independently. To illustrate, as part of group instruction, a teacher may provide a set of guided notes to the entire class because the teacher realizes that one or more students do not know how to detect main from supporting details—a key strategy for successful note taking. As content supports are provided to ensure that content is mastered, the strategies associated with a specific content support (e.g., note taking) can be taught. Similarly, when a CER is used, the specific strategy associated with each CER (e.g., those described in the following section) can be explicitly taught and practiced as part of the content learning experience.

As supports are provided to ensure content area learning and higher-level thinking, strategy instruction is also provided to students so they can eventually apply the strategies independently. These are often higher-level thinking strategies such as those that help students understand a concept, answer important questions, make comparisons, or explain causation. In addition, more general strategies may be taught in the content area classroom. General strategies include those that support paraphrasing, self-questioning, or summarizing. Finally, those general strategies can be cued by the content area teacher if students have been taught those strategies in another setting. All of these strategies may be embedded in content area instruction.

Classroom-Assisted Content Area Interventions

Many content area teachers use interventions that promote the use of assisted learning structures within the content area classroom. Classroom-assisted interventions are designed to provide adult or peer assistance to students in the content area classroom other than those provided by the primary content area teacher. These arrangements can include the use of special-education teachers, paraprofessionals, within-class tutors, and peers. Although assisted learning structures for students with disabilities have not been shown to be as effective in promoting student learning as teacher-directed instruction (H. L. Swanson & Hoskyn, 2001b), content area teachers often use these types of learning structures to individualize instruction. In fact, secondary teachers reported that having students work in groups to learn content was one of the top three instructional strategies that they used in order to individualize instruction to meet the needs of students in an academically diverse group of learners (Lenz, Schumaker, & Deshler, 1991). Teachers therefore need information on effective assisted learning structures that can be used within content area classrooms.

Peer-assisted learning structures have been described in the literature as peer tutoring, student learning teams, and cooperative learning. In peer-assisted learning structures, students are expected to help each other learn content or complete tasks; however, the teacher is expected to plan for and monitor peer-assisted learning activities. Peer-assisted learning structures allow the teacher to shift teaching responsibilities to a student's peers. Although peer-assisted learning structures can be used in many ways to improve content learning outcomes, they are used most often to promote understanding of course content, to provide practice opportunities, or to help students complete assignments or perform tasks (see Bulgren & Schumaker, 2006).

Adult-assisted learning structures are learning activities provided to individuals or small groups of students in which an adult supports content area learning. These activities typically are implemented in supportive co-teaching arrangements in which a special education teacher or paraprofessional helps students learn the content. Content area tutoring is an example of these types of activities frequently found in schools. One model for providing content area tutoring that has demonstrated some empirical support is strategic tutoring (Hock, Pulvers, Deshler, & Schumaker, 2001). In strategic tutoring, the tutor teaches students strategies in how to learn the content for a specific content area class.

Support-Class Content Area Interventions

Another approach to improving content learning outcomes involves interventions that teach learning strategies to students in a support class (e.g., a reading class) or special education class. This approach has generated a considerable amount of research evidence (Schumaker & Deshler, 2010). Proponents of these interventions argue that learning strategies (e.g., paraphrasing, self-questioning, textbook usage, note taking, test preparation, mnemonic strategies) that are taught in a support class (e.g., learning strategies or study skills class) or in special education settings (e.g., resource room) should be directly linked to improving outcomes in the general education content classroom. That is, the teacher should spend instructional time teaching students how to generalize the strategies that they are learning in support classes to their general education content courses (e.g., language arts, history, biology, algebra).

Descriptions of Effective Practices: Content Enhancement Routines

Content Enhancement Routines: Principles, Learning Supports, Procedures, and Research

The term *content enhancements* refers to a type of group accommodation that includes a variety of instructional adjuncts or mediators that teachers can use to facilitate or enhance students' organization, understanding, and remembering of content as part of whole-group instruction. Researchers at the University of Kansas Center for Research on Learning who were designing and studying instructional interventions for use with students with learning disabilities (LD) and other students who were low achieving developed CERs. These researchers found that instructional interventions required systematic, intensive, and explicit instruction sustained over a long period of time in order to be effective (Deshler, Schumaker, & Lenz, 1984). In the following section, we describe the guiding principles, learning supports, procedures, and research associated with CERs.

Content Enhancement Routine Principles

CERs are based on four key principles: (a) content area teachers must select the critical features of the content and then transform that content in a way that promotes learning for academically diverse groups of students, (b) the instruction must meet the needs of both the group and the individuals in the group, (c) the process must not compromise the integrity of content by watering down important ideas, and (d) teachers and students must engage in a co-constructive partnership (i.e., the teacher and student must work together to generate and transform the content) that honors the role of each in the learning process (Bulgren, Deshler, & Lenz, 2007).

Content Enhancement Routine Learning Supports

Several learning supports are common to many of the CERs. Among these are graphic organizers that provide a visual representation of how information may be organized and suggest relationships between chunks of information through the use of geometric shapes and drawing elements. The organization of the shapes shows the relationships among the ideas or chunks of information. Because graphic organizers can only hold a limited amount of information, only the most critical information can be displayed. Thus, the teacher's selections for inclusion in a graphic organizer significantly influence student learning.

The relationships shown in the graphic organizer may or may not be supported by verbal cues provided directly on the graphic organizer. However, Pashler et al. (2007) found that graphic presentations (e.g., graphs, figures, charts, maps) that illustrate key processes and procedures that have the most research support are those used with verbal descriptions and presentations provided by the teacher. Therefore, the provision of explicit instruction is another common learning support provided in CERs. Finally, embedded cognitive learning strategy prompts are common across CERs; most of the embedded strategies are scaffolded by acronyms to facilitate recall and by cueing them on the graphic organizer.

Content Enhancement Routine Procedures

The teaching methods in the CERs are sequenced within three instructional phases: "CUE," "DO," and "REVIEW." The purposes of the phases are summarized in the following list:

- *CUE:* The purpose of CUE is to ensure that students (a) are aware of the graphic organizer unique to each CER; (b) understand the importance of the learning goal; (c) understand how the graphic organizer provides a framework for organizing, understanding, and remembering the information needed to reach the learning goal; and (d) understand expectations for their participation in the co-construction of the organizer and learning. This is a verbal preview led by the teacher using the appropriate blank graphic organizer that has been copied and distributed to each student.

- *DO:* The purpose of DO is to ensure that students (a) understand how to process and organize the information, (b) work with the teacher to co-construct the information that is placed on the graphic organizer, and (c) succeed in achieving the learning goal as a result of participation in a carefully scaffolded learning process. In the DO phase, teachers engage students in a carefully scaffolded learning process that consists of a series of instructional steps to guide learners through the use of a cognitive processing strategy. For example, the strategy steps related to independently analyzing, exploring, and answering a question are presented to students as part of the Question Exploration Routine. The teacher uses these steps to lead the class through this question exploration process, as presented later in this chapter. Each strategy is unique to the learning goals of the CER. The teacher engages students in dialogue and construction to promote understanding at each step in whole-group or small-group instruction, or with support from a special education teacher in the classroom.

- *REVIEW:* The purpose of REVIEW is to ensure that students (a) are aware they have achieved the learning goal and can independently summarize learning, and (b) can describe how the graphic organizer and the strategic process of its development helped them learn and reach the learning goal. The teacher leads the review by asking students to summarize the information in the graphic organizer, how decisions were made that led to the information being recorded on the graphic organizer, and how the graphic organizer might be used to study and learn the information.

The CUE-DO-REVIEW instructional procedures are common to all CERs. However, the major portion of each CER, the DO component, is designed to respond to a unique learning goal (e.g., recall information; understand a concept; manipulate information to make comparisons, determine causation, or answer critical questions).

Content Enhancement Routine Research

The effectiveness of CERs has been tested in inclusive secondary settings such as science, social studies, and English/language arts classes. These were classes that contained groups of students of diverse abilities, including those who were high achieving (HA), average achieving (AA), and low achieving (LA), as well as students with disabilities, including LD. Research conducted at the University of Kansas Center for Research on Learning has occurred across a variety of content topics with a range of experimental designs. Results have shown that teachers can use CERs to enhance students' scores on tests that measure retention of factual information (Bulgren, Deshler, & Schumaker, 1997; Bulgren, Schumaker, & Deshler, 1994), comprehension of conceptual information (Bulgren, Schumaker, & Deshler, 1988), knowledge of a concept by analogy (Bulgren, Deshler, Schumaker, & Lenz, 2000), comparison of critical concepts (Bulgren, Lenz, Schumaker, Deshler, & Marquis, 2002), determining causation and making decisions about competing choices and options (Bulgren et al., 1998), and argumentation and evaluation of a statement of claim (J. D. Ellis & Bulgren, 2009).

To illustrate the types of interventions that might be used to promote content learning, in the following sections we describe two specific CER interventions that can be implemented for large-group instruction in content area classrooms: the Question Exploration Routine and the Recall Enhancement Routine.

The Question Exploration Routine

The Question Exploration Routine (QER) is based on a wealth of previous research. For example, the use of questions and questioning is supported by reviews of empirical literature (Pressley et al., 1992; Rosenshine, Meister, & Chapman, 1996). Researchers support the use of questions to set the stage for reasoning and the eventual application of content knowledge to practical situations (Graesser, Person, & Hu, 2002), provide fundamental guides for basic reasoning (Graesser, Baggett, & Williams, 1996), lead students to integrate ideas (A. King, 1994), help organize knowledge (Graesser et al., 2002), promote deep reasoning (Graesser, McNamara, & VanLehn, 2005), facilitate deeper comprehension (Rouet, Vidal-Abarca, Erboul, & Millogo, 2001), and help students transfer learning from one context to another (Perkins & Salomon, 1992).

Research focusing on the QER specifically showed it is effective in helping students who had disabilities, such as those with LD, as well as LA, AA, and HA students without disabilities, succeed on both quantitative and qualitative assessments (Bulgren, Marquis, Lenz, Deshler, & Schumaker, 2011; Bulgren, Marquis, Lenz, Deshler, & Schumaker, 2009). It is an example of a group accommodation that focuses on student mastery of content that requires higher-level thinking in the form of analysis, synthesis, and generalization.

This routine shows how teachers use a graphic organizer combined with some explicit verbal supports to scaffold learning. The goals associated with the use of the graphic organizer and verbal supports are to promote interactive student–teacher co-construction of learning and to provide a cognitive strategic scaffold that can be used as part of whole-group instruction to more effectively teach content to groups of students of diverse abilities. The QER supports acquisition and retention of content information, understanding about a topic by analysis of a critical question, development of a clear answer, and generalization of what the student has learned.

The Question Exploration Guide

The Question Exploration Guide (QEG) is a graphic organizer teaching device (see Figure 9.2) designed to help teachers lead students through the scaffolded learning experience provided in the QER. Students are prompted to explore and answer questions that teachers have

Figure 9.2   A sample Question Exploration Guide.

Text Reference _____   Name _____
Course _____   Title _____
Critical Question # _____   Unit _____   Date _____
Lesson _____

(1) What is the <u>Critical Question</u>?

(2) What are the <u>Key Terms</u> and explanations?

(3) What are the <u>Supporting Questions</u> and answers?

(4) What is the <u>Main Idea</u> answer?

(5) How can we <u>Use</u> the main idea again?

(6) Is there an <u>Overall Idea</u>? Is there a real-world use?

Source: Bulgren, J. A., Lenz, B. K., Schumaker, J. B., & Deshler, D. D. (2002). *The Concept Comparison Routine* (p. 53). Lawrence, KS: Edge Publications, Inc. Reprinted with permission.

determined to be critical to improving content learning outcomes. Figure 9.3 defines the different sections of a completed QEG for a language arts course focusing on a component of narratives in literature. The guide can be used to launch learning on a topic with a critical question, to record learning tied to the question as a topic is covered, and to confirm that learning tied to the question has occurred. The embedded cognitive strategy is represented by the acronym ANSWER, as described next.

Implementation of the Question Exploration Routine

Effective implementation of the QER is described in detail in the QER guidebook (Bulgren, Lenz, Deshler, & Schumaker, 2001). The QER uses the CUE-DO-REVIEW sequence common to all CERs, but the DO component is uniquely tailored to supporting a strategic approach to answering critical content area questions.

Figure 9.3   Sections defined on a completed Question Exploration Guide from a language arts course.

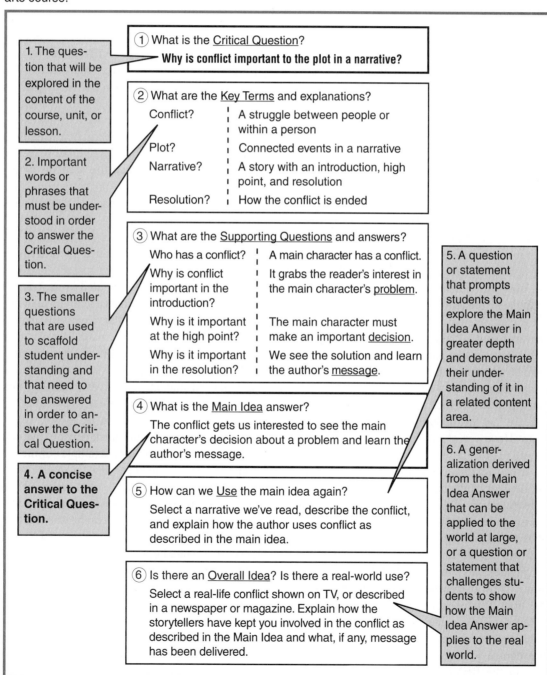

Source: Bulgren, J. A., Lenz, B. K., Deshler, D. D., & Schumaker, J. B. (2001). *The Question Exploration Routine* (p. 7). Lawrence, KS: Edge Publications, Inc. Reprinted with permission.

During the CUE phase, the teacher notes the important question and the importance of understanding and answering it, cues the use of and explains the graphic organizer, and prompts expectations about the students' participation in the co-construction of learning. For example, a teacher might indicate that, as a class, the group will explore why conflict is so important to the plot in a literature narrative, explaining that analysis of conflicts in the plots of short stories, novels, and plays is an important, recurring challenge throughout the course. The teacher will pass out blank QEGs to students and remind them to take notes and participate in a discussion of the important question.

During the DO phase, the part of the routine in which the most time and instructional energy is spent, the teacher and students co-construct the QEG by following a set of six strategic steps, enumerated in Figure 9.3. The six steps are prompted by the acronym ANSWER, which was constructed from the first letter of the first word of each of the six steps: (a) <u>A</u>sk a Critical Question; (b) <u>N</u>ote and explore key terms and basic knowledge needed to answer the Critical Question; (c) <u>S</u>earch for Supporting Questions and answer those Supporting Questions; (d) <u>W</u>ork out or formulate a clear, concise main-idea answer to the Critical Question; (e) <u>E</u>xplore the Main Idea Answer in a related area; and (f) <u>R</u>elate the Main Idea to today's real world. The teacher presents a critical question to the class that is tied to the attainment of specific content standards; the teacher then uses the strategy steps to lead the whole class in the exploration and answering of the question. To further enhance student learning, the teacher might also embed general strategies such as paraphrasing, self-questioning, and summarizing as they proceed through the ANSWER steps. In summary, the acronym ANSWER guides students in learning a higher-order strategy associated with answering a critical question.

The routine was designed so the steps can be flexible in the sense that instruction is often delivered to the whole group. However, depending on teacher preferences, part of the procedures can be developed as small groups or even as individual assignments. The only portion of the development that is largely under teacher control is the selection of the critical question based on standards, assessments, and learning demands. However, when teachers and students become familiar with the routine, teachers can often involve students in developing the critical questions based on their interests or previous questions. Thus, this sequence involves exploring a critical question, developing supporting questions, and answering those questions. It also includes ways for students to apply and transfer or generalize new knowledge both to their course content and the world around them.

Finally, in the REVIEW phase, the teacher and students review both the information covered in the

DO Phase and the process used to answer the Critical Question. For example, the critical understanding is found in the main idea answer: "The conflict gets us interested to see the main character's decision about a problem and learn the author's message." The critical cognitive process is that the steps of the ANSWER strategy allowed the group to carefully develop their understanding; in the early stages of implementation, the teachers may review the steps with the students.

Research on the Question Exploration Routine

Three research studies have been conducted on the QER. One study was conducted in an experimentally controlled setting with instruction delivered by a researcher (Bulgren et al., 2011). Over 100 students, including those with disabilities, in seventh- and eighth-grade science and social studies classes were randomly assigned to experimental or control conditions. Results indicated that students who received instruction with the QER correctly answered a significantly higher percentage of all questions on the tests than did students who received traditional lecture-discussion instruction. Effect sizes were large to very large on each of two tests designed to assess student understanding of a critical question and its answer.

A second study was conducted to determine the feasibility of use of the QER by general education teachers as they taught regularly scheduled content, and the effectiveness of the QER to enhance learning under those conditions (Schumaker, Deshler, Lenz, Bulgren, & Davis, 2006). The study took place in ninth-grade language arts classrooms during instruction on Shakespeare's *Romeo and Juliet*. Over 130 students, including those representing groups of students with diverse abilities, participated. Tests assessed students' ability to explain their understanding of two critical main ideas. Answering the assessment questions required students to indicate overall understanding by providing examples of the main ideas from the play, and to generalize those ideas to other settings. On average, students who received instruction with the QER correctly answered a significantly higher percentage of all questions on both tests than did students who received traditional lecture-discussion instruction. Effect sizes were large on two tests associated with critical questions from the play.

A third study investigated the effects of using the QER to help students of diverse abilities, including those with LD, answer critical essay questions related to content area learning (Bulgren et al., 2009). In this study, researchers randomly assigned 36 students in grades 9 through 12 to experimental or control conditions, and all participated in the instruction about the ozone layer on the first day. On the second day, some students participated in a review using the QER while the other students saw a film that repeated and reinforced all the information from the previous day. Students' responses on an essay were scored in two ways. One assessed students' essays in response to the critical question using the 6-Trait Model of Analysis Scoring, part of the 6-Trait Model of Writing Instruction (Kozlow & Bellamy, 2004). Independent scorers certified in 6-Trait scoring analysis and blind as to which essays were written by students in the experimental or control conditions scored the essays. Results showed statistically significant differences and moderately large effect sizes for students in the experimental condition compared to students in the control condition. The essays were then scored by two independent scorers for accuracy of knowledge and understanding of the

content about the ozone. Results showed significant differences and very large effect sizes for students in the experimental condition compared to students in the control condition with regard to knowledge and comprehension of content about the topic taught.

Examples of how the QEG has been used across additional subject areas (i.e., science, history, and math) are provided in Figures 9.4 through 9.6. As is illustrated in section 3 in Figures 9.4 to 9.6, the supports used in the questioning process to scaffold instruction can be quite varied. In addition, the questions posed on the guide can be whole-course questions that can be revisited across the year, unit questions that can be used to guide learning across the study of topics in a unit, or lesson questions that are posed to guide the discussion of a specific topic or issue that is important for unit- and course-level

Figure 9.4   Completed Question Exploration Guide in science.

① What is the <u>Critical Question</u>?

   Why is a four-chambered heart two pumps in one?

② What are the <u>Key Terms</u> and explanations?

Chamber	An enclosed space.
Heart	A muscle that pumps blood to the lungs through the body.
Pump	A device for moving liquid from one place to another.

③ What are the <u>Supporting Questions</u> and answers?

   A. What are the four chambers?

   What is the function of . . .

   B. The right atrium?
   C. The right ventricle?
   D. The left atrium?
   E. The left ventricle?

④ What is the <u>Main Idea</u> answer?

   The right side of the heart pumps oxygen-poor blood to the lungs, and the left side pumps oxygen-rich blood through the body. (The right side is one pump; the left is the second pump = 2 pumps.)

⑤ How can we <u>Use</u> the main idea again?

   Why do the walls of the left ventricle have to be thicker than the walls of the right ventricle?

⑥ Is there an <u>Overall Idea</u>? Is there a real-world use?

   If a person smokes, which pump is most affected and why?

Source: Bulgren, J. A., Lenz, B. K., Deshler, D. D., & Schumaker, J. B. (2001). *The Question Exploration Routine* (p. 59). Lawrence, KS: Edge Publications, Inc. Reprinted with permission.

Figure 9.5   Completed Question Exploration Guide in history.

① What is the <u>Critical Question</u>?

How has the search for human and civil rights been a major theme of U.S. history?

② What are the <u>Key Terms</u> and explanations?

Human rights	What is due every person as a citizen of the Earth.
Civil rights	What is due every person under law.
Theme	Runs through from beginning to end.

③ What are the <u>Supporting Questions</u> and answers?

What human rights were involved?	Freedom; people are not property.
How is this part of our history?	People violated human rights because of economic and social values (both in North and South).
What civil rights were involved?	Because slaves were property, they were not equal under law. When they were recognized as not being property, it opened the door to being covered by laws and civil rights.
How is this part of our history?	Disagreement over both issues led to war, which allowed progress in gaining more human and civil rights.

④ What is the <u>Main Idea</u> answer?

During the Civil War, our nation struggled over what were the human rights of people being treated as slaves. Protecting human rights opened the door for civil rights.

⑤ How can we <u>Use</u> the main idea again?

The Declaration of Independence states that all people are equal—a major idea of human and civil rights. How does the Declaration of Independence address human and civil rights?

⑥ Is there an <u>Overall Idea</u>? Is there a real-world use?

O.I.: Human rights must be guaranteed before you have civil rights. How do examples from different periods of our history illustrate the relationship between human rights and civil rights?

Source: Bulgren, J. A. (2002). *The Question Exploration Guide: Trainers' Guide* (p. 85). Lawrence, KS: Edge Publications, Inc. Reprinted with permission.

learning. However, regardless of the level, the question answering should be aligned with assessments and ensure that targeted content learning outcomes are achieved. The QER represents a response to instructional needs of all students to engage in higher-level thinking.

The Recall Enhancement Routine

Although higher-order thinking and reasoning are the focus of many of the CERs, the developers also recognized the need to help students acquire, recall, and demonstrate understanding of important information; this was the basis for the development of the Recall Enhancement Routine (RER) (Schumaker, Bulgren, Deshler, & Lenz, 1998). This routine helps students acquire and use a variety of mnemonic devices. Mnemonic devices help students to acquire and store information for use in more complex levels of thinking. The RER is another example of a group accommodation that also focuses on embedding strategy instruction into content area instruction to help students recall important foundational information and prior knowledge. A significant amount of research has been completed supporting the positive effects of mnemonic devices with students with disabilities (e.g., Mastropieri & Scruggs, 1992; Mastropieri, Scruggs, & Fulk, 1990).

Figure 9.6 Completed Question Exploration Guide in math.

---

① What is the <u>Critical Question</u>?

What is the algorithm and an associated acronym for multiplying binomials?

---

② What are the <u>Key Terms</u> and explanations?

Algorithm	A set of steps for performing a math operation.
Binomial	A mathematical expression comprised of two terms joined by a plus sign ($+$) or a minus sign ($-$).
Acronym	A word formed by the first letters of different words.

---

③ What are the <u>Supporting Questions</u> and answers?

What is step 1? F = Multiply the First terms in each binomial
$$(2x-y)(3x+2y) \qquad 2x * 3x = 6x^2$$

What is step 2? O = Multiply the Outside terms in each binomial
$$(2x-y)(3x+2y) \qquad 2x * 2y = 4xy$$

What is step 3? I = Multiply the Inside terms in each binomial
$$(2x-y)(3x+2y) \qquad -y * 3x = -3xy$$

What is step 4? L = Multiply the Last terms in each binomial
$$(2x-y)(3x+2y) \qquad -y * 2y = -2y^2$$

What is step 5? S = Set up and Summarize the answer
$$6x^2 + (4xy - 3xy) - 2y^2 \; = \; 6x^2 + xy - 2y^2$$

---

④ What is the <u>Main Idea</u> answer?

The algorithm contains 5 steps involving multiplying the terms in a sequence and summarizing the answer. The word "FOILS" is an acronym that can be used to remember the steps.

---

⑤ How can we <u>Use</u> the main idea again?

Solve this new problem using the FOILS algorithm. $(3x + 4y)(2x + 2y)$

---

⑥ Is there an Overall Idea? Is there a real-world use?

Explain how the FOILS acronym helps you as a learner. Create your own memory device for another math algorithm.

Source: Bulgren, J. A., Lenz, B. K., Deshler, D. D., & Schumaker, J. B. (2001). *The Question Exploration Routine* (p. 66). Lawrence, KS: Edge Publications, Inc. Reprinted with permission.

Systems to help students remember information can include very simple strategies such as rehearsal. In the early school years, rehearsal is one of the first methods used by teachers to help students remember. For example, teachers often create rhymes, poems, or songs from important information to help young children's recall. As students mature, and as they are expected to remember larger and more complex sets of information, more sophisticated strategies and mnemonic devices can be used to help students develop strategic ways to remember information when it is needed.

The RER illustrates how teachers can help students acquire strategic approaches to recalling small but critical sets of facts needed in content areas. Research on the RER points to a number of elements that teachers should include when embedding mnemonic strategies in large-group content area instruction. These elements include (a) providing information to students regarding the types of mnemonics that can be used and the types of information that are best suited for each type of mnemonic; (b) teaching how content area information should be selected, organized, and effectively applied to the construction of a mnemonic; (c) teaching how information captured by mnemonics is practiced and used to remember the information; and (d) using the principles of direct instruction to ensure that the mnemonic is learned (Schumaker et al., 1998).

The strategic steps associated with the RER include formatting the information, analyzing the information and selecting a device, creating the recall device, and tying the mnemonic together. These steps not only guide instructional procedures and development of the device, but also contain an embedded strategy cued by the acronym FACT. A number of mnemonic devices are taught to the students in the RER. These include variations on mental images or picture devices, keyword devices, stories, symbols or associations, acronyms and acrostics, series or location cues, and other devices such as rhyming and coding in which letters serve as substitutes for numbers.

The Recall Device Sheet

The Recall Device Sheet is used as a central part of the direct instruction process to organize information and practice. Figure 9.7 shows a graphic organizer, the Recall Device Sheet, that teachers and students can use

to approach the use of mnemonics. It extends the FACT acronym to FACTOR to guide students to format the information, analyze the information and select a device, create the recall device, tie it together, organize some questions, and review the plan. Figure 9.8 shows a completed Recall Device Sheet, with a list entitled "Classes of Fishes."

Implementation of the Recall Enhancement Routine

The instructional procedures use the CUE-DO-REVIEW sequence common to all CERs and already illustrated with the QER. After cueing the use of the graphic organizer, the importance of answering the question, and expectations regarding participation and note taking, the DO component is implemented. In the first step, the students and teacher write the important information that needs to be remembered and select the format of the

Figure 9.7   Blank Recall Device Sheet.

Source: Schumaker, J., Bulgren, J., Deshler, D., & Lenz, B. K. (1998). *The Recall Enhancement Routine* (p. 20). Lawrence, KS: The University of Kansas Center for Research on Learning. Reprinted with permission.

Figure 9.8 Completed Recall Enhancement Routine Device Sheet from a science course.

Format the Information   Type of Information: ❑ List ❑ Pair ❑ Trio ❑ Definition ❑ Other

    Classes of Fishes
        Boney
        Jawless
        Cartilage

Analyze the Information & Select a Device

Type of Memory Device: _____*Boxina*_____

Create the Recall Device

B o n e y

J a w l e s s

C a r t i l a g e

Jaw   Bone   Cart   Mrs. Jackson

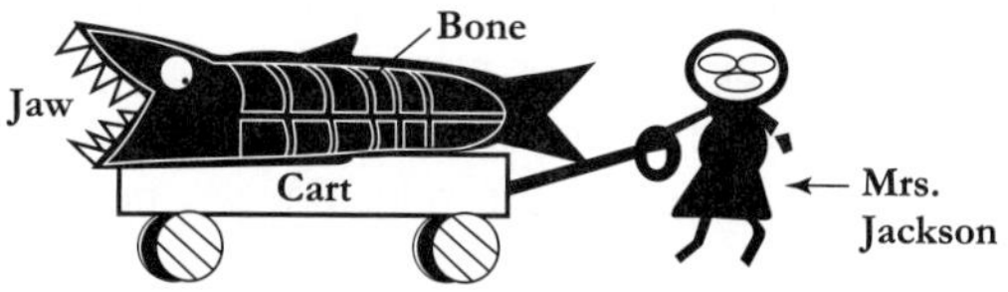

Tie it Together

My husband went fishing and caught a huge shark, a type of fish. He had a big jaw, and we could see his bones. I wanted to show him to all of my students, so I took him to class on a cart. He was too heavy for me to carry. I got the words "jaw," "bone," and "cart" by looking for the little words found in the three items in our list. Be sure to remember the longer words for each of these short words.

Organize Some Questions

What are the three classes of fishes?
Describe the three classes of fishes.
Compare and contrast the three classes of fishes.

Review Plan

Partners will study together on Sept. 15

Source: Schumaker, J., Bulgren, J., Deshler, D., & Lenz, B. K. (1998). *The Recall Enhancement Routine* (p. 20). Lawrence, KS: The University of Kansas Center for Research on Learning. Reprinted with permission.

information. In the next step of the graphic organizer, the student examines the information and selects the best type of mnemonic that might be used to remember the information. Figure 9.8 shows that the students have chosen to use a variation on the keyword method called "boxing" as the appropriate memory device. In this method a key syllable is identified, boxed off from the rest of the word, and used as part of the complex mnemonic that can also involve mental pictures and stories.

To illustrate, the next segment of the graphic organizer shows how the students "boxed" part of each word in the list to identify the key part of the word that would be used in the memory device. Then the students and teachers collaboratively think of a story that links the key words together. Figure 9.8 shows how students draw a picture to help remember the associations. The class then discusses and collaboratively ties this mnemonic together by writing a few sentences that make explicit the connections between the content and the mnemonic used. The students then develop some questions they will use to test the use of the mnemonic and to commit the information to memory. This step also includes the creation of study cards for use during the study process. And in the final steps of the Recall Device Sheet, the teacher guides students to develop a plan related to how and when studying will occur. At the conclusion, the REVIEW step is completed to check on understanding of the information and the process of developing the device.

Research on the RER

Bulgren and co-workers conducted two studies on the RER in inclusive general education classrooms. In the first study conducted on this routine, Bulgren et al. (1994) randomly assigned 41 students with LD and students without disabilities in seventh- and eighth-grade social studies classes to experimental and control groups. All of the students received the same lecture on the history of American journalism in which 40 facts on a social studies unit were embedded. Students in the experimental group collaboratively reviewed 20 important facts in the lecture using mnemonic devices and the RER. The review for the control group included collaborative review of the same important information, but without the mnemonics.

All of the students took a 40-item multiple-choice test (half of the items were related to reviewed facts, and half were related to nonreviewed facts). Results showed that students with LD and without disabilities in experimental classes answered significantly more test items related to reviewed facts when the routine was used than did students in the comparison classes.

Another experimental study on the same routine (Bulgren et al., 1997) showed that nine teachers in secondary (junior high and high school) content area classes could be taught to use the RER at mastery levels in their classrooms after a 3-hour workshop. It also showed that students were more likely to identify the most appropriate type of mnemonic device to be used for particular factual items (e.g., correctly selected devices for recalling listed information when lists were present, selected

visual imagery devices when the information required imagery) when their teacher had used that device in comparison to students in the comparison group.

Evaluation of Content Enhancement Routines

Teachers, administrators, and professional developers can evaluate the effectiveness of a teaching routine and its intended use in a group of students with disabilities along three dimensions, which we will illustrate with evaluation materials for the QER. The first evaluation dimension focuses on the accuracy of the content that is placed in the QEG and whether the information that is provided is appropriately ordered in the question unpacking process. Figure 9.9 provides a checklist that has

Figure 9.9   Question Exploration Routine content checklist for the Question Exploration Guide.

Teacher _____   Observer _____

School _____   Subject _____

Date _____

Directions: Put a checkmark (√) by each component that is present/observed.

Critical Question   **Refer to pp. 7 and 21 in the Question Exploration Routine (QER) guidebook**

_____   is a Big Idea question that students need to answer to succeed in the course (usually a "how" or "why" or broader "what" question).

NOTE: A question may consist of an interrogatory statement signaled by "explain," "describe," etc., but must elicit in-depth consideration as a question would.

Key Term and Explanations   **Refer to pp. 7 and 23–24 in the QER guidebook**

_____   are the important words or phrases (implicit or explicit) that must be understood to discuss and answer the question;

_____   are each explained briefly but clearly.

NOTE: Key terms and explanations may be added at any point in the lesson as needed.

Supporting Questions and Answers   **Refer to pp. 8 and 24–25 in the QER guidebook**

_____   are supporting questions leading to the Main Idea answer to the Critical Question;

_____   are answers for each supporting question that are clearly developed.

NOTE: The answers to the supporting questions, viewed as a sequence of written statements, often represent a coherent short-answer response.

Main Idea Answer   **Refer to pp. 8 and 22 in the QER guidebook**

_____   is a concise answer to the Critical Question that can be used later in a variety of ways.

Use in a Related Area   **Refer to pp. 8 and 25 in the QER guidebook**

_____   is a question prompting students to explore the Main Idea answer in greater depth within the same subject;

_____   results in an application of the Main Idea.

Real-World Use   **Refer to pp. 8 and 25 in the QER guidebook**

_____   is a question prompting students to explore the Main Idea answer as it applies to the real world;

_____   results in a generalization of the Main Idea answer (Overall Idea) OR is a Challenge Question or activity.

Source: Information from Bulgren, J. A., Lenz, B. K., Deshler, D. D., & Schumaker, J. B. (2001). *The Question Exploration Routine.* Lawrence, KS: Edge Publications, Inc.

been used for evaluating the information placed in the device during classroom instruction.

The second evaluation dimension focuses on the degree to which a teacher provides direct, explicit, guided instruction in the CUE-DO-REVIEW process. Because the verbal supports related to using the guide are so important to its effectiveness, the CUE-DO-REVIEW process described earlier is critical to its success. Figure 9.10 provides an example of a checklist for evaluating the teacher's adherence to the process.

The third evaluation dimension focuses on the degree to which the device is used routinely in the course with frequency and intensity. If a teacher is not using the routine over the course of the year, the teacher can be

Figure 9.10 Question Exploration Routine Implementation Checklist.

Teacher _____   Observer _____

Date _____   Subject _____

Question Exploration Routine Implementation Checklist

Cue

The teacher…
_____ named the Question Exploration Guide.
_____ explained how it will help students learn important ideas.
_____ handed out blank guides.
_____ explained expectations for note taking and participation.

Note: Score points only if the teacher writes each item on a Question Exploration Guide that is visible to the students.

Do

Step 1:
The teacher…
_____ announced the Critical Question.

Step 2:
The teacher…
_____ noted Key Terms.
_____ explained or developed explanations for Key Terms with students.

Step 3:
The teacher…
_____ guided discussion of the supporting questions to elicit *all* needed information.
_____ elicited/co-constructed answers to the supporting questions in a logical, sequenced flow.

Step 4:
The teacher…
_____ co-constructed a brief, but concise Main Idea answer with students.

Step 5:
The teacher…
_____ announced or co-constructed a question prompting students to apply the Main Idea answer in a related area.

Step 6:
The teacher…
_____ announced or co-constructed a question prompting students to generalize the Main Idea answer in a real-world or extended area.

Review

The teacher…
_____ asked questions prompting the students to ensure their *understanding* of the Main Idea.
_____ asked questions prompting the students to reflect about and review the *process* of exploring critical questions.

Source: Information from Bulgren, J. A., Lenz, B. K., Deshler, D. D., & Schumaker, J. B. (2001). *The Question Exploration Routine.* Lawrence, KS: Edge Publications, Inc.

judged as not implementing the routine correctly. That is, in order for students to become comfortable with the routine, the teacher must use it sufficiently throughout the course in order for students to become familiar with its use. Some indications that a teacher is using a teaching routine sufficiently include that students immediately recognize the device and how it will be used during the CUE phase, contribute and participate in the completion of information during the DO phase, and can use the device to independently summarize the information included on the device in the REVIEW phase.

Conclusion

The purpose of this chapter has been to discuss approaches that have emerged in the research literature related to promoting content area learning for groups of students of diverse abilities and achievement, including students with disabilities. The content enhancement intervention approaches described here and the methods we have highlighted provide windows on practices that can significantly help students with disabilities learn in content area classrooms. However, the effectiveness of both of these interventions depends on the careful selection of content and the explicit and intentional use of the procedures to address the learning problems of students with disabilities. Ensuring access to content relies on teachers' striking a careful balance between those strategies that students can ultimately use to learn content independently and the critical need to provide teacher-directed supports and instruction for content attainment regardless of students' proficiency in using good learning strategies.

The two highlighted CERs address the content area learning needs of students with disabilities in a number of ways. The use of CERs can be specified in the IEP process as ways to respond to the learning needs of students who may, for example, learn better when information is presented in visual as well as a verbal format. In addition, CERs conform to UDL principles in that they have been designed and tested to be responsive to the learning needs of all students. In terms of instructional procedures, the routines have been developed to be flexible enough that teachers can use them to support learning in small, peer groups as well as large-group instruction.

In addition, CERs incorporate instructional components shown to be effective practices. For example, in terms of learning supports, the graphic organizers used in CERs provide a method of collaboration and efficient communication about important content and thinking when general education teachers work with adult tutors or special education teachers in support classes. In addition, the routines include explicit instruction about learning goals and procedures as well as co-constructive procedures that help all students build understandings based on different sets of prior knowledge. The routines also contain embedded cognitive strategies, both general and higher level, which may be used in different content areas. The goal is that use of integrated sets of routines combined with teacher prompts about using effective strategies will result in increased metacognitive abilities on the part of students. Ultimately, the attention that these routines gives to the selection of proven instructional procedures has been shown to help all students as they acquire, store, and retrieve information; demonstrate their understanding of content information; and engage in the strategic thinking required to improve academic outcomes in content areas.

CHAPTER 10

Strategies for Improving Student Outcomes in Co-Taught General Education Classrooms

Naomi Zigmond | *University of Pittsburgh*

Kathleen Magiera | *State University of NY Fredonia*

Rhea Simmons | *State University of NY Fredonia*

Victoria Volonino | *University of Pittsburgh*

With the 2004 reauthorization of the Individuals with Disabilities Education Act, students with disabilities were mandated not only to have access to the general education curriculum, but also to take the state accountability assessments. This most recent reauthorization of the federal special education law reinforced the provisions of the No Child Left Behind Act of 2001 that emphasized accountability for the performance of all students, with and without disabilities. As general education classrooms have become increasingly populated with diverse learners, all of whom are expected to meet annual achievement benchmarks, co-teaching has been advocated as a way to enhance instruction and facilitate learning for all students, but especially for students with disabilities in general education classrooms. In fact, co-teaching has become the strategic centerpiece of both special and general education reform movements during the past several years (Hyatt, Iddings, & Ober, 2005; Mariage & Patriarca, 2007; Saxon, 2005).

Co-teaching has enormous intuitive appeal and has been widely implemented in schools across the nation. Several state education agencies support the use of co-teaching through statewide policies and teacher trainings (Muller, Friend, & Hurley-Chamberlain, 2009). Nevertheless, research on the instructional validity of co-teaching (i.e., whether it actually provides the assumed instructional benefits) and on student outcomes (i.e., increased student achievement) as a result of its implementation is extremely limited. A review of the literature reveals gaps and omissions in the research evidence for the actual contribution of co-teaching to the teaching–learning process. In this chapter, we provide a brief overview of that literature and research on co-teaching and identify approaches for implementing co-teaching that are based in the research literature and may facilitate attaining improved student outcomes in co-taught classes. We begin with a discussion of definitional issues that have affected both implementation and research on co-teaching.

Co-Teaching Models and Practices

The traditional definition of co-teaching has been described by several researchers (Bauwens, Hourcade, & Friend, 1989; L. Cook & Friend, 1996; Vaughn, Bos, & Schumm, 2006). These authors have noted that co-teaching occurs when a special educator and a general educator teach together in a general education classroom during some portion of the instructional day to accommodate the needs of students with and without disabilities. They also emphasize various formats of the co-teaching model in which students learn within smaller groups (i.e., not whole-class instruction). Recently, in a more "functional" definition of co-teaching, Kloo and Zigmond (2008) reiterated the importance of focusing on the strategic grouping of the students rather than on the interactions between the two teachers. Their "functional" definition suggests that small-group instruction should be the norm in a co-taught classroom.

In this chapter, we focus on co-teaching as a service that is recommended for students with high-incidence disabilities (e.g., learning disabilities [LD], emotional disturbance, mild intellectual disability). Although their individualized education programs (IEPs) typically call for instruction to be adapted, students with high-incidence disabilities are placed in co-taught classes with the expectation that they will participate and make progress in the general education curriculum in content areas such as reading, mathematics, social studies, or science. Co-teaching is also recommended for students with low-incidence disabilities (see Hunt & Goetz, 1997; J. Katz & Mirenda, 2002; Santamaria & Thousand, 2004), but the curricular focus of co-teaching for these students may be more individualized—a topic we do not consider in this chapter. Further, we limit our review of co-teaching to situations in which one general educator and one special educator share responsibility for planning, delivering, and evaluating instruction for a diverse class of students, some of whom are students with disabilities. Typically, the general education teacher instructs students with disabilities in the general education curriculum while the special education teacher provides greater access to that curriculum through accommodations and supports (Thousand & Villa, 1989).

One of the earliest models of co-teaching was described by Friend and Cook (1992). They described the following "traditional" approaches in which either teacher can assume any role:

1. The *one teaching and one assisting* variation requires one teacher to retain the instructional lead in the classroom, while the other teacher circulates through the room providing assistance and support to the students as needed.

2. The *one teaching and one observing* approach requires one educator to assume responsibility for instruction while the other educator actively observes and assesses the learning of target students.

3. *Station teaching* involves students rotating through three instructional groups with each teacher assuming particular instructional responsibility for one group while a third group works independently.

4. *Parallel teaching* requires teachers to jointly plan instruction, but then each teacher delivers the content to half of the students.

5. *Alternative teaching* allows for a large- and small-group configuration with each group led by one of the teachers.

6. *Team teaching* occurs when teachers continually alternate the role of primary instructor within individual lessons.

A model offered by Vaughn, Schumm, and Arguelles (1997) builds on the options of parallel teaching, station teaching, and team teaching, but provides adaptations to enhance the instructional aspects of the one teaching/one assisting approach. In their model, while one teacher leads the class, the other teacher provides brief intensive instruction to individual students, student pairs, or small groups. Walther-Thomas, Korinek, McLaughlin, and Williams (2000) further extended the co-teaching model. They retained the co-teaching options of parallel teaching, station teaching, and alternative teaching, but replaced the option of one teaching/one assisting with a variation referred to as *interactive teaching*. In this interactive teaching format, instruction is presented to the whole group, with the educators alternating the role of instructional leader for periods of 5 to 10 minutes. As the lead teacher role changes frequently, both teachers are afforded several opportunities to serve as the primary educator (Walther-Thomas et al., 2000).

Co-Teaching Research

Given the popularity of co-teaching as a service-delivery model for students with high incidence disabilities, one might expect to find a sizable research base supporting the practice. Unfortunately that is not the case. Most of the published literature on co-teaching is not empirical or evaluative; instead it describes logistics and recommends procedures such as ongoing co-planning, compatibility in teaching philosophy, and strong administrative support (Bauwens et al., 1989; Friend & Cook, 2003;

Gately & Gately, 2001; Reeve & Hallahan, 1994; Vaughn et al., 1997; Walther-Thomas et al., 2000). Some researchers provide rich descriptions of co-teaching implemented in elementary, middle school, or high school classrooms (J. Baker & Zigmond, 1995; Walther-Thomas, 1997; Weiss & Lloyd, 2002), though these studies often focus solely on the one particular arrangement that participating teachers have adopted.

Several authors have reported high levels of satisfaction among all constituents once co-teaching has been implemented (Pugach & Johnson, 1995; Purkey & Smith, 1985; D. L. Voltz, Elliot, & Cobb, 1994). General education teachers, often initially skeptical about sharing their classroom space, generally come to enjoy having a second adult in the classroom who can assist students. On the other hand, special education teachers respond positively to reaching more students in the general education classroom.

Questions remain, however. Does co-teaching work? Does it provide students with high-incidence disabilities more and better instructional opportunities and lead to improved student outcomes? Research on the effectiveness of co-teaching is still emerging (Weiss & Brigham, 2000; Zigmond, 2003), and data on achievement outcomes for students with disabilities in co-taught classes have been particularly elusive. Klingner, Vaughn, Hughes, Schumm, and Elbaum (1998) studied co-teaching at an elementary school that implemented "responsible" inclusion. They followed 25 students with LD assigned into six general education classrooms in one elementary school and calculated gains in academic achievement over one school year using pretests and post-tests. Their study did not include a control group of students with LD taught in general education classrooms without co-teaching or students with LD taught in pullout settings. Although Klingner et al. found that students with disabilities, as well as students at risk for educational failure, made small but significant increases in fall-to-spring reading achievement in co-taught classrooms, the gains were not significant for math achievement.

Welch (2000) completed a descriptive analysis of team teaching using qualitative and quantitative methods in an approach referred to as a "formative experiment" (Reinking & Pickle, 1993). He tracked the progress of eight students with LD, five in one classroom and three in another, and their classmates in two schools implementing co-teaching for 16 to 19 weeks. Again, this study included no control group of students with LD who did not receive co-teaching. Welch found that team teaching improved the reading fluency and word-recognition skills of *all* students in the two elementary-level classrooms, but the overall increase in mean performance of students with LD was not statistically significant.

Rea, McLaughlin, and Walther-Thomas (2002) investigated the relationship between placement in the special education program and academic and behavior outcomes for eighth-grade school students with LD in two middle schools, one providing inclusive, co-taught services (n = 36) and the other providing pullout services (n = 22). They used a retrospective approach, gathering extant data for a cohort of students who had been served in two distinct service-delivery models in the middle schools of a single suburban district. Although students were not randomly assigned to the treatments/schools, several student-level variables established the equivalence of the two groups of students at the start of the study. The authors reported that students with LD taught in the general education classrooms with co-teaching services received higher course grades in language arts, math, science, and social studies than their peers in pullout programs. Rea et al. reported significant findings also favoring co-taught students with LD for scores on the Iowa Test of Basic Skills (ITBS) in language and math, and for attendance. However, the groups earned comparable scores on state achievement tests; comparable scores on the ITBS in reading, science, and social studies; and comparable numbers of school suspensions.

K. C. Fontana (2005) also examined the effect of co-teaching on eighth graders with LD. Students with LD who were randomly assigned to a control group (n = 16) were taught in a traditional one-teacher classroom for English and math. Students with LD who were randomly assigned to the target group (n = 17) were randomly placed in English and math classes co-taught by three general education teachers who volunteered to co-teach. Students with LD in both the control and target groups received one period of resource room support. The only comparisons between the outcomes of the two groups involved English and math grades. Grades (calculated from objective measures such as unit tests and quizzes) of target, co-taught students were significantly higher at the end of eighth grade than they had been at the end of seventh grade. Grades of students with LD in solo-taught eighth-grade classes showed no significant improvement over their previous year's grades.

Murawski (2006) conducted a randomized block design experiment to study outcomes of co-taught, solo-taught, and resource room English classes for 38 ninth graders with LD and 72 students without disabilities in one urban high school. The four experimental conditions included a general education class with no included students with disabilities, two solo-taught inclusive classes, two co-taught inclusive classes, and one special education class. A block design was called for because students with LD were assigned to an inclusive or special education class based on student ability and family preference, not at random. However, students with LD selected for an inclusive class were randomly assigned to a co-taught ($n = 12$) or a solo-taught class ($n = 8$). After co-varying for pretest and ability scores, Murawski found no significant main effects for treatment condition for standardized tests of spelling, math, vocabulary, reading comprehension, or writing after the 10-week intervention for students with LD in resource room, solo-taught, or co-taught classes, and no main effects for students without disabilities in classes with one teacher (with or without included students with LD) or with two teachers (and included students).

In addition to outcomes on academic skills, studies have also evaluated outcomes related to socialization. Co-teaching all day long was not as effective as a consultation/collaborative teaching model of service delivery (with co-teaching for only part of the day) in increasing peer acceptance ratings and overall friendship quality for elementary-aged students with LD. Vaughn and colleagues (Vaughn, Elbaum, Schumm, & Hughes, 1998) found that the number and quality of students' friendships improved when students transitioned from exclusionary educational settings back into the general education classroom, but students in the co-teaching school did not fare as well as those in the comparison school. The authors acknowledge that the results could be attributed to differences in the ratio of students with LD to students without disabilities in the two settings: in the co-teaching school, half the classes of 27 to 35 students were students with LD, while in the consultation/collaborative teaching, only 3 to 8 of the 31 to 37 students in each classroom were students with LD. It was also difficult to separate setting effects from teacher and other home and school effects despite the authors' attempts to match schools in terms of overall achievement scores and ethnicity of the student population.

In a review of the overall research base of co-teaching, Murawski and Swanson (2001) conducted a meta-analysis. Unfortunately, only six quantitative studies that met their inclusion criteria were identified. Only one study (Self, Benning, Marston, & Magnusson, 1991) involved students in kindergarten through third grade, and this study yielded an effect size of 0.95. Two studies (Klingner, Vaughn, Hughes, et al., 1998; Vaughn, Elbaum, et al., 1998) reported on 11 outcome measures for students in grades 3 through 6; the total effect size of 0.19 indicated a low effect for elementary students. Finally, three studies analyzed for their effects on high school students (Lundeen & Lundeen, 1993; Rosman, 1994; J. M. Walsh & Snyder, 1993) yielded a total effect size on nine measures of 0.30. Measures of student outcomes spanned a range of dependent variables that included grades (mean effect size of 0.32), special education referrals (mean effect size of 0.43), attitudes (no effect), and academic achievement in reading (mean effect size of 1.59) and mathematics (mean effect size of 0.45).

Murawski and Swanson (2001) concluded that co-teaching was moderately effective in influencing student outcomes (overall mean effect size of 0.40), although they cautioned that because so little quantitative research evaluated the effectiveness of co-teaching, it is difficult to draw meaningful conclusions about the practice. Further, their meta-analysis did not include the Boudah, Schumaker, and Deshler (1997) landmark study of co-taught classes at the high school level in which academic achievement for students with mild disabilities actually decreased.

The lack of empirical support for co-teaching is not surprising; co-teaching may be a service, but it is not a "treatment" that can be imposed with fidelity on an experimental group and withheld with equal fidelity from a control group. Researchers who have attempted to contrast student outcomes in co-taught vs. solo-taught classrooms or co-taught vs. pullout instruction, whether through quasi-experimental designs or true random assignment of students, assume they have specified the treatment when they claim that co-teaching is occurring, yet the intervention is often defined merely as "a variety of co-teaching methods" (K. C. Fontana, 2005, p. 20).

Collaboration is the process whereby special and general education teachers implement co-teaching (Magiera, Simmons, Marotta, & Battaglia, 2005). Most often, the collaboration is described in terms of the roles assumed by the two teachers. Several descriptive studies have sought to determine whether the potential for co-teaching to provide enhanced learning opportunities actually materializes in co-taught classes. Magiera and Zigmond (2005) studied co-taught and solo-taught classrooms at the middle school level and reported that the instructional experience for students in co-taught classrooms was similar to the instructional experience in solo-taught classrooms. McDuffie, Mastropieri, and Scruggs (2009) found that students with disabilities in four solo-taught classes interacted significantly *more* often with their teachers than did students in four co-taught classes.

In secondary co-taught classes observed by Weiss and Lloyd (2002), and in a later study reported by Zigmond and Matta (2004), researchers failed to observe significantly enhanced instructional experiences. In fact, a recent meta-synthesis of qualitative research on co-teaching by Scruggs, Mastropieri, and McDuffie (2007) showed that true collaboration between co-teachers seldom has been achieved. They found that special educators frequently assume the role of instructional aide and that a variety of factors inhibit their ability to provide specialized instruction within the general education classroom. Further, Scruggs et al. concluded that the benefits of co-teaching services related to "curriculum needs, innovative practice, and appropriate individualization—ha[ve] largely not been met" (p. 412).

Despite the research base providing limited support for co-teaching, proponents continue to emphasize that co-taught classrooms provide a venue for the integration of the complementary skills of general and special educators (Friend & Cook, 2003). That is, the general educator brings to co-teaching content knowledge and group instructional skills, while the special educator brings expertise in the diagnosis and remediation of individual learning problems or challenges. By interfacing these instructional skills, instruction in the general education classroom should be sufficiently enhanced such that the needs of both students with disabilities and those at-risk for educational failure can effectively be met (Kauffman & Hallahan, 2005). However, future researchers will need to specify the actual instructional practices under consideration (e.g., collaboration) in their attempts to document desired student outcomes.

A Key to More Successful Co-Teaching: The Collaboration Process

Teachers require professional socialization to learn to become more collaborative (Friend & Cook, 2003; R. J. Simmons, Magiera, Cummings, & Arena, 2008). Without consistent training and follow-up, teachers make up their own ways of implementing a co-teaching model. For example, R. J. Simmons and Magiera (2007) observed 10 secondary co-taught classes and interviewed 22 co-teachers in three different high schools within the same school district and found strikingly different degrees of implementation of the co-teaching model in this single school district. These findings are consistent with the conclusions of other researchers (e.g., Adelman & Taylor, 2003; Magiera, Smith, Zigmond, & Gebauer, 2005; Salend, Gordon, & Lopez-Vona, 2002; R. J. Simmons & Magiera, 2007) that only a systematic approach to implementing the process of collaboration within a school district will lead to greater access to the general education curriculum for students with disabilities.

Based on previous foundational research and their own studies of co-teaching, Magiera, Simmons, and Hance (2008) have delineated a six-step "quality process" to ensure that co-teachers are truly collaborating. The implementation process begins by establishing a common understanding of co-teaching to be implemented among all co-teachers and administrators. To become more collaborative, several researchers (Caron & McLaughlin, 2002; Magiera et al., 2005; R. J. Simmons & Magiera, 2007) have recommended a tiered approach to professional development (see Figure 10.1). Magiera and her colleagues (2008) suggest that the first step is joint planning meetings involving district leaders, staff development specialists, and higher education partners to establish a vision of co-teaching for the district. A common and consistent framework for co-teaching may be essential for successful collaboration.

Professional development opportunities for administrators and co-teaching pairs are the second step in laying the co-teaching foundation. Essential to this foundational staff development is the establishment of a common vocabulary and a consistent understanding of the co-teaching service for administrators and co-teachers (McLaughlin, 2002). In a large-scale co-teaching initiative involving 132 teachers, Magiera, Simmons, et al.

Figure 10.1   Essential elements for developing a quality collaborative process for co-teaching.

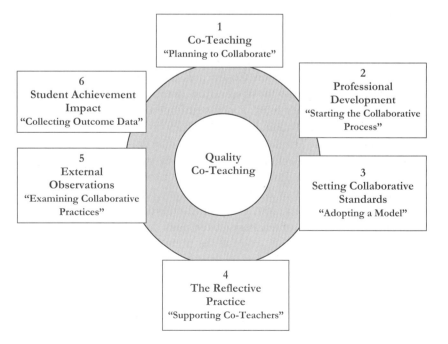

(2005) found administrative and teacher knowledge was critical to establishing a consistent foundation for co-teaching.

Setting collaborative standards is the third step. This involves making transparent and observable the "best practices" of collaborative behaviors that are being fostered (Caron & McLaughlin, 2002; Dieker, 2001; Salend et al., 2002). Caron and McLaughlin (2002) have called for measurable indicators of these practices so that implementation of co-teaching can be monitored and improved. In their work in four elementary and two middle schools involving 12 special education teachers and 17 general education teachers, Caron and McLaughlin identified "critical indicators" related to successful collaboration among special and general education teachers. Following classroom observations of co-teaching, teachers discussed various patterns of collaboration. The researchers found that setting clear expectations for all students including students with disabilities within the context of teaching the general education curriculum was critical to the collaborative process.

A. I. Nevin (2006) has identified three available tools that may help with successful collaboration: the Co-Teacher Relationship Scale (Noonan, McCormick, & Heck, 2003), which focuses on matching up potential co-teaching pairs; the Are We Really Co-Teachers Scale (Villa, Thousand, & Nevin, 2008), which focuses on teaching interactions and behaviors in a co-taught classroom; and finally the Magiera-Simmons Quality Indicator Model of Co-Teaching (Magiera & Simmons, 2005), designed to help teachers become more collaborative in co-taught classrooms. These tools yield formative teacher data critical to ensure that co-teaching implementation goes beyond the "one teach/one assist" as noted by Scruggs et al. (2007).

Setting standards and collecting data are not sufficient. Therefore, the fourth step in establishing collaborative practices is reflection. Co-teachers need time and opportunities to review the observation data, to ask questions, to clarify their roles, and to reinforce their initial learning of the collaborative process. They do this as they plan together. The iterative process of data collection followed by reflection helps co-teaching pairs refine their collaborative instructional practice (Caron & McLaughlin, 2002; Dieker, 2001; Magiera et al., 2008; R. J. Simmons & Magiera, 2007). Dieker (2001) found in a study of nine pairs of teachers (seven pairs at the middle school level and two pairs at the high school level) that student outcome data were used during planning time to guide teachers' selection of the co-teaching support model to be implemented. Teachers valued this planning time and reported that "sanctity" of team planning time was essential to the co-teaching model.

The fifth step involves an examination of collaborative practices with or by an objective, independent evaluation team. This step is highly recommended by Salend and his colleagues (2002) as a useful balance to self-study and self-reflection. Salend et al. (2002) described various sources of evaluation data such as interviews, surveys, best practices checklists, observations, journals, and teaching portfolios to identify strengths and concerns of co-teachers. After reviewing the overall progress of the collaborative processes, the independent evaluation team (often including a higher-education partner) can help guide the school administrators' and teachers' next steps in the implementation process.

Consistent with McLaughlin's work (2002) on the usefulness of collaborative communities, Magiera, Smith, et al. (2005) found in their research that a strong learning community of administrators and special and general educators is the precursor to student success. Supporting co-teachers through ongoing administrative follow-up was key to implementing the co-teaching model with fidelity. Because of the community, co-teaching pairs were actually willing to take risks and more fully implement varied groupings in their classrooms for the benefit of all students, with and without disabilities (Magiera et al., 2008).

The final step for developing a quality collaborative process involves appropriately measuring student outcomes. Murawski and Swanson (2001) in their meta-analysis of co-teaching research found that in the limited number of studies in which teachers provided joint instruction and had common planning time, co-teaching had a positive impact on student achievement, particularly in reading and language arts. Future research in the area of co-teaching should examine the impact of the collaborative process on student achievement. However, while the ultimate goal of collaboration is overall improved student performance, Friend, Hurley-Chamberlain, and Cook (2006) caution against judging the value of a co-teaching service solely on the basis of student outcomes.

Another Perspective on Co-Teaching: Reconfigure the Dance

Collaboration among general and special educators is often described as a delicate dance enacted in a single classroom. Kloo and Zigmond (2008) provide yet another way of framing the co-teaching partnership. They delineate three broad "lesson configurations" made possible when two fully certified teachers are in the classroom co-teaching: (a) both teachers actively instructing a single group of students; (b) each teacher actively instructing their own group of students; and (c) neither teacher involved in group instruction (students working independently, working on group projects, watching a film, etc.). They argue that the purpose and content of the lesson should determine which of these configurations is used, not the preferences or teaching styles of the two teachers involved. Both teachers actively instructing a single group of students works well for teaching content subjects like literature, science, or the social studies. Each teacher actively instructing his or her own group of students fits well with the skills orientation of reading and math instruction. And if students are engaged in independent work, both teachers are mere observers.

Content Subjects: Two Teachers, One Instructional Group

In content subject classes, the norm is a single, whole-class lesson or assignment; classes in science, social studies, or English are generally characterized by large-group lecture or discussion followed by individual or small-group assignments or projects. Small-group *instruction* is not a common practice in content subject classes, particularly at the high school level (Zigmond, 2006; Zigmond & Matta, 2004). Kloo and Zigmond (2008), drawing on the extensive research base on effective instructional techniques for struggling learners, suggest that the job of the special education teacher in content subject instruction is to provide *S-U-P-P-O-R-T,* not only to the students with disabilities in the classroom but also to the general education partner (see Figure 10.2).

Study the Content

To support students' understanding of content, special education teachers should have a working knowledge of the curriculum. They must become familiar with the

Figure 10.2   Activities of the special education teacher in a co-taught content subject class.

> **S**-tudy the content.
>
> **U**-nderstand the Big Ideas.
>
> **P**-rioritize course objectives.
>
> **P**-lan with the general education teacher.
>
> **O**-bserve the students in the class as they listen to instruction.
>
> **R**-ephrase, repeat, redirect.
>
> **T**-each your co-teacher to do it all on her own.

content or relearn concepts and principles of the subject being taught. This is, perhaps, one of the greatest challenges for special education teachers, particularly at the secondary level (Weiss & Lloyd, 2002). However, special education teachers need not become content experts in that classroom.

Understand the Big Ideas; Prioritize Course Objectives

General education teachers plan courses of study for content subjects using logic and experience to determine how much can be accomplished in one grading period, one semester, or one school year. Students with disabilities generally start each school year knowing less than their classmates, have more to learn, and take longer to learn it (Zigmond, 1996). The special education teacher should work collaboratively with the general education teacher to set priorities within the general education curriculum. The curriculum for students with disabilities, as well as for students without disabilities, is often focused on what will be assessed on the statewide test. For students with disabilities who already struggle to learn, the curriculum probably needs to be narrowed even more to allow time for teachers to teach high-priority content deeply and to ensure student mastery (Schumm, Vaughn, & Harris, 1997).

Plan with the General Education Teacher

Lack of co-planning time for special and general educators is one of the major obstacles to successful collaboration (Bauwens & Hourcade, 1995; Walther-Thomas, 1997). To be effective, co-teachers need to learn to work together so that each performs relevant and meaningful tasks that promote student learning (S. C. Trent, 1998). When co-teachers plan together, this agenda moves forward by identifying instructional responsibilities and possible accommodations for the students who will need them (Schumm et al., 1997).

Observe Students in Class as They Listen to Instruction; Rephrase, Repeat, and Redirect, as Needed

In content subject classes, special and general education teachers may take turns leading and supporting instruction. The supporting teacher (often the special education co-teacher) assumes the critical role of observing and evaluating students' learning. The special education teacher actively observes and "diagnoses" student engagement, interest, and understanding. At the first sign of student confusion, the special education teacher redirects the flow of instruction by elaborating and clarifying difficult concepts.

Teach Your Co-Teacher to Do It All on Her Own

None of the advocates for co-teaching (e.g., Bauwens & Hourcade, 1995; L. Cook & Friend, 1996; Vaughn et al., 1997; Walther-Thomas et al., 2000) have proposed that co-teaching is a vehicle for training general education teachers to become strategy specialists, but we do. Part of the job of the special education co-teacher must be to make explicit to the general education partner the rationale for the accommodations provided in the IEPs so that, over time, the general education teacher can make appropriate accommodations decisions on her own.

Skill Subjects: Two Teachers, Two Instructional Groups

Educational researchers have long known that to increase students' learning of skill subjects like reading and mathematics, teachers need to increase students' opportunities to respond to and engage in the instruction (Shulman, 1985). In a co-taught classroom, two teachers are available to monitor student engagement and provide corrective feedback. As a result, Kloo and Zigmond (2008) suggest that when two teachers are in the classroom and a basic skills lesson is being taught (i.e., reading, writing, spelling, mathematics), the job of the special education teacher would be to *T-E-A-C-H* (see Figure 10.3). Small-group instruction, rather than whole-class instruction, should be the norm with increased use of parallel teaching, station teaching, or alternative teaching.

Target the Skills and Strategies a Particular Student Needs to Learn

Ample evidence indicates that most students with disabilities in general education classrooms are far behind their peers in the mastery of basic skills and are unlikely

Figure 10.3   Activities of the special education teacher in a co-taught skills-based class.

> **T**-arget the skills and strategies a particular student needs to learn.
>
> **E**-xpress enthusiasm and optimism.
>
> **A**-dapt the instructional environment.
>
> **C**-reate opportunities for small-group or individual, direct, intensive instruction.
>
> **H**-elp student apply skills learned to content classes.

to benefit from large-group skill instruction moving at a normal pace (Thurlow, Altman, & Vang, 2009). These students are also unlikely to cover the entire curriculum for that grade level in the time available (U.S. Department of Education, 2007). Kloo and Zigmond (2008) recommend that the special education teacher in a co-taught class help target the skills and strategies a particular student with a disability needs to learn and, in collaboration with the general education teacher, help set curricular priorities.

Express Enthusiasm and Optimism

Students with disabilities need to work longer and harder than students without disabilities. However, the learning environment and their own learning histories often prevent them from investing vigorously in their learning (Guthrie & Davis, 2003; Margolis & McCabe, 2004). F. J. Brigham, Scruggs, and Mastropieri (1992) demonstrated that a teacher's positive attitude, high expectations, and high levels of enthusiasm can turn around students' negative reactions to learning. Brigham et al. taught each of two classes using both enthusiastic and unenthusiastic presentations in a cross-over design in which each classroom received both presentation styles in counterbalanced order. After 2 weeks of enthusiastic and unenthusiastic teaching, they reported that students learned more and had been on task more when enthusiastic teaching variables were employed. Additionally, independent observers viewing randomly selected videotape segments rated students much higher on learning and motivations variables when those students were taught in the enthusiastic condition.

Adapt the Instructional Environment

General education classrooms are often noisy and confusing settings, not conducive to focused, intensive, teacher-directed instruction. One major drawback to the inclusive classroom may well be the high level of distraction (J. Baker & Zigmond, 1995). Special education teachers in co-taught classrooms must take the lead in adapting the instructional environment, the seating arrangements, and the instructional dynamics to maximize instructional outcomes for students with disabilities.

Create Opportunities for Small-Group or Individual, Direct, Intensive Instruction

Students with disabilities need to learn more in less time in order to make up lost ground (Tomlinson, 1999). The special and general education teachers should collaborate to create opportunities for small-group or intensive teacher-directed instruction. In a review of the research literature, Vaughn and colleagues conclude that small groups produce better learning outcomes than whole-class instruction by increasing students' opportunities for responding and for receiving corrective feedback (Vaughn, Hughes, Moody, & Elbaum, 2001).

Help Students Apply Skills Learned to Content Classes

Multiple research studies have shown that students with disabilities often fail to apply effective learning strategies across relevant learning contexts but can be taught to do so. For example, Chan and Cole (1986) taught 11-year-old students with LD to remember what they read by learning to ask a question about the text and/or underline interesting words in the text. Schumaker and Deshler (1992) build explicit instruction for generalization into their learning strategies teaching model so that teachers will facilitate student application of a newly learned strategy in other academic and nonacademic settings. This is an important role for the special education teacher in a co-taught skills class.

Kloo and Zigmond (2008) contend that efforts to evaluate the effectiveness of co-teaching on student learning outcomes will be fruitless until teachers understand more precisely what they are supposed to be doing and researchers can be assured of some fidelity of treatment implementation in their research designs. Although Kloo and Zigmond provide a research base to support each component in their TEACH/SUPPORT suggestions, it is important to remember that to date no empirical data support the effectiveness of their service-delivery model.

Conclusion and Directions for Future Research

Co-teaching should be planned deliberately and implemented dynamically. It should also marry the science of specially designed instruction and effective pedagogy with the art of reorganizing resources.

Developing collaborative skills among co-teachers requires a strategic process involving administrators and co-teaching partners. Based on empirical data collected in case studies of six exemplary schools, Caron and McLaughlin (2002) suggest that co-teaching helps to foster a strong "professional community" (p. 307) by building capacity among school personnel that will ensure that collaborative partnerships are sustained over time. In McLaughlin's introduction to the special issue of the *Journal of Educational and Psychological Consultation* that reports on the Beacons of Excellence research projects, she observes that, when co-teaching is implemented well, the impact can be far greater than that of two individual teachers simply sharing a common task (McLaughlin, 2002).

Large-scale, long-term research is needed that explicitly defines co-teaching practices and carefully monitors fidelity of implementation. Ideally, also needed are controlled experimental research designs using random assignment to co-taught and solo-taught comparison classrooms to examine academic and behavioral outcomes for students with disabilities.

Co-teaching is an example of a service that has been embraced by some researchers and practitioners as a solution to the problem of access and mastery of the general education curriculum by students with disabilities. However, the research base is limited in its support of effective co-teaching instruction. Future research must uncover the collaborative practices that lead to "added value" in the educational experiences of students with disabilities.

References

Adams, M. J. (1990). *Beginning to read: Thinking and learning about print.* Cambridge, MA: MIT Press.

Adelman, H. S., & Taylor, L. (2003). On sustainability of project innovation as systemic change. *Journal of Educational and Psychological Consultation, 14*(1), 1–25.

Al Otaiba, S., & Fuchs, D. (2002). Characteristics of children who are unresponsive to early literacy intervention: A review of the literature. *Remedial and Special Education, 23,* 300–316.

Al Otaiba, S., & Fuchs, D. (2006). Who are the young children for whom best practices in reading are ineffective? An experimental and longitudinal study. *Journal of Learning Disabilities, 39,* 414–418.

Al Otaiba, S., Schatschneider, C., & Silverman, E. (2005). Tutor assisted intensive learning strategies in kindergarten: How much is enough? *Exceptionality, 13,* 195–208.

Al Otaiba, S., & Torgesen, J. K. (2007). Effects from intensive standardized kindergarten and first grade interventions for the prevention of reading difficulties. In S. R. Jimerson, M. K. Burns, & A. M. VanDerHeyden (Eds.), *Handbook of response to intervention: The science and practice of assessment and intervention* (pp. 212–222). New York: Springer.

Allor, J. H., Mathes, P. G., Champlin, T., & Cheatham, J. P. (2009). Research-based techniques for teaching early reading skills to students with intellectual disabilities. *Education and Training in Developmental Disabilities, 44,* 356–366.

Allor, J. H., Mathes, P. G., Jones, F. G., Champlin, T., & Cheatham, J. P. (2010). Individualized research-based reading instruction for students with intellectual disabilities. *Teaching Exceptional Children, 42,* 6–12.

Allor, J. H., Mathes, P. G., Roberts, J. K., Cheatham, J., & Champlin, T. (2010). Comprehensive reading instruction for students with intellectual disabilities: Findings from the first three years of a longitudinal study. *Psychology in the Schools, 47,* 445–466.

Allor, J. H., Mathes, P. G., Roberts, K. R., Jones, F. G., & Champlin, T. (2010). Teaching students with moderate intellectual disabilities to read: An experimental examination of a comprehensive reading intervention. *Education and Training in Autism and Developmental Disabilities, 45,* 3–22.

Alves, A. J., & Gottlieb, J. (1986). Teacher interactions with mainstreamed handicapped students and their nonhandicapped peers. *Learning Disability Quarterly, 9,* 77–83.

Anderson, R. C., Hiebert, E. F., Scott, J. A., & Wilkinson, L. A. (1985). *Becoming a nation of readers: The report of the Commission on Reading.* Washington, DC: The National Institute of Education.

Arreaga-Mayer, C., Terry B. J., & Greenwood C. R. (1998). Classwide peer tutoring. In K. Topping & S. Ehly (Eds.), *Peer-assisted learning* (pp, 105–119). Mahwah, NJ: Erlbaum.

Arunachalam, V. (2001). The science behind tradition. *Current Science, 80,* 1272–1275.

Association for Supervision and Curriculum Development. (ASCD). (2002). *Teaching students with learning disabilities: Using learning strategies* [DVD]. Alexandria, VA: Author.

Baker, J., & Zigmond, N. (1995). The meaning and practice of inclusion for students with learning disabilities. *The Journal of Special Education, 29,* 163–180.

Baker, L., & Brown, A. C. (1984). Metacognitive skills and reading. In P. D. Pearson, M. Kamil, R. Barr, & P. Mosenthal (Eds.), *Handbook of reading research* (Vol. 1, pp. 353–394). White Plains, NY: Longman.

Baker, S., Gersten, R., & Lee, D. (2002). A synthesis of empirical research on teaching mathematics to low-achieving students. *The Elementary School Journal, 103,* 51–73.

Baker, S. K., Chard, D. J., Ketterlin-Geller, L. R., Apichatabutra, C., & Doabler, C. (2009). Teaching writing to at-risk students: The quality of evidence for self-regulated strategy development. *Exceptional Children, 75,* 303–318.

Baker, S. K., Simmons, D. C., & Kame'enui, E. J. (1995). *Vocabulary acquisition: Synthesis of the research.* (Tech. Rep. No. 13). Eugene: University of Oregon, National Center to Improve the Tools of Educators.

Ball, D., & Bass, H. (2003). Making mathematics reasonable in school: What research says about the NCTM Standards. In J. Kilpatrick, G. Martin, & D. Schifter (Eds.), *A research companion to principles and standards for school mathematics* (pp. 27–44). Reston, VA: National Council of Teachers of Mathematics.

Barker, L. (2003). Computer-assisted vocabulary acquisition: The CSLU vocabulary tutor in oral-deaf education. *Journal of Deaf Studies and Deaf Education, 8,* 187–198.

Baumann, J. F., Edwards, E. C., Boland, E. M., Olejnik, S., & Kame'enui, E. J. (2003). Vocabulary tricks: Effects of instruction in morphology and context on fifth-grade students' ability to derive and infer word meanings. *American Educational Research Journal, 40,* 447–494.

Baumann, J. F., Edwards, E. C., Font, G., Tereshinski, C. A., Kame'enui, E. J., & Olejnik, S. F. (2002). Teaching morphemic and contextual analysis to fifth-grade students. *Reading Research Quarterly, 37,* 150–176.

Bauwens, J., & Hourcade, J. J. (1995). *Cooperative teaching: Rebuilding the schoolhouse for all students.* Austin, TX: Pro-Ed.

Bauwens, J., Hourcade, J., & Friend, M. (1989). Cooperative teaching: A model for general and special education integration. *Remedial and Special Education, 10,* 17–22.

Beals, V. L. (1983). *The effects of large group instruction on the acquisition of specific learning strategies by learning disabled adolescents.* Unpublished doctoral dissertation, University of Kansas, Lawrence, KS.

Beck, I. L., & McKeown, M. G. (1991). Conditions of vocabulary acquisition. In R. Barr, M. Kamil, P. Mosenthal, & P. D. Pearson (Eds.), *Handbook of reading research* (Vol. 2, pp. 789–814). New York: Longman.

Beck, I. L., & McKeown, M. G. (2007). Increasing young low-income children's oral vocabulary repertoires through rich and focused instruction. *The Elementary School Journal, 107,* 251–271.

Beck, I. L., McKeown, M. G., & Kucan, L. (2002). *Bringing words to life: Robust vocabulary instruction.* New York: Guilford Press.

Beirne-Smith, M. (1991). Peer tutoring in arithmetic for children with learning disabilities. *Exceptional Children, 57,* 330–337.

Berninger, V., Mizokawa, D., & Bragg, R. (1991). Theory-based diagnosis and remediation of writing disabilities. *Journal of School Psychology, 29,* 57–79.

Berninger, V. W., Winn, W. D., Stock, P., Abbott, R. D., Eschen, K., Lin, S., et al. (2008). Tier 3 specialized writing instruction for students with dyslexia. *Reading and Writing, 21,* 95–129.

Boardman, A. G., Arguelles, M. E., Vaughn, S., Hughes, M. T., & Klingner, J. (2005). Special education teachers' views of research-based practices. *Journal of Special Education, 39,* 168–180.

Boone, R., & Higgins, K. (1993). Hypermedia basal readers: Three years of school-based research. *Journal of Special Education Technology, 12,* 86–106.

Bos, C. S., & Vaughn, S. (2006). *Strategies for teaching students with learning and behavior problems* (6th ed.). Upper Saddle River, NJ: Pearson/ Allyn & Bacon.

Bosseler, A., & Massaro, D. (2003). Development and evaluation of a computer-animated tutor for vocabulary and language learning in children with autism. *Journal of Autism and Developmental Disorders, 33,* 653–672.

Boudah, D., Schumaker, J., & Deshler, D. (1997). Collaborative instruction: Is it an effective option for inclusion in secondary classrooms? *Learning Disability Quarterly, 20,* 293–316.

Breznitz, Z. (2006). *Fluency in reading: Synchronization of processes.* Mahwah, NJ: Erlbaum.

Brigham, F. J., Scruggs, T. E., & Mastropieri, M. A. (1992). The effect of teacher enthusiasm on the learning and behavior of learning disabled students. *Learning Disabilities Research & Practice, 7,* 68–73.

Brophy, J., & Good, T. L. (1986). Teacher behavior and student achievement. In M. C. Wittrock (Ed.), *Handbook of research on teaching* (3rd ed., pp. 328–375). New York: Macmillan.

Brown, A. L., & Palincsar, A. S. (1987). Reciprocal teaching of comprehension strategies. In J. D. Day & J. G. Borkowski (Eds.), *Intelligence and*

exceptionality: New directions for theory, assessment, and instructional practice (pp. 81–132). Norwood, NJ: Ablex.

Bryant, D. P., Bryant, B. R., Gersten, R., Scammacca, N., & Chavez, M. (2008). Mathematics intervention for first- and second-grade students with mathematics difficulties: The effects of tier 2 intervention delivered as booster lessons. *Remedial and Special Education, 29*(1), 20–32.

Bryant, D. P., Bryant, B. R., Gersten, R., Scammacca, N., Funk, C., & Winter, A. (2008). The effects of tier 2 intervention on first-grade mathematics performance. *Learning Disability Quarterly, 31*(2), 47–63.

Bryant, D., Goodwin, M., Bryant, B., & Higgins, K. (2003). Vocabulary instruction for students with learning disabilities: A review of the research. *Learning Disability Quarterly, 26,* 117–128.

Bryant, D. P., Vaughn, S., Linan-Thompson, S., Ugel, N., Hamff, A., & Hougen, M. (2000). Reading outcomes for students with and without reading disabilities in general education middle-school content area classes. *Learning Disability Quarterly, 23,* 238–252.

Buikema, J. L., & Graves, M. F. (1993). Teaching students to use context cues to infer word meanings. *Journal of Reading, 36,* 450–457.

Bulgren, J. A. (2002). *The Question Exploration Guide: Trainers' Guide.* Lawrence, KS: Edge Publications.

Bulgren, J. Deshler, D. D., & Lenz, B. K. (2007). Engaging adolescents with LD in higher order thinking about history concepts using integrated content enhancement routines. *Journal of Learning Disabilities, 40,* 121–133.

Bulgren, J. A., Deshler, D. D., & Schumaker, J. B. (1997). Use of a recall enhancement routine and strategies in inclusive secondary classes. *Learning Disabilities Research and Practice, 12,* 198–208.

Bulgren, J. A., Deshler, D. D., & Schumaker, J. B. (1998). *Reasoning strategies and teaching routines for use in mainstream content classrooms.* Final research report submitted to the U.S. Department of Education, Special Education Services.

Bulgren, J. A., Deshler, D. D., Schumaker, J. B., & Lenz, B. K. (2000). The use and effectiveness of analogical instruction in diverse secondary content classrooms. *Journal of Educational Psychology, 92,* 426–441. doi:10.1037/0022-0663.92.3.426

Bulgren, J. A., Lenz, B. K., Deshler, D. D., & Schumaker, J. B. (2001). *The question exploration routine.* Lawrence, KS: Edge.

Bulgren, J. A., Lenz, B. K., Schumaker, J. B., & Deshler, D. D. (2002). *The Concept Comparison Routine.* Lawrence, KS: Edge Publications.

Bulgren, J. A., Lenz, B. K., Schumaker, J. B., Deshler, D. D., & Marquis, J. G. (2002). The use and effectiveness of a comparison routine in diverse secondary content classrooms. *Journal of Educational Psychology, 94,* 356–371. doi:10.1037/0022-0663.94.2.356

Bulgren, J. A., Marquis, J. G., Lenz, B. K., Deshler, D. D., & Schumaker, J. B. (2009). Effectiveness of question exploration to enhance students' written expression of content knowledge and comprehension. *Reading and Writing Quarterly, 25,* 271–289.

Bulgren, J. A., Marquis, J. G., Lenz, B. K., Deshler, D. D., & Schumaker, J. B. (2011). The effectiveness of a question exploration routine for enhancing the content learning of secondary students. *Journal of Educational Psychology 103,* 578–593.

Bulgren, J. A., & Schumaker, J. B. (2006). Teaching practices that optimize curriculum access. In D. D. Deshler & J. B. Schumaker (Eds.), *Teaching adolescents with disabilities: Accessing the general education curriculum* (pp. 79–120). Thousand Oaks, CA: Corwin Press.

Bulgren, J. A., Schumaker, J. B., & Deshler, D. D. (1988). Effectiveness of a concept teaching routine in enhancing the performance of LD students in secondary-level mainstream classes. *Learning Disabilities Quarterly, 11*(1), 3–17. Bulgren, J. A., Schumaker, J. B., & Deshler, D. D. (1994). The effects of a recall enhancement routine on the test performance of secondary students with and without learning disabilities. *Learning Disabilities Research & Practice, 9*(1), 2–11.

Burns, M., & Scholin, S. (2012). Response to Intervention: School-wide prevention of academic difficulties. In B. G. Cook & M. Tankersley (Eds.), *Research-based practices in special education.* Upper Saddle River, NJ: Pearson.

Burns, M. K., & Ysseldyke, J. E. (2009). Reported prevalence of evidence-based instructional practices in special education. *Journal of Special Education, 43,* 3–11.

Bus, A. G., van Ijzendoorn, M. H., & Pellegrini, A. D. (1995). Joint book reading makes for success in learning to read. A meta-analysis on intergenerational transmission of literacy. *Review of Educational Research, 65,* 1–21.

Cain, K., Oakhill, J., & Elbro, C. (2003). The ability to learn new word meanings from context by school-age children with and without language comprehension difficulties. *Journal of Child Language, 30,* 681–694.

Calhoon, B., Al Otaiba, S., Greenberg, D., King, A., & Avalos, A. (2006). Boosting the intensity of reading instruction for culturally diverse first grade students: The promise of Peer-Assisted Learning Strategies. *Learning Disabilities: Research & Practice, 21,* 261–272.

Carlisle, J. F., Fleming, J., & Gudbrandsen, B. (2000). Incidental word learning in science classes. *Contemporary Educational Psychology, 25,* 184–211.

Carlo, M. S., August, D., Snow, C. E., Lively, T. J., & White, C. E. (2004). Closing the gap: Addressing the vocabulary needs of English-language learners in bilingual and mainstream classrooms. *Reading Research Quarterly, 39,* 188–215.

Carnine, D. (1997). Bridging the research-to-practice gap. *Exceptional Children, 63,* 513–521.

Carnine, D. (2000). *Why education experts resist effective practices: And what it would take to make education more like medicine.* Washington, DC: Thomas B. Fordham Foundation. Carnine, D., & Stein, M. (1981). Organisational strategies and practice procedures for teaching basic facts. *Journal of Research in Mathematics Education, 12*(1), 65–69.

Caron, E. A., & McLaughlin, M. J. (2002). Indicators of beacons of excellence: What do they tell us about collaborative practices? *Journal of Educational and Psychological Consultation, 13,* 285–314.

Case, L. P., Harris, K. R., & Graham, S. (1992). Improving the mathematical problem-solving skills of students with learning disabilities: Self-regulated strategy development. *Journal of Special Education, 26,* 1–19.

Cassel, J., & Reid, R. (1996). Use of a self-regulated strategy intervention to improve word problem-solving skills of students with mild disabilities. *Journal of Behavioral Education, 6,* 153–172.

Chabris, C., & Simons, D. (2010). *The invisible gorilla: And other ways our intuitions deceive us.* New York: Crown.

Chall, J. (1983). *Learning to read: The great debate.* New York: McGraw-Hill.

Chan, L. K. S., & Cole, P. G. (1986). The effects of comprehension monitoring training on learning disabled and regular class students. *Remedial and Special Education, 7*(4), 43–40.

Chard, D., Ketterlin-Geller, L. R., Baker, S. K., Doabler, C., & Apichatabutra, C. (2009). Repeated reading interventions for students with learning disabilities: Status of the evidence. *Exceptional Children, 75,* 263–281.

Chard, D. J., Pikulski, J. J., & McDonagh, S. (2006). Fluency: The link between decoding and comprehension for struggling readers. In T. Rasinski, C. Blachowicz, & K. Lems (Eds.), *Teaching reading fluency* (pp. 39–61). New York: Guilford.

Christ, T., & Davie, J. (2009). Empirical evaluation of Read Naturally effects. A randomized control trial. Retrieved from http://www.readnaturally.com/pdf/UofMnReadNaturallyStudy.pdf

Christou, C., & Philippou, G. (1999). Role of schemas in one-step word problems. *Educational Research and Evaluation, 5*, 269–289.

Chung, K. H., & Tam, Y. H. (2005). Effects of cognitive-based instruction on mathematical problem solving by learners with mild intellectual disabilities. *Journal of Intellectual and Developmental Disability, 30,* 207–216.

Cohen, J. (1988). *Statistical power analysis for the behavioral sciences* (2nd ed.). Hillsdale, NJ: Erlbaum.

Conley, D. T. (2008). *Rethinking college readiness. New Directions for Higher Education,* 3–13. doi: 10.1002/he.321

Conley, M. W. (2008). Cognitive strategy instruction for adolescents: What we know about the promise, what we don't know about the potential. *Harvard Educational Review, 78,* 84–106.

Cook, B. G., Landrum, T. J., Tankersley, M., & Kauffman, J. M. (2003). Bringing research to bear on practice: Effecting evidence-based instruction for students with emotional or behavioral disorders. *Education and Treatment of Children, 26*, 325–361.

Cook, B. G., & Schirmer, B. R. (2006). An overview and analysis of the role of evidence-based practices in special education. In B. G. Cook & B. R. Schirmer (Eds.), *What is special about special education: The role of evidence-based practices* (pp. 175–185). Austin, TX: Pro-Ed.

Cook, B. G., & Smith, G. J. (2012). Leadership and instruction: Evidence-based practices in special education. In J. B. Crockett, B. S. Billingsley, & M. L. Boscardin (Eds.), *Handbook of leadership and administration for special education.* London: Routledge.

Cook, B. G., Tankersley, M., Cook, L., & Landrum, T. J. (2008). Evidence-based practices in special education: Some practical considerations. *Intervention in School & Clinic, 44*(2), 69–75.

Cook, B. G., Tankersley, M., & Harjusola-Webb, S. (2008). Evidence-based special education and professional wisdom: Putting it all together. *Intervention in School and Clinic, 44,* 105–111.

Cook, L., Cook, B. G., Landrum, T. J., & Tankersley, M. (2008). Examining the role of group experimental research in establishing evidenced-based practices. *Intervention in School & Clinic, 44*(2), 76–82.

Cook, L., & Friend, M. (1996). Coteaching: Guidelines for creating effective practices. In E. L. Meyer, G. A. Vergason, & R. J. Whelan (Eds.), *Strategies for teaching exceptional children in inclusive settings* (pp. 309–330). Denver, CO: Love.

Coughlin, J., & Montague, M. (2011). The effects of cognitive strategy instruction on the mathematical problem solving of students with spina bifida. *Journal of Special Education, 45,* 171–183.

Council for Exceptional Children. (2009). *What every special educator must know: Ethics, standards, and guidelines* (6th ed.). Arlington, VA: Council for Exceptional Children.

Coyne, M. D., Kame'enui, E. J., & Simmons, D. C. (2001). Prevention and intervention in beginning reading: Two complex systems. *Learning Disabilities: Research & Practice, 16*, 62–73.

Coyne, M. D., McCoach, B., & Kapp, S. (2007). Vocabulary intervention for kindergarten students: Comparing extended instruction to embedded instruction and incidental exposure. *Learning Disability Quarterly, 30,* 74–89.

Coyne, M. D., McCoach, D. B., Loftus, S., Zipoli, R., & Kapp, S. (2009). Direct vocabulary instruction in kindergarten: Teaching for breadth versus depth. *The Elementary School Journal, 110*, 1–18.

Coyne, M. D., Simmons, D., Kame'enui, E., & Stoolmiller, M. (2004). Teaching vocabulary during shared storybook readings: An examination of differential effects. *Exceptionality, 12,* 145–162.

Coyne, M. D., Simmons, D., Kame'enui, E., Stoolmiller, M., Santoro-Edwards, L., Smith, S. B., & Kaufman, N. (2007). Attributes of effective and efficient kindergarten reading intervention: An examination of instructional time and design specificity. *Journal of Learning Disabilities, 40,* 331–347.

Crain-Thoreson, C., & Dale, P. (1999). Enhancing linguistic performance: Parents and teachers as book reading partners for children with language delays. *Topics in Early Childhood Special Education, 19*, 28–39.

Cramer, K. A., Post, T. R., & del Mas, R. C. (2002). Initial fraction learning by fourth- and fifth-grade students: A comparison of the effects of using commercial curricula with the effects of using the rational number project curriculum, *Journal for Research in Mathematics Education, 33*, 111–144.

Crowe, L., Norris, J., & Hoffman, P. (2000). Facilitating storybook interactions between mothers and their preschoolers with language impairment. *Communications Disorders Quarterly, 21*, 131–146.

Cumming, J., & Elkins, J. (1999). Lack of automaticity in the basic addition facts as a characteristic of arithmetic learning problems and instructional needs. *Mathematical Cognition, 5*, 149–180.

Cunningham, A. E., & Stanovich, K. E. (1997). Early reading acquisition and its relationship to reading experience and ability 10 years later. *Developmental Psychology, 33*, 934–945.

Curtis, M. E. (1987). Vocabulary testing and vocabulary instruction. In M. G. McKeown & M. E. Curtis (Eds.), *The nature of vocabulary acquisition.* Hillsdale, NJ: Erlbaum.

Cutler, L., & Graham, S. (2008). Primary grade writing instruction: A national survey. *Journal of Educational Psychology, 100*, 907–919.

Dacy, B. J. S., Nihalani, P. K., Cestone, C. M., & Robinson, D. H. (2011). (Lack of) support for prescriptive statements in teacher education textbooks. *The Journal of Educational Research, 104*, 1–6.

Dalton, B., & Proctor, C. P. (2008). The changing landscape of text and comprehension in the age of new literacies. In J. Coiro, M. Knobel, C. Lankshear, & D. Leu (Eds.), *Handbook of research on new literacies* (pp. 297–324). Mahweh, NJ: Erlbaum.

Dammann, J. E., & Vaughn, S. (2001). Science and sanity in special education. *Behavioral Disorders, 27,* 21–29.

Daniel, G. E. (2003). *Effects of cognitive strategy instruction on the mathematical problem solving of middle school students with learning disabilities.* Unpublished doctoral dissertation, Ohio State University.

De La Paz, S. (2001). Teaching writing to students with attention deficit disorder and specific language impairment. *The Journal of Educational Research, 95,* 37–47.

De La Paz, S., & MacArthur, S. (2003). Knowing the how and why of history: Expectations for secondary students with and without learning disabilities. *Learning Disability Quarterly, 26,* 142–154.

Debarbyshe, B. (1993). Joint picture-book reading correlates of early oral language skills. *Journal of Child Language, 20,* 455–461.

Delquadri, J., Greenwood, C. R., Whorton, D., Carta, J. J., & Hall, R. V. (1986). Classwide peer tutoring. *Exceptional Children, 52,* 535–542.

Deno, S. L. (2006). Developments in curriculum-based measurement. In B. G. Cook & B. R. Schirmer (Eds.), *What is special about special education: The role of evidence-based practices* (pp. 100–112). Austin, TX: Pro-Ed.

Deshler, D. D., & Schumaker, J. B. (2006). *Teaching adolescents with disabilities: Accessing the general education curriculum.* Thousand Oaks, CA: Corwin Press.

Deshler, D. D., Schumaker, J. B., & Lenz, B. K. (1984). Cognitive and academic interventions for learning disabled adolescents: Part I. *Journal of Learning Disabilities, 17,* 108–116.

Deshler, D. D., Schumaker, J. B., Lenz, B. K., Bulgren, J. A., Hock, M. F., Knight, J., & Ehren, B. J. (2001). Ensuring content-area learning by secondary students with learning disabilities. *Learning Disabilities Research and Practice, 16*(2), 96–108.

Dewitz, P., Jones, J., & Leahy, S. (2009). Comprehension strategy instruction in core reading programs. *Reading Research Quarterly, 44,* 102–126.

Dickson, D. (2003). Let's not get too romantic about traditional knowledge. *Science Development Network.* Retrieved from http://www.scidev.net/en/editorials/lets-not-get-too-romantic-about-traditional-knowl.html

Dieker, L. A. (2001). What are the characteristics of "effective" middle and high school co-taught teams for students with disabilities? *Preventing School Failure, 46*(1), 14–23.

Dole, J. A., Duffy, G. G., Roehler, L. R., & Pearson, P. D. (1991). Moving from the old to the new: Research on reading comprehension instruction. *Review of Educational Research, 61,* 239–264.

Dowell, H. A., Storey, K., & Gleason, M. (1994). A comparison of programs designed to improve the descriptive writing of students labeled learning disabled. *Developmental Disabilities Bulletin, 22,* 73–91.

Doyle, W. (1986). Classroom organization and management. In M. C. Wittrock (Ed.), *Handbook of research on teaching* (3rd ed., pp. 392–431). New York: Macmillan.

Durkin, D. (1978–1979). What classroom observations reveal about reading comprehension instruction. *Reading Research Quarterly, 14,* 481–533.

Eads, J. R. (1991). *Classroom teacher mediated generalization of a sentence writing strategy to the regular classroom by nine middle school students with learning disabilities.* Unpublished educational specialist thesis, Northeast Missouri State University, Kirksville, MO.

Ebbers, S. M., & Denton, C. A. (2008). A root awakening: vocabulary instruction for older students with reading difficulties. *Learning Disabilities Research and Practice, 23,* 90–102.

Edens, K., & Potter, E. (2006). How students "unpack" the structure of a word problem: Graphic representations and problem solving. *School Science and Mathematics, 108,* 184–196.

Edmonds, M. S., Vaughn, S., Wexler, J., Reutebuch, C., Cable, A., Tackett, K. K., & Schnakenberg, J. W. (2009). Synthesis of reading interventions and effects on reading outcomes for older struggling readers. *Review of Educational Research, 79,* 262–300.

Ehri, L. C. (1997). Sight word learning in normal readers and dyslexics. In B. Blachman (Ed.), *Foundations of reading acquisition and dyslexia* (pp. 163–189). Mahwah, NJ: Erlbaum.

Ehri, L. C. (2002). Phases of acquisition in learning to read words and implications for teaching. *British Journal of Educational Psychology: Monograph Series, 1,* 7–28.

Elbro, C., & Arnbak, E. (1996). The role of morpheme recognition and morphological awareness in dyslexia. *Annals of Dyslexia, 46,* 209–240.

Elkind, J., Cohen, K., & Murray, C. (1993). Using computer-based readers to improve reading comprehension in students with dyslexia. *Annals of Dyslexia, 43,* 238–259.

Elley, W. (1989). Vocabulary acquisition from listening to stories. *Reading Research Quarterly, 24,* 174–187.

Ellis, J. D., & Bulgren, J. (2009). *Improving teaching of scientific argumentation skills.* Paper presented at the annual meeting of the Association for Science Teacher Educators, Hartford, CT.

Engelmann, S., & Carnine, D. W. (1982). *Theory of instruction: Principles and applications.* New York: Irvington.

Englert, C. S., & Thomas, C. C. (1987). Sensitivity to text structure in reading and writing: A comparison between learning disabled and non-learning disabled students. *Learning Disability Quarterly, 10,* 93–105.

First, C. G. (1994). *The effects of sentence combining on the written expression skills of students with serious emotional disturbances.* Unpublished doctoral dissertation, University of the Pacific, Stockton, CA.

Fitzgerald, G., Koury, K., & Mitchem, K. (2008). Research on computer-mediated instruction for students with high incidence disabilities. *Journal of Educational Computing Research, 38*(2), 201–233.

Flavell, J. H. (1979). Metacognition and cognitive monitoring: A new area of cognitive developmental inquiry. *American Psychologist, 34,* 906–911.

Fontana, K. C. (2005). The effects of co-teaching on the achievement of eighth grade students with learning disabilities. *The Journal of At-Risk Issues, 11,* 17–23.

Fore, III, C., Hagan-Burke, S., Burke, M., Boon, R., & Smith, S. (2008). Academic achievement and class placement: Do students with specific learning disabilities achieve more in one class placement than another? *Education and Treatment of Children, 31*, 1–18.

Freedman, D. H. (2010). *Wrong: Why experts keep failing us—and how to know when not to trust them.* New York: Little, Brown.

Friend, M., & Cook, L. (1992). *Interactions: Collaboration skills for school professionals.* New York: Longman.

Friend, M., & Cook, L. (2003). *Interactions: Collaboration skills for school professionals* (4th ed.). Upper Saddle River, NJ: Pearson/Allyn & Bacon.

Friend, M., Hurley-Chamberlain, D., & Cook, L. (2006, April). *NCLB and IDEA: Disaster or golden opportunity for co-teaching?* Paper presented at the convention of the Council for Exceptional Children, Salt Lake City, UT. from the evolution of self-regulated strategy development. *Learning Disability Quarterly, 22,* 251–262.

Fuchs, D., & Fuchs, L. S. (1998). Researchers and teachers working together to adapt instruction for diverse learners. *Learning Disabilities Research and Practice, 13,* 126–137.

Fuchs D., & Fuchs, L. S. (2005). Peer-assisted learning strategies: Promoting word recognition, fluency, and reading comprehension in young children. *Journal of Special Education, 39,* 34–44.

Fuchs, D., Fuchs, L. S., & Burish, P. (2000). Peer-assisted learning strategies: An evidence-based practice to promote reading achievement. *Learning Disabilities Research and Practice, 15,* 85–91.

Fuchs, D., Fuchs, L. S., Mathes, P. G., & Simmons, D. C. (1997). Peer-assisted learning strategies: Making classrooms more responsive to academic diversity. *American Educational Research Journal, 34,* 174–206.

Fuchs, D., Fuchs, L. S., Svenson, E., Thompson, A., Yen, L., McMaster, K. N., Al Otaiba, S., & Yang, N. J. (2000). *Peabody peer assisted learning strategies: First grade reading.* Unpublished training manual, Vanderbilt University, Nashville, TN.

Fuchs, D., Fuchs, L. S., Thompson, A., Al Otaiba, S., Yen, L., & Braun, M. (2000). Peer-assisted learning strategies: Kindergarten: A teacher's manual. Unpublished training manual, Vanderbilt University, Nashville, TN.

Fuchs, D., Fuchs, L. S., Thompson, A., Svenson, E., Al Otaiba, S., Yang, N., . . . Saenz, L. (2001). Peer-assisted learning strategies in reading: Extensions to kindergarten/first grade and high school. *Remedial and Special Education, 22,* 15–21.

Fuchs, L. S., & Fuchs, D. (2003). Enhancing the mathematical problem solving of students with mathematics disabilities. In H. L. Swanson, K. R. Harris, & S. E. Graham (Eds.), *Handbook on learning disabilities* (pp. 306–322). New York: Guilford.

Fuchs, L. S., Fuchs, D., Craddock, C., Hollenbeck, K. N., Hamlett, C. L., & Schatschneider, C. (2008). Effects of small-group tutoring with and without validated classroom instruction on at-risk students' math problem solving: Are two tiers of prevention better than one? *Journal of Educational Psychology, 100,* 491–509.

Fuchs, L. S., Fuchs, D., Finelli, R., Courey, S. J., & Hamlett, C. L. (2004). Expanding schema-based transfer instruction to help third graders solve real-life mathematical problems. *American Educational Research Journal, 41,* 419–445.

Fuchs, L. S., Fuchs, D., Hamlett, C. L., & Appleton, A. C. (2002). Explicitly teaching for transfer: Effects on the mathematical problem-solving performance of students with mathematics disabilities. *Learning Disabilities Research & Practice, 17,* 90–106.

Fuchs, L. S., Fuchs, D., & Kazdan, S. (1999). Effects of peer-assisted learning strategies on high-school students with serious reading problems. *Remedial and Special Education, 20,* 309–318.

Fuchs, L. S., Powell, S. R., Seethaler, P. M., Cirino, P. T., Fletcher, J. M., Fuchs, D., Hamlett, C. L., & Zumeta, R. O. (2009). Remediating number combination and word problem deficits among students with mathematics difficulties: A randomized control trial. *Journal of Educational Psychology, 101,* 561–576.

Fuchs, L. S., Seethaler, P. M., Powell, S. R., Fuchs, D., Hamlett, C. L., & Fletcher, J. M. (2008). Effects of preventative tutoring on the mathematical problem solving of third-grade students with math and reading difficulties. *Exceptional Children, 74,* 155–173.

Fukkink, R. G., & deGlopper, K. (1998). Effects of instruction in deriving word meaning from context: A meta-analysis. *Review of Educational Research, 68,* 450–469.

Fuson, K. C., & Willis, G. B. (1989). Second graders' use of schematic drawings in solving addition and subtraction word problems. *Journal of Educational Psychology, 81,* 514–520.

Gajria, M., Jitendra, A. K., Sood, S., & Sacks, S. (2007). Comprehension of expository text in students with LD: A research synthesis. *Journal of Learning Disabilities, 40,* 210–225.

Gallimore, R., & Tharp, R. (1990). Teaching mind in society. In L. C. Moll (Ed.), *Vygotsky and education* (pp. 175–205). New York: Cambridge Press.

Gately, S., & Gately, F., Jr. (2001). Understanding co-teaching components. *TEACHING Exceptional Children, 33,* 40–47.

Geary, D. C. (1990). A componential analysis of an early learning deficit in mathematics. *Journal of Exceptional Child Psychology, 33,* 386–404.

Geary, D. (1994). *Children's mathematical development.* Washington, DC: American Psychological Association.

Gersten, R., Beckmann, S., Clarke, B., Foegen, A., Marsh, L., Star, J. R., & Witzel, B. (2009). *Assisting students struggling with mathematics: Response to Intervention (RtI) for elementary and middle schools* (NCEE 2009-4060). Washington, DC: National Center for Education Evaluation and Regional Assistance, Institute of Education Sciences, U.S. Department of Education. Retrieved from http://ies.ed.gov/ncee/wwc/publications/practiceguides/

Gersten, R., Chard, D., & Baker, S. (2000). Factors enhancing sustained use of research-based instructional practices. *Journal of Learning Disabilities, 33,* 445–457.

Gersten, R., Chard, D., Jayanthi, M., Baker, S., Morphy, P., & Flojo, J. (2009). Mathematics instruction for students with learning disabilities: A meta-analysis of instructional components. *Review of Educational Research, 79,* 1202–1242.

Gersten, R., Compton, D., Connor, C. M., Dimino, J., Santoro, L., Linan-Thompson, S., & Tilly, W. D. (2008). Assisting students struggling with reading: Response to Intervention and multi-tier intervention for reading in the primary grades. A practice guide. (NCEE 2009-4045). Washington, DC: National Center for Education Evaluation and Regional Assistance, Institute of Education Sciences, U.S. Department of Education. Retrieved from http://ies.ed.gov/ncee/wwc/publications/practiceguides/

Gersten, R., Fuchs, L. S., Compton, D. L., Coyne, M. D., Greenwood, C. R., & Innocenti, K. S. (2005). Quality indicators for group experimental and quasi-experimental research in special education. *Exceptional Children, 71,* 149–164.

Gersten, R., Fuchs, L. S., Williams, J. P., & Baker, S. (2001). Teaching reading comprehension strategies to students with learning disabilities: A review of research. *Review of Educational Research, 71,* 279–320.

Goerss, B. L., Beck, I. L., & McKeown, M. G. (1999). Increasing remedial students' ability to derive word meaning from context. *Reading Psychology, 20,* 151–175.

Gough, P. B. (1996). How children learn to read and why they fail. *Annals of Dyslexia, 46,* 3–20.

Graesser, A. C., Baggett, W., & Williams, K. (1996). Question-driven explanatory reasoning. *Applied Cognitive Psychology, 10*(7), 17–31. doi:10.1002/(SICI)1099-0720(199611)10:7<17::AID-ACP435>3.0.CO;2-7

Graesser, A. C., McNamara, D. S., & VanLehn, K. (2005). Scaffolding deep comprehension strategies through point & query, autotutor, and iSTART. *Educational Psychologist, 40,* 225–234. doi:10.1207/s15326985ep4004_4

Graesser, A. C., Person, N. K., & Hu, X. (2002). Improving comprehension through discourse processing. In D. F. Halpern & M. D. Hakel (Eds.), *Applying the science of learning to university teaching and beyond: New directions for teaching and learning* (pp. 33–44). San Francisco, CA: Wiley Periodicals.

Graham, S. (1990). The role of production factors in learning disabled students' compositions. *Journal of Educational Psychology, 82,* 781–791.

Graham, S. (1999). Handwriting and spelling instruction for students with learning disabilities: A review. *Learning Disabilities Quarterly, 22,* 78–98.

Graham, S. (2006). Strategy instruction and the teaching of writing: A meta-analysis. In C. MacArthur, S. Graham, & J. Fitzgerald (Eds.), *Handbook of writing research* (pp. 187–207). New York: Guilford. Graham, S., & Harris, K. R. (2003). Students with learning disabilities and the process of writing: A meta-analysis of SRSD studies. In H. L. Swanson, K. R. Harris, & S. Graham (Eds.), *Handbook of learning disabilities* (pp. 323–344). New York: Guilford Press.

Graham, S., & Harris, K. R. (2006). Preventing writing difficulties: Providing additional handwriting and spelling instruction to at-risk children in first grade. *Teaching Exceptional Children, 39,* 64–66.

Graham, S., & Harris, K. R. (2009). Almost 30 years of writing research: Making sense of it all with the *Wrath of Khan. Learning Disabilities Research & Practice, 24,* 58–68.

Graham, S., Harris, K. R., & Fink, B. (2000). Is handwriting causally related to learning to write? Treatment of handwriting problems in beginning writers. *Journal of Educational Psychology, 92,* 620–633.

Graham, S., Harris, K. R., & Fink-Chorzempa, B. (2002). Contributions of spelling instruction to the spelling, writing, and reading of poor spellers. *Journal of Educational Psychology, 94,* 669–686.

Graham, S., Harris, K. R., & Loynachan, C. (1996). The directed spelling thinking activity: Applications with high frequency words. *Learning Disabilities Research and Practice, 11,* 34–40.

Graham, S., Harris, K. R., & Mason, L. (2005). Improving the writing performance, knowledge, and motivation of struggling young writers: The effects of self-regulated strategy development. *Contemporary Educational Psychology, 30,* 207–241.

Graham, S., Harris, K. R., Mason, L. H., Fink-Chorzempa, B., Moran, S., & Saddler, B. How do primary grade teachers teach handwriting? (2008). *Reading and Writing: An Interdisciplinary Journal, 21,* 49–69.

Graham, S., Loynachan, C., & Harris, K. R. (1993). The basic spelling vocabulary list. *Journal of Educational Research, 86,* 363–368.

Graham, S., & MacArthur, C. (1988). Improving learning disabled students' skills at revising essays produced on a word processor: Self-instructional strategy training. *The Journal of Special Education, 22,* 133–152.

Graham, S., Morphy, P., Harris, K., Fink-Chorzempa, B., Saddler, B., Moran, S., & Mason, L. (2008). Teaching spelling in the primary grades: A national survey of instructional practices and adaptations. *American Educational Research Journal, 45,* 796–825.

Graham, S., & Perin, D. (2007). A meta-analysis of writing instruction for adolescent students. *Journal of Educational Psychology, 99,* 445–476.

Graves, A. W., Gersten, R., & Haager, D. (2004). Literacy instruction in multiple language first-grade classrooms: Linking student outcomes to observed instructional practice. *Learning Disabilities: Research & Practice, 19,* 262–272.

Graves, M. F. (2006). *The vocabulary book: Learning and instruction.* New York: Teachers College Press.

Greenwood, C. R., & Abbott, M. (2001). The research-to-practice gap in special education. *Teacher Education and Special Education, 24,* 276–289.

Greenwood, C. R., Carta, J. J., & Hall, R. V. (1988). The use of peer-tutoring strategies in classroom management and educational instruction. *School Psychology Review, 17,* 258–275.

Guthrie, J. T., & Davis, M. H. (2003). Motivating struggling readers in middle school through an engagement model of classroom practice. *Reading & Writing Quarterly, 19*(1), 59–86.

Guthrie, J. T., & Wigfield, A. (2000). Engagement and motivation in reading. In M. Kamil, R. Barr, P. Mosenthal, & P. D. Pearson (Eds.), *Handbook of reading research* (Vol. 3, pp. 403–422). New York: Longman.

Hall, T. E., Hughes, C. A., & Filbert, M. (2000). Computer assisted instruction in reading for students with learning disabilities: A research synthesis. *Education and Treatment of Children, 23*, 173–193.

Hargrave, A., & Senechal, M. (2000). A book reading intervention with preschool children who have limited vocabularies: The benefits of regular reading and dialogic reading. *Early Childhood Research Quarterly, 15*, 75–90.

Harris, A., & Jacobson, M. (1980). A comparison of the Fry, Spache, and Harris-Jacobson Readability formulas for primary grades. *The Reading Teacher, 33*(8), 920–924.

Harris, C. A., Miller, S. P., & Mercer, C. D. (1995). Teaching initial multiplication skills to students with disabilities in general education classrooms. *Learning Disabilities Research & Practice, 10*, 180–195.

Harris, K. R., & Graham, S. (1999). Programmatic intervention research: Illustrations from the evolution of self-regulated strategy development. *Learning Disability Quarterly, 22*, 251–262.

Harris, K. R., & Graham, S. (2007). Marconi invented the television so people who couldn't afford radio could hear the news: The research on teaching powerful composition strategies we have, and the research we need. In M. Pressley (Ed.), *Shaping literacy achievement: Research we have, research we need* (pp. 175–198). New York: Guilford.

Harris, K. R., & Graham, S. (2009). Self-regulated strategy development in writing: Premises, evolution, and the future. *British Journal of Educational Psychology Monograph Series II, Number 6—Teaching and Learning Writing, 1*(1), 113–135.

Harris, K. R., Graham, S., Brindle, M., & Sandmel, K. (2009). Metacognition and children's writing. In D. Hacker, J. Dunlosky, & A. Graesser (Eds.), *Handbook of metacognition in education*. Mahwah, NJ: Erlbaum.

Harris, K. R., Graham, S., & Mason, L. (2003). Self-regulated strategy development in the classroom: Part of a balanced approach to writing instruction for students with disabilities. *Focus on Exceptional Children, 35*, 1–16.

Harris, K. R., Graham, S., & Mason, L. (2006). Improving the writing, knowledge, and motivation of struggling young writers: Effects of Self-Regulated Strategy Development with and without peer support. *American Educational Research Journal, 43*, 295–340.

Harris, K. R., Graham, S., Mason, L. H., & Friedlander, B. (2008). *Powerful writing strategies for all students*. Baltimore: Brookes.

Harris, T., & Hodges, R. (1985). *The literacy dictionary*. Newark, DE: International Reading Association.

Hasbrouck, J. E., Ihnot, C., & Rogers, G. (1999). Read Naturally: A strategy to increase oral reading fluency. *Reading Research and Instruction, 39*(1), 27–37.

Hebert, B., & Murdock, J. (1994). Comparing three computer-aided instruction output modes to teach vocabulary words to students with learning disabilities. *Learning Disabilities Research & Practice, 9*, 136–141.

Hegarty, M., & Kozhevnikov, M. (1999). Types of visual-spatial representations and mathematical problem solving. *Journal of Educational Psychology, 91*, 684–689.

Hegarty, M., Mayer, R. E., & Monk, C. A. (1995). Comprehension of arithmetic word problems: A comparison of successful and unsuccessful problem solvers. *Journal of Educational Psychology, 87*, 18–32.

Heller, R., & Greenleaf, C. (2007). *Literacy instruction in the content areas: Getting to the core of middle and high school improvement*. Washington, DC: Alliance for Excellent Education.

Henry, M. (1993). Morphological structure: Latinate and Greek roots and affixes as upper grade code strategies. *Reading and Writing: An Interdisciplinary Journal, 5*, 227–241.

Hess, F., & Petrilli, M. (2006). *No Child Left Behind primer*. New York: Peter Lang.

Hiebert, E. H. (2009). *Reading more, reading better*. New York: Guilford Press.

Hiebert, J. (2003). What research says about the NCTM Standards. In J. Kilpatrick, G. Martin, & D. Schifter (Eds.), *A research companion to principles and standards for school mathematics* (pp. 5–26). Reston, VA: National Council of Teachers of Mathematics.

Higgins, E. L., & Raskind, M. H. (2005). The compensatory effectiveness of the Quicktionary Reading Pen II on the reading comprehension of students with learning disabilities. *Journal of Special Education Technology, 20*, 31–39.

Hock, M. F., Pulvers, K. A., Deshler, D. D., & Schumaker, J. B. (2001). The effects of an after-school tutoring program on the academic performance of at-risk students and students with LD. *Remedial and Special Education, 22*, 172–186.

Hogue, A., Henderson, C. E., Dauber, S., Barajas, P. C., Fried, A., & Liddle, H. A. (2008). Treatment adherence, competence, and outcome in individual and family therapy for adolescent behavior problems. *Journal of Consulting and Clinical Psychology, 76*, 544–555.

Horner, R. H., Carr, E. G., Halle, J., McGee, G., Odom, S., & Wolery, M. (2005). The use of single-subject research to identify evidence-based practice in special education. *Exceptional Children, 71*, 165–179.

Hudson, R. F., Mercer, C. D., & Lane, H. B. (2000). *Exploring reading fluency: A paradigmatic overview*. Unpublished manuscript, University of Florida, Gainesville.

Hunt, P., & Goetz, L. (1997). Research on inclusive educational programs, practices, and outcomes for students with severe disabilities, *Journal of Special Education, 31*(1), 3–29.

Hutchinson, N. L. (1993). Effects of cognitive strategy instruction on algebra problem solving of adolescents with learning disabilities. *Learning Disability Quarterly, 16,* 34–63.

Hyatt, K. J., Iddings, A. C. D., & Ober, S. (2005). Inclusion: A catalyst for school reform. *Teaching Exceptional Children Plus, 1*(3). Retrieved from *http://escholarship.bc.edu/cgi/ viewcontent.cgi?article=1078& context=education/tecplus*

Individuals with Disabilities Education Improvement Act of 2004, Pub. L. No. 108-446 C.F.R. 20 U.S.C. § 1415 *et seq.* (2004).

Isaacs, A., & Carroll, W. (1999). Strategies for basic fact instruction. *Teaching Children Mathematics, 5,* 508–515.

Janvier, C. (1987). *Problems of representation in the teaching and learning of mathematics.* Hillsdale, NJ: Erlbaum.

Jaspers, M. W. M., & Van Lieshout, E. C. D. M. (1994). The evaluation of two computerized instruction programs for arithmetic word-problem solving by educable mentally retarded children. *Learning and Instruction, 4,* 193–215.

Jenkins, J. R., Matlock, B., & Slocum, T. A. (1989). Approaches to vocabulary instruction: The teaching of individual word meanings and practice deriving word meaning from context. *Reading Research Quarterly, 24,* 215–235.

Jenkins, J. R., Vadasy, P. F., Firebaugh, M., & Profilet, C. (2000). Tutoring first-grade struggling readers in phonological reading skills. *Learning Disabilities: Research & Practice, 15,* 75–84.

Jimenez, R. T., Garcia, G. E., & Pearson, P. D. (1995). Three children, two languages, and strategic reading: Case studies in bilingual/monolingual reading. *American Educational Research Journal, 32,* 67–97.

Jitendra, A. K. (2007). *Solving math word problems: Teaching students with learning disabilities using schema-based instruction.* Austin, TX: Pro-Ed.

Jitendra, A. K. (2008). Using schema-based instruction to make appropriate sense of word problems. *Perspectives on Language and Literacy,* 20–24.

Jitendra, A. K., DiPipi, C. M., & Perron-Jones, N. (2002). An exploratory study of word problem-solving instruction for middle school students with learning disabilities: An emphasis on conceptual and procedural understanding. *Journal of Special Education, 36,* 23–38.

Jitendra, A. K., Edwards, L. L., Sacks, G., & Jacobson, L. A. (2004). What research says about vocabulary instruction for students with learning disabilities. *Exceptional Children, 70,* 299–322.

Jitendra, A. K., Griffin, C., Haria, P., Leh, J., Adams, A., & Kaduvetoor, A. (2007). A comparison of single and multiple strategy instruction on third grade students' mathematical problem solving. *Journal of Educational Psychology, 99,* 115–127.

Jitendra, A. K., Griffin, C., McGoey, K., Gardill, C., Bhat, P., & Riley, T. (1998). Effects of mathematical word problem solving by students at risk or with mild disabilities. *Journal of Educational Research, 91,* 345–356.

Jitendra, A. K., & Hoff, K. (1996). The effects of schema-based instruction on mathematical word problem solving performance of students with learning disabilities. *Journal of Learning Disabilities, 29,* 422–431.

Jitendra, A. K., Hoff, K., & Beck, M. (1999). Teaching middle school students with learning disabilities to solve multistep word problems using a schema-based approach. *Remedial and Special Education, 20,* 50–64.

Jitendra, A. K., Star, J., Starosta, K., Leh, J., Sood, S., Caskie, G., … & Mack, T. (2009). Improving students' learning of ratio and proportion problem solving: The role of schema-based instruction. *Contemporary Educational Psychology, 34,* 250–264.

Jitendra, A., & Xin, A. (1997). Mathematical word problem solving instruction for students with mild disabilities and students at risk for failure: A research synthesis. *Journal of Special Education, 30,* 412–438.

Johnson, C. S. (2005). Teaching sentence writing preskills to middle school students with mild to moderate disabilities. Unpublished master's thesis, California State University, Fullerton, CA.

Johnson, D. W., & Johnson, R. (1989). *Cooperation and competition: Theory and research.* Edina, MN: Interaction Book Company.

Johnson, D. W., & Johnson, R. (2009). An educational psychology success story: Social interdependence theory and cooperative learning. *Educational Researcher, 38,* 365–380.

Johnson, D. W., Johnson, R., & Holubec, E. (2008). *Cooperation in the classroom* (8th ed.). Edina, MN: Interaction Book Company.

Jones, M. L. (2009). A study of novice special educators' views of evidence-based practices. *Teacher Education and Special Education, 32*(2), 101–120.

Juel, C. (1988). Learning to read and write: A longitudinal study of 54 children from first through fourth grades. *Journal of Educational Psychology, 80,* 443–447.

Kaestle, C., Campbell, A., Finn, J., Johnson, S., Mikulecky, L. (2001). *Adult literacy and education in America.* Washington, DC: National Center for Education Statistics.

Kalyuga, S. (2006). Rapid cognitive assessment of learners' knowledge structures. *Learning and Instruction, 16,* 1–11.

Katz, J., & Mirenda, P. (2002) Including students with developmental disabilities in general education classrooms: Educational benefits, *International Journal of Special Education, 17*(2), 14–24.

Katz, L. A., & Carlisle, J. F. (2009). Teaching students with reading difficulties to be close readers: A feasibility study. *Language, Speech and Hearing Services in Schools, 40,* 325–340.

Kauffman, J. M. (1996). Research to practice issues. *Behavioral Disorders, 22,* 55–60.

Kauffman, J. M., & Hallahan, D. P. (2005). *Special education: What it is and why we need it.* Boston: Allyn & Bacon.

Kavale, K. A., & Reese, J. H. (1992). The character of learning disabilities. *Learning Disability Quarterly, 15,* 74–94.

Kennedy, M., & Deshler, D. (2010). Literacy instruction, technology, and students with learning disabilities: Research we have, research we need. *The Free Library.* Retrieved from http://www.thefreelibrary.com/ Literacy instruction, technology, and students with learning . . . -a0242754548

Kim, A., Vaughn, S., Klingner, J. K., Woodruf, A. L., Reutebuch, C. K., & Kouzekanani, K. (2006). Improving the reading comprehension of middle school students with disabilities through computer-assisted collaborative strategic reading. *Remedial and Special Education, 27,* 235–249.

Kim, A., Vaughn, S., Wanzek, J., & Wei, S. (2004). Graphic organizers and their effects on the reading comprehension of students with LD. *Journal of Learning Disabilities, 37,* 105–118.

Kindler, A. (2002). *Survey of the states' limited English proficient students and available educational programs and services, 2000–2001 summary report.* Washington, DC: National Clearinghouse for English Language Acquisition and Language Instruction Educational Programs.

King, A. (1994). Guiding knowledge construction in the classroom: Effects of teaching children how to question and how to explain. *American Educational Research Journal, 31,* 358-368. doi:10.3102/00028312031002338

King, F. J., Goodson, L., & Rohani, F. (1998). *Higher order thinking skills.* Center for Advancement and Learning. Retrieved from http://www.cala .fsu.edu/portfolio?chosen_service= Assessment+and+Test+Development

Kiuhara, S., Graham, S., & Hawken, L. (2009). Teaching writing to high school students:

Klingner, J. K. (2004). Assessing reading comprehension. *Assessment for Effective Intervention, 29,* 59–70.

Klingner, J., Arguelles, M. E., Hughes, M. T., & Vaughn, S. (2001). Examining the school-wide "spread" of research-based practices. *Learning Disability Quarterly, 24,* 221–234.

Klingner, J., Urbach, J., Golos, D., Brownell, M., & Menon, S. (2008, April). *How do special education teachers promote reading comprehension?* Paper presented at the annual meeting of the American Educational Research Association, New York.

Klingner, J. K., & Vaughn, S. (1996). Reciprocal teaching of reading comprehension strategies for students with learning disabilities who use English as a second language. *Elementary School Journal, 96,* 275–293.

Klingner, J. K., & Vaughn, S. (1999). Promoting reading comprehension, content learning, and English acquisition through collaborative strategic reading (CSR). *The Reading Teacher, 52,* 738–747.

Klingner, J. K., & Vaughn, S. (2000). The helping behaviors of fifth graders while using collaborative strategic reading during ESL content classes. *TESOL Quarterly, 34,* 69–98.

Klingner, J. K., Vaughn, S., Arguelles, M. E., Hughes, M. T., & Leftwich, S. A. (2004). Collaborative strategic reading: Real world lessons from classroom teachers. *Remedial and Special Education, 25,* 291–302. Klingner, J. K., Vaughn, S., & Boardman, A. (2007). *Teaching reading comprehension to students with learning difficulties.* New York: Guilford Press.

Klingner, J. K., Vaughn, S., Boardman, A. G., & Swanson, E. (in press). *Up with literacy: Improving comprehension with Collaborative Strategic Reading,* San Francisco, CA: Jossey-Bass.

Klingner, J. K., Vaughn, S., Dimino, J., Schumm, J. S., & Bryant, D. (2001). *Collaborative strategic reading: Strategies for improving comprehension.* Longmont, CO: Sopris West.

Klingner, J. K., Vaughn, S., Hughes, M. T., & Arguelles, M. E. (1999). Sustaining research-based practices in reading: A 3-year follow-up. *Remedial and Special Education, 20,* 263–274.

Klingner, J. K., Vaughn, S., Hughes, S. T., Schumm, J. S., & Elbaum, B. (1998). Outcomes for students with and without learning disabilities in inclusive classrooms. *Learning Disabilities Research and Practice, 13,* 153–161.

Klingner, J. K., Vaughn, S., & Schumm, J. S. (1998). Collaborative strategic reading during social studies in heterogeneous fourth-grade classrooms. *The Elementary School Journal, 99,* 3–22.

Kloo, A., & Zigmond, N. (2008). Coteaching revisited: Redrawing the blueprint. *Preventing School Failure, 52*(2), 12–20.

Kolich, E. M. (1991). Effects of computer assisted vocabulary training on word knowledge. *Journal of Educational Research, 84,* 177–182.

Kozlow, M., & Bellamy, P. (2004). *Experimental study on the impact of the 6+1 Trait Writing Model on student achievement.* Portland, OR: Northwest Regional Educational Laboratory.

Kuhn, M. R., & Stahl, S. A. (1998). Teaching children to learn word meanings from context: A synthesis and some questions. *Journal of Literacy Research, 30,* 119–138.

LaBerge, D., & Samuels, S. A. (1974). Toward a theory of automatic information processing. *Cognitive Psychology, 6,* 293–323.

Landrum, T. J., Cook, B. G., Tankersley, M. T., & Fitzgerald, S. (2002). Teachers' perceptions of the trustworthiness, useability, and accessibility of information from different sources. *Remedial and Special Education, 23*(1), 42–48.

Landrum, T. J., Cook, B. G., Tankersley, M., & Fitzgerald, S. (2007). Teacher perceptions of the usability of intervention information from personal versus data-based sources. *Education and Treatment of Children, 30,* 27–42.

Landrum, T. J., & McDuffie, K. A. (2010). Learning styles in the age of differentiated instruction. *Exceptionality, 18,* 6–17.

Landrum, T. J., & Tankersley, M. (2004). Science at the schoolhouse: An uninvited guest. *Journal of Learning Disabilities, 37,* 207–212.

Lane, K., Harris, K. R., Graham, S., Weisenbach, J., Brindle, M., & Morphy, P. (2008). The effects of self-regulated strategy development on the writing performance of second grade students with behavioral and writing difficulties. *Journal of Special Education, 41,* 234–253.

Langer, J., & Applebee, A. N. (1987). *How writing shapes thinking.* Urbana, IL: National

learning strategies by learning disabled adolescents. Unpublished doctoral dissertation, University of Kansas, Lawrence, KS.

Lembke, E., Hampton, D., & Hendricker, E. (2012). Data-based decision-making in academics using curriculum-based measurement. In B. G. Cook & M. Tankersley (Eds.), *Research-based practices in special education.* Upper Saddle River, NJ: Pearson.

Lenz, B. K., & Bulgren, J. A. (1995). Promoting learning in the content areas. In P. A. Cegelka & W. H. Berdine (Eds.), *Effective instruction for students with learning problems* (pp. 385–417). Needham Heights, MA: Allyn & Bacon.

Lenz, B. K., Schumaker, J. B., & Deshler, D. D. (1991, March). *Planning in the face of academic diversity: Whose questions should we be answering?* Paper presented at the American Educational Research Association Conference, Chicago.

Lenz, B. K., Schumaker, J. B., Deshler, D. D., & Beals, V. L. (1984). *The word identification strategy* (Learning Strategies Curriculum). Lawrence, KS: University of Kansas.

Leu, D. J., Jr., Kinzer, C. K., Coiro, J., & Cammack, D. (2004). Toward a theory of new literacies emerging from the Internet and other information and communication technologies. In R. B. Ruddell & N. Unrau (Eds.), *Theoretical models and processes of reading* (5th ed., pp. 1568–1611). Newark: International Reading Association.

Lithner, J. (2008). A research framework for creative and imitative reasoning. *Educational Studies in Mathematics, 67,* 255–276.

Lloyd, J. W., Pullen, P. C., Tankersley, M., & Lloyd, P. A. (2006). Critical dimensions of experimental studies and research syntheses that help define effective practice. In B. G. Cook & B. R. Schirmer (Eds.), *What is special about special education? Examining the role of evidence-based practices* (pp. 136–153). Austin, TX: Pro-Ed.

Lloyd, J., Saltzman, N. J., & Kauffman, J. M. (1981). Predictable generalization in academic learning as a result of preskills and strategy training. *Learning Disability Quarterly, 4,* 203–216.

Locke, W. R., & Fuchs, L. S. (1995). Effects of peer-mediated reading instruction on the on-task behavior and social interactions of children with behavior disorders. *Journal of Emotional and Behavioral Disorders, 3,* 92–99.

Logan, G. D. (1988). Toward an instance theory of automatization. *Psychological Review, 95,* 492–527.

Lovett, M. W., Lacerenza, L., & Borden, S. L. (2000). Putting struggling readers on the PHAST track: A program to integrate phonological and strategy-based remedial reading instruction and maximize outcomes. *Journal of Learning Disabilities, 33,* 458–476.

Lovett, M. W., Steinbach, K. A., & Frijters, J. C. (2000). Remediating the core deficits of developmental reading disability: A Double-Deficit perspective. *Journal of Learning Disabilities, 33,* 334–358.

Lundeen, C., & Lundeen, D. (1993, November). *Effectiveness of mainstreaming with collaborative teaching* Paper presented at the annual convention of the American Speech–Language-Hearing Association, Anaheim, CA (ERIC Document Reproduction Service No. ED 368 127).

Lyon, G. R. (1998). Why reading is not a natural process. *Educational Leadership, 55*(6), 14–18.

MacArthur, C., Schwartz, S., & Graham, S. (1991). Effects of a reciprocal peer revision strategy in special education classrooms. *Learning Disability Research and Practice, 6,* 201–210.

Maccini, P., Gagnon, J. C., & Hughes, C. A. (2002). Technology-based interventions for secondary students with learning disabilities. *Learning Disability Quarterly, 25,* 247–262.

Madelaine, A., & Wheldall, K. (2005). Identifying low-progress readers: Comparing teacher judgment with a curriculum-based measurement procedure. *International Journal of Disability, Development and Education, 52,* 33–42.

Magiera, K. A., & Simmons, R. J. (2005). *The Magiera-Simmons quality indicator model of co-teaching.* Fredonia, NY: Excelsior Educational Service.

Magiera, K., Simmons, R., & Hance, S. (2008). Secondary co-teaching: A quality process. *Impact on Instructional Improvement, 34*(1), 18–25.

Magiera, K., Simmons, R., Marotta, A., & Battaglia, B. (2005). A co-teaching model: A response to students with disabilities and their performance on NYS assessments. *School Administrators Association of New York Journal, 34*(2), 9–12.

Magiera, K., Smith, C., Zigmond, N., & Gebauer, K. (2005). Benefits of co-teaching in secondary mathematics classes. *Teaching Exceptional Children, 37*(3), 20–24.

Magiera, K., & Zigmond, N. (2005). Co-teaching in middle school classrooms under routine conditions: Does the instructional experience differ for SWDs in co-taught and solo-taught classes? *Learning Disabilities Research and Practice, 20,* 79–85.

Malouf, D. B., & Schiller, E. P. (1995). Practice and research in special education. *Exceptional Children, 61,* 414–424.

Margolis, H., & McCabe, P. (2004). Resolving struggling readers' homework difficulties: a social cognitive perspective. *Reading Psychology, 25,* 225–260.

Mariage, T., & Patriarca, L. (2007). Meeting the spirit of AYP through school reform: Systems of individuation and differentiation are needed to meet all stakeholders' needs, *Focus on Results, 9*(4), GATA 07-01.

Marshall, S. P. (1995). *Schemas in problem solving.* New York: Cambridge University Press.

Marvin, C., & Mirenda, P. (1993). Home literacy experiences of preschoolers enrolled in head start and special education programs. *Journal of Early Intervention, 17,* 351–367.

Mason, L. (2008). Teaching spelling in the primary grades: A national survey of instructional practices and adaptations. *American Educational Research Journal, 45,* 796–825.

Mason, L. H. (2010). Literacy instruction for students with special needs. In E. Baker, B. McGaw, & P. Peterson (Eds.), *International encyclopedia of education* (3rd ed., pp. 759–766). Oxford, UK: Elsevier.

Mason, L. H., & Graham, S. (2008). Writing instruction for adolescents with learning disabilities: Programs of intervention research. *Learning Disabilities Research and Practice, 23,* 103–112.

Mason, L. H., & Shriner, J. G. (2008). Self-regulated strategy development for writing an opinion essay: Effects for six students with emotional/behavioral disorders. *Reading and Writing: An Interdisciplinary Journal, 21,* 71–93.

Mastropieri, M. A., & Scruggs, T. E. (1992). Science for students with disabilities. *Review of Educational Research, 62,* 377-411. doi: 10.3102/00346543062004377

Mastropieri, M. A., Scruggs, T. E., Bakken, J. P., & Whedon, C. (1996). Reading comprehension: A synthesis of research in learning disabilities. In T. E. Scruggs & M. A. Mastropieri (Eds.), *Advances in learning and behavioral disabilities* (pp. 277–303). Greenwich, CT: JAI Press.

Mastropieri, M. A., Scruggs, T. E., & Fulk, B. M. (1990). Teaching abstract vocabulary with the keyword method: Effects on recall and comprehension. *Journal of Learning Disabilities, 23*(2), 92–96, 107.

Mastropieri, M. A., Scruggs, T. E., & Graetz, J. E. (2003). Reading comprehension instruction for secondary students: Challenges for struggling students and teachers. *Learning Disability Quarterly, 26,* 103–116.

Mathes, P. G., & Babyak, A. O. (2001). The effects of peer-assisted literacy strategies for first-grade readers with and without additional mini-skills lessons. *Learning Disabilities: Research & Practice, 16,* 28–44.

Mathes, P. G., Denton, C. A., Fletcher, J. M., Anthony, J. L., Francis, D. J., & Schatschneider, C. (2005). The effects of theoretically different instruction and student characteristics on the skills of struggling readers. *Reading Research Quarterly, 40*(2), 148–182.

Mathes, P. G., Howard, J. K., Allen, S. H., & Fuchs, D. (1998). Peer-assisted learning strategies for first grade readers: Responding to the needs of diverse learners. *Reading Research Quarterly, 33,* 62–94.

Mathes, P. G., Kethley, C., Nimon, K., Denton, C. A., & Ware, P. (2009). *A test of proven early intervention in high poverty schools: Do results generalize to more challenging contexts?* Unpublished manuscript.

Mathes, P. G., & Torgesen, J. K. (2005). *Early interventions in reading, Level 1.* Columbus, OH: SRA/McGraw-Hill. Mathes, P. G., Torgesen, J. K., Allen, S. H., & Allor, J. H. (2001). *First-grade PALS: Peer-assisted literacy strategies.* Longmont, CO: Sopris West.

Mathes, P. G., Torgesen, J. K., & Allor, J. H. (2001). The effects of peer-assisted learning strategies for first grade readers with and without additional computer assisted instruction in phonological awareness. *American Educational Research Journal, 38,* 371–410.

Mathes, P. G., Torgesen, J. K., & Clancy-Menchetti, J. (2001). *K-PALS: Kindergarten peer-assisted literacy strategies.* Longmont, CO: Sopris West.

Mattingly, J. C., & Bott, D. A. (1990). Teaching multiplication facts to students with learning problems. *Exceptional Children, 56,* 438–450.

Mayer, R. E. (1985). Mathematical ability. In R. J. Sternberg (Ed.), *Human abilities: Information processing approach* (pp. 127–150). San Francisco, CA: Freeman.

Mayer, R. E. (1999). *The promise of educational psychology Vol. I: Learning in the content areas.* Upper Saddle River, NJ: Merrill/Pearson.

Mayer, R. E., & Hegarty, M. (1996). The process of understanding mathematics problems. In R. J. Sternberg & T. Ben-Zeev (Eds.), *The nature of mathematical thinking* (pp. 29–53). Hillsdale, NJ: Erlbaum.

McDuffie, K. A., Landrum, T. J., & Gelman, J. (2008). Co-teaching and students with emotional and behavioral disorders. *Beyond Behavior, 17*(2), 11–16.

McDuffie, K. A., Mastropieri, M. A., & Scruggs, T. E. (2009). Differential effects of peer tutoring in co-taught and non co-taught classes: Results for content learning and student-teacher interactions. *Exceptional Children, 75,* 493–510.

McIntosh, R., Vaughn, S., Schumm, J. S., Haager, D., & Lee, O. (1993). Observations of students with learning disabilities in general education classrooms. *Exceptional Children, 60,* 249–262.

McIntyre, S. B., Test, D. W., Cooke, N. L., & Beattie, J. (1991). Using count-bys to increase multiplication facts fluency. *Learning Disability Quarterly, 14,* 82–88.

McKeown, M. G. (1986). The acquisition of word meaning from context by children of high and low ability. *Reading Research Quarterly, 20,* 482–496.

McLaughlin, M. J. (2002). Examining special and general education collaborative practices in exemplary schools. *Journal of Educational and Psychological Consultation, 13,* 279–284.

McMaster, K. L., Fuchs, D., & Fuchs, L. S. (2007). Promises and limitations of peer-assisted learning strategies in reading. *Learning Disabilities: A Contemporary Journal, 5,* 97–112.

McMaster, K. L., Fuchs, D., Saenz, L., Lemons, C., Kearns, D., Yen, L., ... & Fuchs, L. S. (2010). Scaling up PALS: The importance of implementing evidence-based practice with fidelity and flexibility. *New Times for DLD, 28*(1), 1–3. Retrieved from http://www.teachingld.org/pdf/NewTimes_ScalingUpPals2010.pdf

Meyer, A., & Rose, D. H. (1998). *Learning to read in the computer age.* Cambridge, MA: Brookline.

Miller, S. P., & Mercer, C. D. (1993). Using data to learn about concrete-semiconcrete-abstract instruction for students with math disabilities. *Learning Disabilities Research & Practice, 8,* 89–96.

Montague, M. (1992). The effects of cognitive and metacognitive strategy instruction on mathematical problem solving of middle school students with learning disabilities. *Journal of Learning Disabilities, 25,* 230–248.

Montague, M. (2003). *Solve it: A mathematical problem-solving instructional program.* Reston, VA: Exceptional Innovations.

Montague, M., & Applegate, B. (1993). Mathematical problem-solving characteristics of middle school students with learning disabilities. *Journal of Special Education, 27,* 175–201.

Montague, M., Applegate, B., & Marquard, K. (1993). Cognitive strategy instruction and mathematical problem-solving performance of students with learning disabilities. *Learning Disabilities Research and Practice, 29,* 251–261.

Montague, M., & Bos, C. (1986). The effect of cognitive strategy training on verbal math problem solving performance of learning disabled adolescents. *Journal of Learning Disabilities, 19,* 26–33.

Montague, M., & Dietz, S. (2009). Evaluating the evidence base for cognitive strategy instruction and mathematical problem solving. *Exceptional Children, 75,* 285–382.

Montague, M., Enders, C., & Dietz, S. (2009). [The effects of Solve It! on middle school students' math problem solving and math self-efficacy]. Unpublished raw data.

Montague, M., Enders, C., & Dietz, S. (2010, February). *The effects of Solve It! on middle school students' math problem solving.* Paper presented at the Pacific Coast Research Conference, Coronado, CA.

Montali, J., & Lewandowski, L. (1996). Bimodal reading: Benefits of a talking computer for average and less skilled readers. *Journal of Learning Disabilities, 29,* 271–279.

Moore, M., & Calvert, S. (2000). Brief report: Vocabulary acquisition for children with autism: Teacher or computer instruction. *Journal of Autism and Developmental Disorders, 30,* 359–362.

Moran, M. R., Schumaker, J. B., & Vetter, A. F. (1981). *Teaching a paragraph organization strategy to learning disabled adolescents* (Research Report No. 54). Lawrence, KS: Institute for Research in Learning Disabilities.

Morris, R. D., Lovett, M., Wolf, M., Sevcik, R., Steinbeach, K., Frijters, J. C., & Shapiro, M. B. (2010). Multiple-component remediation for developmental reading disabilities: IQ, socioeconomic status, and race as factors in remedial outcome. *Journal of Learning Disabilities,* doi:10.1177/0022219409355472

Mostert, M. P. (Ed.). (2010). Empirically unsupported interventions in special education [Special issue]. *Exceptionality, 18*(1).

Mostert, M. P., & Crockett, J. B. (2000). Reclaiming the history of special education for more effective practice. *Exceptionality, 8,* 133–143.

Muller, E., Friend, M., & Hurley-Chamberlain, D. (2009). State-level approaches to co-teaching. *In Forum Brief Policy Analysis,* 1–7.

Murawski, W. W. (2006). Student outcomes in co-taught secondary English classes: How can we improve? *Reading and Writing Quarterly, 22,* 227–247.

Murawski, W. W., & Swanson, H. L. (2001). A meta-analysis of co-teaching research: Where are the data? *Remedial and Special Education, 22,* 258–267.

Nagy, W. E. (2007). Metalinguistic awareness and the vocabulary-comprehension connection. In R. K. Wagner, A. E. Muse, & K. R. Tannenbaum (Eds.), *Vocabulary acquisition: Implications for reading comprehension* (pp. 52–77). New York: Guilford

Nagy, W. E., & Anderson, R. C. (1984). The number of words in printed school English. *Reading Research Quarterly, 19,* 304–330.

Nagy, W. E., & Scott, J. A. (2000). Vocabulary processes. In M. L. Kamil, P. B. Mosenthal, P. D. Pearson, & R. Barr (Eds.), *Handbook of reading research* (Vol. 3, pp. 269–284). Mahwah, NJ: Erlbaum.

Nash, H., & Snowling, M. (2006). Teaching new words to children with poor existing vocabulary knowledge: A controlled evaluation of the definition and context methods. *International Journal of Language and Communication Disorders, 41,* 335–354.

Nathan, M. J., & Kim, S. (2009). Regulation of teacher elicitations in the mathematics classroom. *Cognition and Instruction, 27,* 91–120.

Nathan, R. G., & Stanovich, K. E. (1991). The causes and consequences in differences in reading fluency. *Theory in Practice, 30*(3), 176–184.

National Assessment of Educational Progress. (2009). *The nation's report card.* Washington, DC: Author.

National Assessment of Educational Progress, National Center for Education Statistics. (2007). *The nation's report card: Reading 2007.* Washington, D.C: National Center for Education Statistics.

National Center on Educational Restructuring and Inclusion. (1995). *National study of inclusive education* (2nd ed.) New York: Author.

National Commission on Writing. (2007). *2007 survey: Learning to write.* Retrieved from www.collegeboard.com

National Council of Teachers of Mathematics. (2000). *Principles and standards for school mathematics.* Reston, VA: Author.

National Council of Teachers of Mathematics. (2006). *Curriculum focal points.* Reston, VA: Author.

National Council of Teachers of Mathematics. (2009). *Focus in Grade 1.* Reston, VA: Author.

National Early Literacy Panel. (2008). *Executive summary. Developing early literacy: Report of the National Early Literacy Panel (NELP).* Louisville, KY: National Institute for Literacy.

National Institute of Child Health and Human Development. (2000). *Report of the National Reading Panel: Teaching children to read: An evidence-based assessment of the scientific research literature on reading and its implications for reading instruction: Reports of the sub-groups.* Washington, DC: U.S. Department of Health and Human Services, National Institute on Health.

National Mathematics Advisory Panel. (2008). *Foundations for success: The final report of the National Mathematics Advisory Panel.* Washington, DC: U.S. Department of Education.

National Reading Panel. (2000). Teaching children to read: An evidence-based assessment of the scientific research literature on reading and its implications for reading instruction

(NIH Pub. No. 00-4769). Washington, DC. National Institute for Child Health and Development.

National Research Council. (2001). Adding it up: Helping children learn mathematics. In J. Kilpatrick, J. Swafford, & B. Findell (Eds.), *Mathematics Learning Study Committee, Center for Education, Division of Behavioral and Social Sciences and Education*. Washington, DC: National Academy Press.

National Research Council. (2009). *Mathematic learning in early childhood: Paths toward excellence and equity*. Washington, DC: Author.

Nelson, J. R., Benner, G. J., & Gonzalez, J. (2003). Learner characteristics that influence the treatment effectiveness of early literacy interventions: A meta-analytic review. *Learning Disabilities: Research & Practice, 18,* 255–267.

Nevin, A. I. (2006). Can co-teaching provide quality education? Let the data tell us [Review of the book *The Magiera-Simmons quality indicator model of co-teaching* by K. A. Magiera & R. J. Simmons]. *Remedial and Special Education, 27,* 250–251.

No Child Left Behind Act of 2001, Pub. L. No. 107-110, 115 Stat. 1425 *et seq.* (2001).

Nolet, V., & McLaughlin, M. J. (2000). *Accessing the general curriculum: Including students with disabilities in standards-based reform*. Thousand Oaks, CA: Corwin Press.

Noonan, M. J., McCormick, L., & Heck, R. (2003). The co-teacher relationship scale: Applications for professional development. *Education and Training in Developmental Disabilities, 38,* 113–120.

Nunes, T., & Bryant, P. (Eds.). (2006). *Improving literacy by teaching morphemes*. London: Routledge.

O'Connor, R. E., Notari-Syverson, A., & Vadasy, P. F. (1998). *Ladders to literacy: A kindergarten activity book*. Baltimore, MD: Brookes.

Office of Special Education Programs. (2009). *28th Annual Report to Congress on the Implementation of the Individuals with Disabilities Education Act, 2006*, Vol. 2. Washington, DC: Author.

Olson, R. K., & Wise, B. W. (1992). Reading on the computer with orthographic and speech feedback: An overview of the Colorado Remedial Reading Project. *Reading and Writing: An Interdisciplinary Journal, 4,* 107–144.

Owen, R. L., & Fuchs, L. S. (2002). Mathematical problem-solving strategy instruction for third-grade students with learning disabilities. *Remedial and Special Education, 23,* 268–278.

Palincsar, A. S. (1986). The role of dialogue in providing scaffolded instruction. *Educational Psychologist, 21,* 73–98.

Palincsar, A. S., & Brown, A. L. (1984). The reciprocal teaching of comprehension-fostering and comprehension-monitoring activities. *Cognition and Instruction, 1,* 117–175.

Palincsar, A. S., & Brown, D. S. (1987). Enhancing instructional time through attention to metacognition. *Journal of Learning Disabilities, 20*(2), 66–75.

Paris, A. H., Lipson, M. Y., & Wixson, K. K. (1983). Becoming a strategic reader. *Contemporary Educational Psychology, 8,* 293–316.

Paris, A. H., Wasik, B. A., & Turner, J. C. (1991). The development of strategic readers. In R. Barr, M. L. Kamil, B. P. Mosenthal, & P. D. Pearson (Eds.), *Handbook of reading research* (Vol. 2, pp. 609–640). New York: Longman.

Pashler, H., Bain, P. M., Bottge, B. A., Graesser, A., Koedinger, K., McDaniel, M., & Metcalfe, J. (2007). *Organizing instruction and study to improve student learning*. IES Practice Guide (NCER 2007-2004). Jessup, MD: National Center for Education Research.

Passolunghi, M. C., & Siegel, L. S. (2001). Short-term memory, working memory, and inhibitory control in children with specific arithmetic learning disabilities. *Journal of Experimental Child Psychology, 80,* 44–57.

Patberg, J. P., Graves, M. F., & Stibbe, M. A. (1984). Effects of active teaching and practice in facilitating students' use of context clues. In J. A. Niles & L. A. Harris (Eds.),

Changing perspectives on research in reading/language processing and instruction: Thirty-third Yearbook of the National Reading Conference (pp. 146–151). Rochester, NY: National Reading Conference.

Perfetti, C. A. (1977). Language comprehension and fast decoding: Some psycholinguistic prerequisites for skilled reading comprehension. In J. T. Guthrie (Ed.), *Cognition, curriculum and comprehension* (pp. 20–41). Newark, DE: International Reading Association.

Perfetti, C. (1985). *Reading ability*. New York: Oxford University Press. Perfetti, C. A., Landi, N., & Oakhill, J. (2005). The acquisition of reading comprehension skill. In M. J. Snowling & C. Hulme (Eds.), *The science of reading: A handbook* (pp. 227–247). Oxford: Blackwell.

Perkins, D., & Salomon, G. (1992). *Transfer of learning: Contribution to the international encyclopedia of education* (2nd ed.). Oxford, England: Pergamon Press.

Pikulski, J. J., & Chard, D. J. (2005). Fluency: Bridge between decoding and reading comprehension. *Reading Teacher, 58,* 510–519.

Pinnell, G. S., Pikulski, J. J., Wizson, K. K., Campbell, J. R., Gough, P. B., & Beatty, A. S. (1995). *Listening to children read aloud*. Washington, DC: Office of Educational Research and Improvement, U.S. Department of Education.

Porter, A., McMaken, J., Hwang, J., & Yang, R. (2011). Common core standards: The new U.S. intended curriculum. *Educational Researcher, 40*(3), 103–116.

Pressley, M. (2002). Conclusion: Improving comprehension strategy instruction: A path for the future. In C. C. Block, L. B. Gambrel, & M. Pressley (Eds.), *Improving comprehension instruction* (pp. 385–399). San Francisco: Jossey-Bass.

Pressley, M. (2006). *Reading instruction that works: The case for balanced teaching* (3rd ed.). New York: Guilford Press.

Pressley, M., & Afferbach, P. (1995). *Verbal protocols of reading: The nature of constructively responsive reading*. Hillsdale, NJ: Erlbaum.

Pressley, M., Borkowski, J. G., & Schneider, W. (1987). Cognitive strategies: Good strategy users coordinate metacognition and knowledge. In R. Vasta & G. Whitehurst (Eds.), *Annals of child development* (Vol. 5, pp. 89–98). New York: JAI Press.

Pressley, M., El-Dinary, P. B., Gaskins, I., Schuder, T., Bergman, J., Almasi, J., & Brown, R. (1992). Beyond direct explanation: Transactional instruction of reading comprehension strategies. *The Elementary School Journal, 92*, 513–555.

Pressley, M., Wood, E., Woloshyn, V. E., Martin, V., King, A., & Menke, D. (1992). Encouraging mindful use of prior knowledge: Attempting to construct explanatory answers facilitates learning. *Educational Psychologist, 27*(1), 91–109. doi:10.1207/s15326985ep2701_7

Proctor, C. P., Dalton, B., & Grisham, D. (2007). Scaffolding English language learners and struggling readers in a multimedia hypertext environment with embedded strategy instruction and vocabulary support. *Journal of Literacy Research, 39*, 71–93.

Proctor, C. P., Uccelli, P., Dalton, B., & Snow, C. E. (2009). Understanding depth of vocabulary online with bilingual and monolingual children. *Reading and Writing Quarterly, 25*, 311–333.

Pugach, M. C., & Johnson., L. J. (1989). The challenge of implementing collaboration between general and special education. *Exceptional Children, 56*, 232–236.

Purkey, S. C., & Smith, M. S. (1985). School reform: The district policy implications of the effective schools literature. *Elementary School Journal, 85*, 353–389.

RAND Reading Study Group. (2002). *Reading for understanding: Towards an R & D program in reading comprehension.* Santa Monica, CA: RAND. Retrieved from http://www.rand.org/pubs/monograph_reports/2005/MR1465.pdf

Rasinski, T. V., Rueztel, D. R., Chard, D., & Linan-Thompson, S. (2010). Reading fluency. In M. L. Kamil, P. D., Pearson, E. Birr Moje, & P. P. Afflerbach (Eds.), *Handbook of READING RESEARCH* (Vol. 4, pp. XX–XX). New York: Routledge.

Rea, P. J., McLaughlin, V. L., & Walther-Thomas, C. (2002). Outcomes for students with learning disabilities in inclusive and pullout programs. *Exceptional Children, 68*, 203–222.

Reeve, P., & Hallahan, D. (1994). Practical questions about collaboration between general and special educators. *Focus on Exceptional Children, 26*, 1–12.

Reinking, D., & Pickle, J. M. (1993). Using a formative experiment to study how computers affect reading and writing in classrooms. In D. J. Leu & C. K. Kinzer (Eds.), *Examining central issues in literacy research, theory, and practice* (pp. 263–270). Chicago: National Reading Conference.

Robbins C., & Ehri, L. C. (1994). Reading storybooks to kindergartners helps them learn new vocabulary words. *Journal of Educational Psychology, 86*, 54–64.

Roberts, G., Torgesen, J. K., Boardman, A., & Scammacca, N. (2008). Evidence-based strategies for reading instruction in older students with learning disabilities. *Learning Disabilities Research and Practice, 23*, 63–69.

Robinson, C., Menchetti, B., & Torgesen, J. (2002). Toward a two-factor theory of one type of mathematics disabilities. *Learning Disabilities Research & Practice, 17*, 81–89.

Rogers, L., & Graham, S. (2008). A meta-analysis of single subject design writing intervention research. *Journal of Educational Psychology, 100*, 879–906.

Root, P. (1996). *Mrs. Potter's pig.* Cambridge, MA: Candelwick.

Rose, D., & Meyer, A. (2002). *Teaching every student the digital age.* Alexandria, VA: ASCD.

Rosenberg, M., Bott, D., Majsterek, D., Chiang, B., Gartland, D., Wesson, C., . . . & Wilson, R. (1992). Minimum standards for the description of participants in learning disabilities research. *Learning Disability Quarterly, 15*, 65–70.

Rosenshine, B., Meister, C., & Chapman, S. (1996). Teaching students to generate questions: A review of the intervention studies. *Review of Educational Research, 66*(2), 181–221. doi:10.2307/1170607

Rosenshine, B., & Stevens, R. (1986). Teaching functions. In M. C. Wittrock (Ed.), *Handbook of research on teaching* (3rd ed.). New York, Macmillan.

Rosman, N. J. S. (1994). *Effects of varying the special educator's role within an algebra class on math attitude and achievement.* Master's thesis, University of South Dakota, Vermillion. (ERIC Document Reproduction Service No. ED 381 993)

Rouet, J. F., Vidal-Abarca, E., Erboul, A. B., & Millogo, V. (2001). Effects of information search tasks on the comprehension of instructional text. *Discourse Processes, 31*(2), 163–186. doi:10.1207/S15326950DP3102_03

Rudell, R. B., & Unrau, N. J. (Eds.). (2004). *Theoretical models and processes of reading.* (5th ed.). Newark, DE: International Reading Association.

Sáenz, L. M., Fuchs, L. S., & Fuchs, D. (2005). Peer-assisted learning strategies for English language learners with learning disabilities. *Exceptional Children, 71*, 231–247.

Sagan, C. (1996). *The demon-haunted world: Science as a candle in the dark.* New York: Ballantine Books.

Salahu-Din, D., Persky, H., & Miller, J. (2008). *The Nation's Report Card: Writing 2007* (NCES 2008-468). National Center for Education Statistics, Institute of Education Sciences, U.S. Department of Education, Washington, DC.

Salend, S. J., Gordon, J., & Lopez-Vona, K. (2002). Evaluating cooperative teaching teams. *Intervention in School and Clinic, 37*, 195–200.

Sandmel, K., Brindle, M., Harris, K. R., Lane, K., Graham, S., Little, A., Nackel, J., & Mathias, R. (2009). Making it work: Differentiating tier two writing instruction with self-regulated strategies development in tandem with schoolwide positive behavioral support for second graders. *Teaching Exceptional Children, 42*(2), 22–33.

Santamaría, L. J., & Thousand, J. S. (2004). Collaboration, co-teaching, and differentiated instruction: a process-oriented approach to whole schooling. *International Journal of Whole Schooling 1*(1), 13–27.

Saxon, K. (March 22, 2005). Co-teaching and school reform: A case study. *Academic Exchange Quarterly*. Retrieved from http://goliath.ecnext.com/coms2/gi_0199-4327562/Co-teaching-and-school-reform.html

Scarborough, H. S., & Dobrich, W. (1994). On the efficacy of reading to preschoolers. *Developmental Review, 14*, 245–302.Schmidt, J. L., Deshler, D. D., Schumaker, J. B., & Alley, G. R. (1988). Effects of generalization instruction on the written language performance of adolescents with learning disabilities in the mainstream classroom. *Reading, Writing, and Learning Disabilities, 4*, 291–309.

Schumaker, J., Bulgren, J., Deshler, D., & Lenz, B. K. (1998). *The recall enhancement routine.* Lawrence, KS: The University of Kansas Center for Research on Learning.

Schumaker, J. B., & Deshler, D. D. (1992). Validation of learning strategy interventions for students with LD: Results of a programmatic research effort. In Y. L. Wong (Ed.), *Contemporary intervention research in learning disabilities: An international perspective.* New York: Springer-Verlag.

Schumaker, J. B., & Deshler, D. D. (2003). Can students with LD become competent writers? *Learning Disabilities Quarterly, 26*, 129–141.

Schumaker, J. B., & Deshler, D. D. (2009). Adolescents with learning disabilities as writers: Are we selling them short? *Learning Disabilities Research and Practice, 24*, 81–92.

Schumaker, J. B., & Deshler, D. D. (2010). Using a tiered intervention model in secondary schools to improve academic outcomes in subject-area courses. In M. Shinn & H. Walker (Eds.), *Interventions for achievement and behavior problems in a three-tier model including RTI* (pp. 609–632). Bethesda, MD: National Association of School Psychologists.

Schumaker, J. B., Deshler, D. D., Lenz, B. K., Bulgren, J. B., & Davis, B. (2006). *Strategies for helping adolescents with disabilities access the general education curriculum.*

Lawrence, KS: University of Kansas Center for Research on Learning.

Schumaker, J. B., Deshler, D. D., & McKnight, P. (2002). Ensuring success in the secondary general education curriculum through the use of teaching routines. In M. A. Shinn, H. M. Walker, & G. Stoner (Eds.), *Interventions for academic and behavior problems II: Preventive and remedial approaches* (pp. 791–823). Bethesda, MD: NASP Publications.

Schumaker, J. B., & Lyerla, K. D. (1991). *The paragraph writing strategy: Instructor's manual.* Lawrence, KS: The University of Kansas Center for Research on Learning. Schumaker, J. B., & Sheldon, J. (1985). *Proficiency in the sentence writing strategy: Instructor's manual.* Lawrence, KS: The University of Kansas Center for Research on Learning.

Schumm, J. S., Vaughn, S., & Harris, J. (1997). Pyramid power for cooperative planning. *Teaching Exceptional Children, 29*, 62–66.

Scruggs, T. E., & Mastropieri, M. A. (2000). The effectiveness of mnemonic instruction for students with learning and behavior problems: An update and research synthesis. *Journal of Behavioral Education, 10*, 163–173.

Scruggs, T. E., & Mastropieri, M. A. (2013). Teaching students with high-incidence disabilities. In B. G. Cook & M. Tankersley (Eds.), *Research-based practices in special education.* Columbus, OH: Pearson.

Scruggs, T. E., Mastropieri, M. A., & Casto, G. (1987). The quantitative synthesis of single subject research: Methodology and validation. *Remedial and Special Education, 8*, 24–33.

Scruggs, T. E., Mastropieri, M. A., & McDuffie, K. A. (2007). Co-teaching in inclusive classrooms: A metasynthesis of qualitative research. *Exceptional Children, 73*, 392–416.

Self, H., Benning, A., Marston, D., & Magnusson, D. (1991). Cooperative teaching project: A model for students at risk. *Exceptional Children 58*, 26–33.

Senechal, M. (1997). The differential effect of storybook reading on preschoolers' acquisition of expressive and receptive vocabulary. *Journal of Child Language, 24*, 123–138.

Shermer, M. (2002). *Why people believe weird things.* New York: Henry Holt.

Shulman, L. (1985). On teaching problem-solving and the solving of the problems of teaching. In E. A. Silver (Ed.), *Teaching and learning mathematical problem solving: Multiple research perspectives* (pp. 439–450). Hillsdale, NJ: Erlbaum.

Siegler, R. S. (2007). Cognitive variability. *Developmental Science, 10*, 104–109.

Silver, E. A. (1985). Research on teaching mathematical problem solving: Some underrepresented themes and needed directions. In E.A. Silver (Ed.), *Teaching and learning mathematical problem solving: Multiple research perspectives* (pp. 247–266). Hillsdale, NJ: Erlbaum.

Simmons, D., Fuchs, L., & Fuchs, D. (1995). Effects of explicit teaching and peer-mediated instruction on the reading achievement of learning disabled and low-performing students. *Elementary School Journal, 95*, 387-407.

Simmons, D. C., Fuchs, L. S., Fuchs, D., Mathes, P. G., & Hodge, J. (1995). Effects of explicit teaching and peer-mediated instruction on the reading achievement of learning disabled and low performing students. *Elementary School Journal, 95,* 387–408.

Simmons, D., Fuchs, D., Fuchs, L. S., Pate, J., & Mathes, P. (1994). Importance of instructional complexity and role reciprocity to classwide peer tutoring. *Learning Disabilities Research and Practice, 9,* 203–212.

Simmons, R. J., & Magiera, K. (2007). Evaluation of co-teaching in three high schools within one school district: How do you know when you are TRULY co-teaching? *Teaching Exceptional Children Plus, 3*(3) Article 4. Retrieved July from http://escholarship.bc.edu/education/tecplus/vol3/iss3/art4

Simmons, R. J., Magiera, K., Cummings, B., & Arena, M. (2008). Co-teaching in secondary mathematics: How the special education teacher fits into the equation. *New York State Mathematics Teachers' Journal, 58*(1), 12–25.

Smith, A. (2003). Scientifically based research and evidence-based education: A federal policy context. *Research and Practice for Persons with Severe Disabilities, 28*, 126–132.

Snow, C. E., Burns, M. S., & Griffin, P. (Eds.). (1998). *Preventing reading difficulties in young children.* Washington, DC: National Academy Press.

Sonntag, C. M., & McLaughlin, T. F. (1984). The effects of training students in paragraph writing. *Education & Treatment of Children, 7,* 49–59.

Stading, M., Williams, R. L., & McLaughlin, T. F. (1996). Effects of a copy, cover, and compare procedure on multiplication facts mastery with a third grade girl with learning disabilities in a home setting. *Education & Treatment of Children, 19*(4), 425–434. Stanovich, K. E. (1986). Matthew effects in reading: Some consequences in individual differences in the acquisition of literacy. *Reading Research Quarterly, 21,* 360–407.

Starr, M. S., Kambe, G., Miller, B., & Keith, R. (2002). Basic functions of language, reading and reading disability. In E. Witruk, A. D. Friederici, & T. Lachmann (Eds.), *Neuropsychology and cognition* (Vol. 20, pp. 121–136). Dordrecht, Netherlands: Kluwer Academic. Stecker, S. K., Roser, N. L., & Martinez, M. G. (1998). Understanding oral reading fluency. In T. Shanahan & F. V. Rodrigues-Brown (Eds.), *47th Yearbook of the National Reading Conference* (pp. 295–310). Chicago: National Reading Conference.

Stein, M., Kinder, D., Silbert, J., & Carnine, D. W. (2006). *Designing effective mathematics instruction: A direct instruction approach* (4th ed.). Upper Saddle, NJ: Prentice Hall.

Sternberg, R. (1985). *Beyond IQ.* Cambridge, MA: Cambridge University.

Stoddard, B., & MacArthur, C. A. (1993). A peer editor strategy: Guiding learning-disabled students in response and revision. *Research in the Teaching of English, 27,* 76–103.

Strangman, N., & Dalton, B. (2005). Technology for struggling readers: A review of the research. In D. Edyburn, K. Higgins, & R. Boone (Eds.), *Handbook of special education technology research and practice* (pp. 549–569). Whitefish Bay, WI: Knowledge by Design.

Sulzby, E. (1985). Children's emergent reading of favorite storybooks: A developmental study. *Reading Research Quarterly, 20,* 458–481.

Swanson, E. A., Wexler, J., & Vaughn, S. (2009). Text reading and students with learning difficulties. In E. H. Hiebert (Ed.), *Reading more, reading better* (pp. 210–230). New York: Guilford Press.

Swanson, H. L. (1990). Instruction derived from the strategy deficit model: Overview of principles and procedures. In T. E. Scruggs & B. Y. L. Wong (Eds.), *Intervention research in learning disabilities* (pp. 34–65). New York: Springer-Verlag.

Swanson, H. L. (1993). Principles and procedures in strategy use. In L. Meltzer (Ed.), *Strategy assessment and instruction for students with learning disabilities* (pp. 61–92). Austin, TX: Pro-Ed.

Swanson, H. L. (1999). *Interventions for students with learning disabilities: A meta-analysis of treatment outcomes.* New York: Guilford Press.

Swanson, H. L., & Beebe-Frankenberger, M. (2004). The relationship between working memory and mathematical problem solving in children at risk and not at risk for math disabilities. *Journal of Education Psychology, 96,* 471–491.

Swanson, H. L., & Deshler, D. D. (2003). Instructing adolescents with learning disabilities: Converting a meta-analysis to practice. *Journal of Learning Disabilities, 36*(2), 124–135. doi:10.1177/002221940303600205

Swanson, H. L., & Hoskyn, M. (2001a). Instructing adolescents with learning disabilities: A component and composite analysis. *Learning Disabilities Research & Practice, 16,* 109–119.

Swanson, H. L., & Hoskyn, M. (2001b). A meta-analysis of intervention research for adolescent students with learning disabilities. *Learning Disabilities Research & Practice, 16,* 109–119.

Swanson, H. L., Hoskyn, M., & Lee, C. (1999). *Interventions for students with learning disabilities: A meta-analysis of treatment outcomes.* New York: Guilford Press.

Swanson, H. L., & Sachs-Lee, C. (2000). A meta-analysis of single-subject-design intervention research for students with LD. *Journal of Learning Disabilities, 33,* 114–136. Sweet, A. P., & Snow, C. (2002). Reconceptualizing reading comprehension. In C. C. Block, L. B. Gambrell, & M. Pressley (Eds.), *Improving reading comprehension instruction: Rethinking research, theory, and classroom practice* (pp. 17–53). San Francisco, CA: Jossey-Bass.

Sweller, J. (2005). Implications of cognitive load theory for multimedia learning. In R. Mayer (Ed.), *Cambridge handbook of multimedia learning* (pp. 19–30). New York: Cambridge University Press.

Sweller, J., Chandler, P., Tierney, P., & Cooper, M. (1990). Cognitive load as a factor in the structuring of technical material. *Journal of Experimental Psychology: General, 119,* 176–192.

Taft, R., & Mason, L. H. (2011). Examining effect of writing interventions: Spotlighting results for students with primary disabilities other than learning disabilities. *Remedial and Special Education, 32,* 359–370.

Talbott, E., Lloyd, J. W., & Tankersley, M. (1995). Effects of reading comprehension interventions with students with learning disabilities. *Learning Disability Quarterly, 17,* 223–232.

Tankersley, M., Harjusola-Webb, S., & Landrum, T. J. (2008). Using single-subject research to establish the evidence base of special education. *Intervention in School and Clinic, 44,* 83–90.

Tawney, J. W., & Gast, D. L. (1984). *Single subject research in special education.* Columbus, OH: Charles E. Merrill Publishing Company.

Therrien, W. J. (2004). Fluency and comprehension gains as a result of repeated reading: A meta-analysis. *Remedial and Special Education, 25,* 252–261.

Thevenot, C., Devidal, M., Barrouillet, P., & Fayol, M. (2007). Why does placing the question before an arithmetic word problem improve performance? A situation model account. *The Quarterly Journal of Experimental Psychology, 60,* 43–56.

Thousand, J. S., & Villa, R. A. (1989). Enhancing success in heterogeneous schools. In S. Stainback, W. Stainback, & M. Forest (Eds.), *Educating all students in the mainstream of regular education* (pp. 89–103). Baltimore, MD: Brookes.

Thurlow, M., Altman, J., & Vang, M. (2009). *Annual performance report: 2006–2007 State assessment data*, Minneapolis, MN: University of Minnesota National Center on Educational Outcomes (NCEO). Retrieved from http://www.cehd.umn.edu/nceo/OnlinePubs/APRreport2006-2007.pdf

Tomesen, M., & Aarnoutse, C. (1998). Effects of an instructional programme for deriving word meanings. *Educational Studies, 24*, 107–128.

Tomlinson, C. (1999). *The differentiated classroom: Responding to the needs of all learners*. Alexandria, VA: ASCD.

Torgesen, J. K. (1998). Catch them before they fall: Identification and assessment to prevent reading failure in young children. *American Educator, 22*, 32–39.

Torgesen, J. K., Alexander, A. W., Wagner, R. K., Rashotte, C. A., Voeller, K. K. S., & Conway, T. (2001). Intensive remedial instruction for children with severe reading disabilities: Immediate and long-term outcomes from two instructional approaches. *Journal of Learning Disabilities, 34,* 33–58, 78.

Torgesen, J. K., & Licht, B. (1983). The learning disabled child as an inactive learner: Restrospect and prospects. In J. D. McKineey & L. Feagans (Eds.), *Current topics in learning disabilities* (Vol. 1, pp. 3–32). Norwood, NJ: Ablex.

Torgesen, J. K., Rashotte, C. A., & Alexander, A. W. (2001). Principles of fluency instruction in reading: Relationships with established empirical outcomes. In M. Wolf (Ed.), *Dyslexia, fluency, and the brain* (pp. 307–331). Timonium, MD: York Press.

Tournaki, N. (2003). The differential effects of teaching addition through strategy instruction versus drill and practice to students with and without learning disabilities. *Journal of Learning Disabilities, 36*, 449–558.

Trent, S. C. (1998). False starts and other dilemmas of a secondary general education collaborative teacher. *Journal of Learning Disabilities, 31*, 503–514.

Turnbull, H. R., III. (2005). Individuals with Disabilities Education Act Reauthorization: Accountability and personal responsibility. *Remedial and Special Education, 26*, 320–326.

U.S. Department of Education. (2006). *26th Annual (2004) Report to Congress on the Implementation of the Individuals with Disabilities Education Act, Vol. 1.* Washington, DC: Author. Retrieved from http://www.ed.gov/about/reports/annual/osep/2004/26th-vol-1-front.pdf

U.S. Department of Education. (2007). *Modified academic achievement standards: Non-regulatory guidance.* Washington, DC: Author. Retrieved September 10, 2007, from http://www.ed.gov/policy/speced/guid/nclb/twopercent.doc

U.S. Department of Education, Office of Special Education and Rehabilitative Services, Office of Special Education Programs. (2009). *28th Annual Report to Congress on the Implementation of the Individuals with Disabilities Education Act, 2006, Vol. 2.*

Vadasy, P. F., Jenkins, J. R., Antil, L. R., Wayne, S. K., & O'Connor, R. E. (1997). Community-based early reading intervention for at-risk first graders. *Learning Disabilities: Research & Practice, 12*, 29–39.

Vadasy, P. F., Jenkins, J. R., & Pool, K. (2000). Effects of tutoring in phonological and early reading skills on students at risk for reading disabilities. *Journal of Learning Disabilities, 33*, 579–590.

Vadasy, P. F., Sanders, E. A., & Abbott, R. D. (2008). Effects of supplemental early reading intervention at 2-year follow up: Reading skill growth patterns and predictors. *Scientific Studies of Reading, 12*(1), 51–89.

Vadasy, P. F., Sanders, E. A., & Peyton, J. A. (2006). Code-oriented instruction for kindergarten students at risk for reading difficulties: A randomized field trial with paraeducator implementers. *Journal of Educational Psychology, 98*, 508–528.

Vadasy, P. F., Wayne, S. K., O'Connor, R. E., Jenkins, J. R., Pool, K., Firebaugh, M., . . . Peyton, J. (2004). *Sound Partners: A supplementary, one-to-one tutoring program in phonics based early reading skills.* Longmont, CO: Sopris West.

Van Dijk, T., & Kintsch, W. (1983). *Strategies of discourse comprehension.* New York: Academic Press.

van Garderen, D., & Montague, M. (2003). Visual-spatial representation, mathematical problem solving, and students of varying abilities. *Learning Disabilities Research & Practice, 18*, 246–254.

Vaughn, S., Bos, C., & Schumm, J. (2006). *Teaching exceptional, diverse, and at-risk students in the general education classroom* (3rd ed.). Upper Saddle River, NJ: Allyn & Bacon/Pearson.

Vaughn, S., Chard, D. J., Bryant, D. P., Coleman, M., Tyler, B., Linan-Thompson, S., & Kouzekanani, K. (2000). Fluency and comprehension interventions for third-grade students. *Remedial and Special Education, 21*, 325–335.

Vaughn, S., Cirino, P. T., Linan-Thompson, S., Mathes, P. G., Carlson, C. D., Cardenas-Hagan, . . . Francis, D. (2006). Effectiveness of a Spanish intervention and an English intervention for English-Language Learners at risk for reading problems. *American Educational Research Journal, 43*, 449–479.

Vaughn, S., Elbaum, B. E., Schumm, J. S., & Hughes, M. T. (1998). Social outcomes for students with and without learning disabilities in inclusive classrooms. *Journal of Learning Disabilities, 31*, 428–436.

Vaughn, S., Gersten, R., & Chard, D. J. (2000). The underlying message in learning disabilities intervention research: Findings from research syntheses. *Exceptional Children, 67*, 99–114.

Vaughn, S., Hughes, M. T., Moody, S., & Elbaum, B. (2001). Instructional grouping for reading for students with LD: Implications for practice, *Intervention in School and Clinic, 36*(3), 131–137.

Vaughn, S., Hughes, M. T., Schumm, J. S., & Klingner, J. K. (1998).

A collaborative effort to enhance reading and writing instruction in inclusion classrooms. *Learning Disability Quarterly, 21*, 57–74.

Vaughn, S., Mathes, P., Linan-Thompson, S., Cirino, P., Carlson, C., Pollard-Durodola, S., . . . & Francis, D. (2006). Effectiveness of an English intervention for first-grade English language learners at risk for reading problems. *The Elementary School Journal, 107*, 153–180.

Vaughn, S., Schumm, J. S., & Arguelles, M. E. (1997). The ABCDE's of co-teaching. *TEACHING Exceptional Children, 30*(2), 4–10.

Vellutino, F. R., Scanlon, D. M., Sipay, E. R., Small, S. G., Pratt, A., Chen, R., & Denckla, M. B. (1996). Cognitive profiles of difficult-to-remediate and readily remediated poor readers: Early intervention as a vehicle for distinguishing between cognitive and experiential deficits as basic causes of specific reading disability. *Journal of Educational Psychology, 88*(4), 601–638.

Villa, R., Thousand, J., & Nevin, A. (2008). *A guide to co-teaching: Practical tips for facilitating student learning* (2nd ed.). Thousand Oaks, CA: Corwin Press.

Voltz, D. L., Elliot, R. N., Jr., & Cobb, H. B. (1994) Collaborative teacher roles: Special and general educators. *Journal of Learning Disabilities, 27*, 527–535.

Vygotsky, L. S. (1978). *Mind in society.* Cambridge, MA: Harvard University Press.

Wagner, R. K., Muse, A. E., & Tannenbaum, K. R. (2007). Promising avenues for better understanding: Implications of vocabulary development for reading comprehension. In R. K. Wagner, A. E. Muse, & K. R. Tannenbaum (Eds.), *Vocabulary acquisition: Implications for reading comprehension.* New York: Guilford.

Wallace, G. W., & Bott, D. A. (1989). Statement-pie: A strategy to improve the paragraph writing skills of adolescents with learning disabilities. *Journal of Learning Disabilities, 22*, 541–553.

Walsh, J. M., & Snyder, D. (1993, April). *Cooperative teaching: An effective model for all students.* Paper presented at the annual convention of the Council for Exceptional Children, San Antonio, TX. (ERIC Document Reproduction Service No ED 361 930)

Walther-Thomas, C. S. (1997). Co-teaching experiences: The benefits and problems that teachers and principals report over time. *Journal of Learning Disabilities, 30*, 395–408.

Walther-Thomas, C., Korinek, L., McLaughlin, V., & Williams, B. (2000). *Collaboration for inclusive education: Developing successful programs.* Needham Heights, MA: Allyn & Bacon.

Wasik, B., Bond, M. A., & Hindman, A. (2006). The effects of a language and literacy intervention on head start children and teachers. *Journal of Educational Psychology, 98*, 63–74.

Weiss, M. P. (2004). Co-teaching as science in the schoolhouse: More questions than answers. *Journal of Learning Disabilities, 37*, 218–223.

Weiss, M. P., & Brigham, F. J. (2000). Co-teaching and the model of shared responsibility: What does the research support. In T. E. Scruggs & M. A. Mastropieri (Eds.), *Advances in learning and behavioral disabilities: Educational interventions* (pp. 217–246). Stamford, CT: JAI Press.

Weiss, M., & Lloyd, J. (2002). Congruence between roles and actions of secondary special educators in co-taught and special education settings. *The Journal of Special Education, 36*(2), 58–68.

Welch, M. (2000). Descriptive analysis of team teaching in two elementary classrooms: A formative experimental approach, *Remedial and Special Education, 21*, 366–376.

What Works Clearinghouse. (2006, September). *WWC intervention report: Enhanced proactive reading. A practice guide.* Washington, DC: National Center for Education Evaluation and Regional Assistance, Institute of Education Sciences, U.S. Department of Education. Retrieved from http://ies.ed.gov/ncee/wwc/

Whitby, P. (2009). *The effects of a modified learning strategy on the multiple step mathematical word problem solving ability of middle school students with high-functioning autism or Aspergers' disorder.* Unpublished doctoral dissertation, University of Central Florida.

Whitehurst, G. J., Arnold, D., Epstein, J., Angell, A., Smith, M., & Fischel, J. (1994). A picture book reading intervention in day care and home for children from low-income families. *Developmental Psychology, 30*, 679–689.

Williams, D. M., & Collins, B. C. (1994). Teaching multiplication facts to students with learning disabilities: Teacher-selected versus student-selected material prompts within the delay procedure. *Journal of Learning Disabilities, 27*, 589–597.

Williams, J. P. (1998). Improving comprehension of disabled readers. *Annals of Dyslexia, 48*, 213–238.

Williams, J. P. (2000). *Strategic processing of text: Improving reading comprehension for students with learning disabilities* (Report No. EDO-EC-00-8). Reston, VA: Council for Exceptional Children. (ERIC Document Reproduction Service No. ED 449596)

Wise, B., Olson, R., Anstett, M., Andrews, L., Terjak, M., Schneider, V., & Kostuch, J. (1989). Implementing a long-term computerized remedial program with synthetic speech feedback: Hardware, software, and real-world issues. *Behavior Research Methods, Instruments, and Computers, 21*, 173–189.

Wise, B., Ring, J., & Olson, R. K. (2000). Individual differences in gains from computer assisted-remedial reading with more emphasis on phonological analysis or accurate reading in context. *Journal of Experimental Child Psychology, 77*, 197–235.

Wolf, M., Barzillai, M., Gottwald, S., Miller, L., Spencer, K., Norton, E., Lovett, M., & Morris, R. (2009). The RAVE-O intervention: Connecting neuroscience to the classroom. *Mind Brain and Education, 3*(2), 84–93.

Wolf, M., & Bowers, P. (1999). The "Double-Deficit Hypothesis" for the developmental dyslexias. *Journal of Educational Psychology, 91*(3), 1–24. Wolf, M., & Bowers, P. (2000). The question of naming-speed deficits in developmental reading disability: An introduction to the Double-Deficit hypothesis. *Journal of Learning Disabilities, 33,* 322–324.

Wolf, M., Bowers, P. G., & Biddle, K. (2000). Naming speed processes, timing, and reading: A conceptual review. *Journal of Learning Disabilities, 33,* 387–407.

Wolf, M., Gottwald, S., & Orkin, M. (2009). Serious word play: How multiple linguistic emphases in RAVE-O instruction improve multiple reading skills. *Perspectives on Language Literacy,* 21–24.

Wolf, M., & Katzir-Cohen, T. (2001). Reading fluency and its intervention. *Scientific Studies of Reading.* (Special Issue on Fluency. E. Kame'enui & D. Simmons, Eds.), *5,* 211–238.

Wolf, M., Miller, L., & Donnelly, K. (2000). RAVE-O: A comprehensive fluency-based reading intervention program. *Journal of Learning Disabilities, 33,* 375–386.

Wong, B. Y. L., Harris, K. R., Graham, S., & Butler, D. L. (2003). Cognitive strategies instruction research in learning disabilities. In H. L. Swanson, K. R. Harris, & S. Graham (Eds.). *Handbook of learning disabilities* (pp. 383–402). New York: Guilford Press.

Wood, D., Frank, A., & Wacker, D. (1998). Teaching multiplication facts to students with learning disabilities. *Journal of Applied Behavior Analysis, 31,* 323–338.

Wood, L. & Hood, E. (2004). Shared storybook readings with who have little or no functional speech: A language intervention tool for students who use augmentative and alternative communication. *Perspectives in Education, 22,* 101–114.

Woodward, J. (2006). Developing automaticity in multiplication facts: Integrating strategy instruction with timed practice drills. *Learning Disability Quarterly, 29,* 269–289.

Woodward, J., & Rieth, H. (1997). An historical review of technology research in special education. *Review of Educational Research, 67,* 503–536.

Xin, J., & Rieth, H. (2001). Video-assisted vocabulary instruction for elementary school students with learning disabilities. *Information Technology in Childhood Education Annual 13,* 87–143. Xin, Y. P. (2008). The effects of schema-based instruction in solving mathematics word problems: An emphasis on prealgebraic conceptualization of multiplicative relations. *Journal for Research in Mathematics Education, 39,* 526–551.

Xin, Y. P., Jitendra, A. K., & Deatline-Buchman, A. (2005). Effects of mathematical word problem solving instruction on students with learning problems. *Journal of Special Education, 39,* 181–192.

Xin, Y. P., Wiles, B., & Lin, Y.-Y. (2008). Teaching conceptual model based word problem story grammar to enhance mathematics problem solving. *Journal of Special Education, 42,* 163–178.

Xin, Y. P. & Zhang, D. (2009). Exploring a conceptual model-based approach to teaching situated word problems.

Journal of Educational Research, 102, 427–441.

Zawaiza, T. B. W., & Gerber, M. M. (1993). Effects of explicit instruction on community college students with learning disabilities. *Learning Disabilities Quarterly, 16,* 64–79.

Zigmond, N. (1996). Organization and management of general education classrooms. In D. Speece & B. Keogh (Eds.), *Research on classroom ecologies: Implications for inclusion of children with learning disabilities* (pp. 163–190). Hillsdale, NJ: Erlbaum.

Zigmond, N. (2003). Where should SWDs receive special education services? Is one place better than another? *Journal of Special Education, 37,* 193–199.

Zigmond, N. (2006). Reading and writing in co-taught secondary school social studies classrooms: A reality check. *Reading and Writing Quarterly, 22,* 249–268.

Zigmond, N., & Magiera, K. (2001). Co-teaching. *Current Practice Alerts, 6,* 1–4.

Zigmond, N., & Matta, D. (2004). Value added of the special education teacher on secondary school co-taught classes. In T. E. Scruggs & M. A. Mastropieri (Eds.), *Research in secondary schools: Advances in learning and behavioral disabilities* (Vol. 17, pp. 55–76). Oxford, UK: Elsevier Science/JAI.

Zinth, J. D. (2007). *Standard graduation requirements.* Denver, CO: Education Commission of the States. Retrieved from http://mb2.ecs.org/reports/Report.aspx?id=735

Name Index

Aarnouste, C., 49, 50, 56
Abbott, M., 6
Abbott, R. D., 13
Adams, M. J., 9
Adelman, H. S., 117
Afferbach, P., 22
Alexander, A. W., 22
Allen, S. H., 11, 12
Alley, G. R., 89
Allor, J. H., 12, 16, 17, 18, 20
Al Otaiba, S., 9, 11, 12, 19
Altman, J., 120
Alves, A. J., 32
Anderson, R. C., 45, 49
Antil, L. R., 13
Apichatabutra, C., 22, 93
Applebee, A. N., 83
Applegate, B., 77, 79
Appleton, A. C., 74
Arguelles, M. E., 6, 35, 36, 114
Arnbak, E., 49
Arreaga-Mayer, C., 23, 25
Arunachalam, V., 2
Association for Supervision and Curriculum
    Development, 93
August, D., 51

Babyak, A. O., 11
Baggett, W., 101
Baker, J., 115, 120
Baker, L., 50
Baker, S., 18, 32, 49, 60, 68
Baker, S. K., 22, 71, 93, 94
Bakken, J. P., 32
Ball, D., 71, 72
Barker, L., 52
Barrouillet, P., 71
Barzillai, M., 26, 27, 28
Bass, H., 71, 72
Battaglia, B., 116
Baumann, J. F., 49, 50, 51, 55, 56
Bauwens, J., 114, 119, 120
Beals, V. L., 35, 89
Beattie, J., 66
Beck, I. L., 22, 44, 45, 47, 48, 49, 51, 55, 56
Beck, M., 74
Beckmann, S., 61, 66, 68, 72
Beebe-Frankenberger, M., 59, 60
Beirne-Smith, M., 61, 63, 64, 68
Bellamy, P., 104
Benner, G. J., 12
Benning, A., 116
Berninger, V., 84

Berninger, V. W., 49
Biddle, K., 22
Boardman, A. G., 6, 30, 33, 45
Boland, E. M., 50
Bond, M. A., 47
Boon, R., 96
Boone, R., 53
Borden, S. L., 49
Borkowski, J. G., 77
Bos, C. S., 79, 84, 114
Bosseler, A., 52
Bott, D. A., 61, 62, 64, 89
Boudah, D., 116
Bowers, P. G., 22, 27
Bragg, R., 84
Breznitz, Z., 28
Brigham, F. J., 115, 120
Brindle, M., 93
Brophy, J., 5
Brown, A. C., 50
Brown, A. L., 25, 33
Brownell, M., 31
Bryant, B. R., 45, 68
Bryant, D. P., 33, 35, 37, 41, 42, 45, 68
Bryant, P., 49, 50, 51, 55
Buikema, J. L., 49
Bulgren, J., 101, 106
Bulgren, J. A., 98, 100, 101, 102, 103, 104,
    106, 107, 108, 109, 110, 111
Bulgren, J. B., 104
Burish, P., 25
Burke, M., 96
Burns, M., 9
Burns, M. K., 6
Burns, M. S., 8, 30
Bus, A. G., 46
Butler, D. L., 81

Cain, K., 49
Calhoon, B., 11
Calvert, S., 52
Cammack, D., 55
Campbell, A., 30
Carlisle, J. F., 44, 50, 55
Carlo, M. S., 51, 55
Carnine, D. W., 5, 16, 34, 60, 63
Caron, E. A., 117, 118, 121
Carroll, W., 61
Carta, J. J., 10, 35
Case, L. P., 79
Cassel, J., 79
Casto, G., 89
Cestone, C. M., 6

Chabris, C., 1
Chall, J., 9
Champlin, T., 16, 17, 18
Chan, L. K. S., 121
Chandler, P., 71
Chapman, S., 101
Chard, D. J., 18, 21, 22, 32, 33, 35, 61, 93
Chavez, M., 68
Cheatham, J. P., 17, 18, 20
Christ, T., 24
Christou, C., 71
Chung, K. H., 79
Cirino, P. T., 16, 17
Clancy-Menchetti, J., 12
Cobb, H. B., 115
Cohen, J., 93
Cohen, K., 53
Coiro, J., 55
Cole, P. G., 121
Collins, B. C., 61, 64
Compton, D. L., 20
Conley, D. T., 96
Conley, M. W., 43, 95
Cook, B. G., 1, 4, 5, 6
Cook, L., 4, 114, 117, 118, 120
Cooke, N. L., 66
Cooper, M., 71
Coughlin, J., 80
Council for Exceptional Children (CEC), 2
Coyne, M. D., 16, 46, 47, 48, 55
Crain-Thoreson, C., 46, 47
Cramer, K. A., 61
Crockett, J. B., 2
Crowe, L., 46
Cumming, J., 61
Cunningham, A. E., 44, 45
Curtis, M. E., 47
Cutler, L., 84

Dacy, B. J. S., 6
Dale, P., 46, 47
Dalton, B., 52, 53
Dammannn, J. E., 2, 6
Daniel, G. E., 79
Davie, J., 24
Davis, B., 104
Davis, M. H., 120
Deatline-Buchman, A., 74
DeBaryshe, B., 46
deGlopper, K., 49
De La Paz, S., 32, 90
del Mas, R. C., 61
Delquadri, J., 35

143

Leahy, S., 31
Lee, C., 60, 84
Lee, D., 60
Lee, O., 32
Leftwich, S. A., 35
Lenz, B. K., 35, 98, 99, 100, 101, 102, 103, 104,
    105, 106, 107, 108, 109, 110, 111
Leu, D. J., Jr., 55
Lewandowski, L., 53
Licht, B., 32
Lin, Y.-Y., 74
Linan-Thompson, S., 21
Lipson, M. Y., 32
Lithner, J., 70, 71
Lively, T. J., 51
Lloyd, J., 66, 115, 116, 119
Lloyd, J. W., 3, 32
Lloyd, P. A., 3
Locke, W. R., 26
Loftus, S., 47
Logan, G. D., 21, 22
Lopez-Vona, K., 117
Lovett, M. W., 27, 49
Loynachan, C., 85, 86
Lundeen, C., 116
Lundeen, D., 116
Lyerla, K. D., 88
Lyon, G. R., 28

MacArthur, C., 90
MacArthur, C. A., 94
MacArthur, S., 32
Maccini, P., 32
Madelaine, A., 3
Magiera, K., 116, 117, 117–118, 118
Magiera, K. A., 117, 118
Magnusson, D., 116
Malouf, D. B., 2
Mann, Thomas, 89
Margolis, H., 120
Mariage, T., 113
Marotta, A., 116
Marquard, K., 79
Marquis, J. G., 101, 102
Marshall, S. P., 71, 74
Marston, D., 116
Martinez, M. G., 21
Marvin, C., 46
Mason, L., 84, 90, 93, 94
Mason, L. H., 83, 87, 90, 93, 94
Massaro, D., 52
Mastropieri, M. A., 5, 32, 43, 65, 89, 106, 116, 120
Mathes, P., 17, 23
Mathes, P. G., 11, 12, 13, 16, 17, 18, 20
Matlock, B., 45
Matta, D., 116, 119
Mattingly, J. C., 61, 62, 64
Mayer, R. E., 72, 77
McCabe, P., 120
McCoach, B., 47
McCoach, D. B., 47
McCormick, L., 118
McDonagh, S., 21
McDuffie, K. A., 2, 116
McIntosh, R., 32
McIntyre, S. B., 66
McKeown, M. G., 22, 44, 45, 47, 48, 49, 51,
    55, 56
McKnight, P., 98
McLaughlin, M. J., 98, 117, 118, 121
McLaughlin, T. F., 61, 89
McLaughlin, V., 114
McLaughlin, V. L., 115
McMaken, J., 99
McMaster, K. L., 5, 10

McNamara, D. S., 101
Meister, C., 101
Menchetti, B., 69
Menon, S., 31
Mercer, C. D., 21, 61, 65, 66
Meyer, A., 52, 98
Mikulecky, L., 30
Miller, B., 31
Miller, J., 83
Miller, L., 27, 28
Miller, S. P., 61, 65, 66
Millogo, V., 101
Milne, A. A., 85
Mirenda, P., 46, 114
Mitchem, K., 52
Mizokawa, D., 84
Monk, C. A., 72
Montague, M., 77, 78, 79, 80, 81
Montali, J., 53
Moody, S., 121
Moore, M., 52
Moran, M. R., 89
Morris, R. D., 27
Mostert, M. P., 2
Muller, E., 113
Murawski, W. W., 115, 116, 118
Murdock, J., 52, 53, 55
Murray, C., 53
Muse, A. E., 44

Nagy, W. E., 45, 49
Nash, H., 49, 51, 56
Nathan, M. J., 70
Nathan, R. G., 22
National Assessment of Educational Progress
    (NAEP), 8, 58
National Center for Educational Statistics, 8
National Commission on Writing, 83
National Council of Teachers of Mathematics
    (NCTM), 59, 61, 66, 69, 70
National Early Literacy Panel (NELP), 8, 10,
    16, 18
National Institute of Child Health and Human
    Development (NICHD), 8, 31, 32
National Mathematics Advisory Panel
    (NMAP), 58, 60, 61, 66
National Reading Panel (NRP), 8, 10, 13, 16,
    18, 44, 48, 51
National Research Council (NRC), 59,
    70, 82
Nelson, J. R., 12
Nevin, A., 118
Nevin, A. I., 118
Nihalani, P. K., 6
Nimon, K., 17
No Child Left Behind Act, 15
Nolet, V., 98
Noonan, M. J., 118
Norris, J., 46
Notari-Syverson, A., 11
Nunes, T., 49, 50, 51, 55

Oakhill, J., 9, 49
Ober, S., 113
O'Connor, R. E., 11, 13
Olejnik, S., 50
Olson, R. K., 53
Owen, R. L., 74, 75

Palincsar, A. S., 25, 33
Paris, A. H., 32
Pashler, H., 100
Passolunghi, M. C., 59
Patberg, J. P., 49
Pate, J., 23

Patriarca, L., 113
Pearson, P. D., 31
Pellegrini, A. D., 46
Perfetti, C., 21
Perfetti, C. A., 9
Perin, D., 84, 87, 93, 94
Perkins, D., 101
Perron-Jones, N., 74
Persky, H., 83
Person, N. K., 101
Petrilli, M., 2
Peyton, J. A., 13
Philippou, G., 71
Pickle, J. M., 115
Pikulski, J. J., 21
Pinnell, G. S., 21
Pool, K., 13
Porter, A., 99
Post, T. R., 61
Potter, E., 71
Pressley, M., 22, 31, 32, 33, 77, 101
Proctor, C. P., 52, 53, 54, 55, 56
Profliet, C., 13
Pugach, M. C., 115
Pullen, P. C., 3
Pulvers, K. A., 100
Purkey, S. C., 115

RAND Reading Study Group, 30, 48
Rashotte, C. A., 22
Rasinski, T. V., 21
Raskind, M. H., 53, 55
Rea, P. J., 115
Reese, J. H., 30
Reeve, P., 115
Reid, R., 79
Reinking, D., 115
Rieth, H., 52, 53, 59
Ring, J., 53
Robbins, C., 46
Roberts, G., 45, 49
Roberts, J. K., 17, 20
Roberts, K. R., 16, 17, 20
Robinson, C., 69
Robinson, D. H., 6
Roehler, L. R., 31
Rogers, G., 22
Rogers, L., 84, 89, 93, 94
Rohani, F., 95
Root, P., 47
Rose, D., 98
Rose, D. H., 52
Rosenberg, M., 69
Rosenshine, B., 34, 101
Roser, N. L., 21
Rosman, N. J. S., 116
Rouet, J. F., 101
Rudell, R. B., 31
Rueztel, D. R., 21

Sacks, G., 45
Sacks, S., 32
Sáenz, L. M., 24, 26
Sagan, C., 4
Salahu-Din, D., 83
Salend, S. J., 117, 118
Salomon, G., 101
Samuels, S. A., 21
Sanders, E. A., 13
Sandmel, K., 92, 93
Santamaria, L. J., 114
Saxon, K., 113
Scammacca, N., 45, 68
Scarborough, H. S., 46
Schatschneider, C., 9

Subject Index

Academic skills outcomes
    arithmetic combinations and, 58–69
    content areas and, 95–112
    co-teaching and, 113–121
    early literacy instruction and, 8–20
    mathematics reasoning and, 70–82
    reading comprehension and, 30–43
    reading fluency and, 21–29
    research-based practices in, 7
    research-to-practice gap and, 6
    vocabulary and, 44–57
    written expression and, 83–94
ADHD. *See* Attention deficit hyperactivity
    disorder (ADHD)
Adult-assisted learning structures, 99–100
Alphabetic principle
    early literacy instruction and, 8, 9, 12, 18
    reading comprehension and, 30–31
    reading fluency and, 22
Alphabet Practice activities, 85
Alternative explanations, determining effective
    practices, 4
Are We Really Co-Teachers Scale, 118
Arithmetic combinations
    instructional practices for, 60–69
    instruction-related difficulties with, 59–60
    mathematical achievement and, 58–59
    rationale and theoretical framework for
        teaching, 60–61
Asperger's syndrome, 80, 94
Assessment, research-based practices in, 7
At-risk students
    Early Interventions in Reading, 16–17
    Peer-Assisted Learning Strategies, 25
    Self-Regulated Strategy Development
        model, 93–94
    Sound Partners, 14
    vocabulary instruction for, 44–48, 48–51,
        51–57
Attention, illusions of, 1–2
Attention deficit hyperactivity disorder
    (ADHD)
    cognitive strategy instruction and, 77
    schema-broadening instruction focusing on
        transfer and, 75, 76
    Self-Regulated Strategy Development
        model and, 93–94
Autism
    cognitive strategy instruction and, 80
    Self-Regulated Strategy Development
        model and, 94
    technological aids for vocabulary
        learning, 52

Automaticity and automatic retrieval. *See also*
    Retrieval, Automaticity, Vocabulary,
    Engagement with Language, and
    Orthography (RAVE-O)
    arithmetic combinations and, 59–60, 61,
        66, 69
    early literacy instruction and, 9, 16
    mathematics reasoning and, 78, 81
    reading comprehension and, 31
    reading fluency and, 27
    vocabulary and, 54

BD. *See* Behavior disorders (BD)
Behavioral outcomes, research-based
    practices in, 7
Behavioral theory, 60
Behavior disorders (BD), Peer-Assisted
    Learning Strategies, 25–26

CAI (computer-assisted instruction), 52
CASL. *See* Center on Accelerated Student
    Learning (CASL) Handwriting/
    Spelling Program
CAST (Center for Applied Special
    Technology), 54
Causality, 1–2, 4
CCC (Copy-Cover-Compare) technique,
    62–63
CEC (Council for Exceptional Children), 2
Center for Applied Special Technology
    (CAST), 54
Center on Accelerated Student Learning
    (CASL) Handwriting/Spelling
    Program
  implementation, 86
  improving written expression, 84
  lesson activities overview, 85–86
  research on, 87
CERs. *See* Content Enhancement Routines
    (CERs)
Classical conditioning, 60
Classroom-assisted content area interventions,
    97, 98, 99–100
Classwide Peer Tutoring, 23
Click and Clunk strategy, 38, 41
Close reading, 50
CMI (computer-mediated instruction), 52
Cognitive cues, 60
Cognitive psychology, 33
Cognitive strategy instruction (CSI)
  description of, 76–77
  problem solving and, 77–79
  recommendations for practice, 81–82

research on, 79–81
  Solve It!, 77–81
Cognitive theory, 77
Cold readings, 23
Collaboration process, 116–118
Collaborative Strategic Reading (CSR)
  cooperative learning group roles, 39–40, 42
  description of, 33
  introducing, 38–43
  materials, 42–43
  as reading comprehension intervention, 31,
    33–43
  reading cue cards, 41, 42–43
  research on, 34–36
  sample reading passage, 37
  selecting text for, 43
  techniques for teaching, 36–38
  theoretical foundation, 33–34
Colleagues, personal experiences of, 1, 3
Common Core Standards, 95
Composing strategies, Self-Regulated Strategy
    Development model, 90
Composition skills
  Self-Regulated Strategy Development
    model for, 89–94
  Strategic Instruction Model for, 87–89
Comprehension. *See also* Reading
    comprehension
  Early Interventions in Reading, 16, 17
  as early literacy intervention component,
    8–9
  Peer-Assisted Learning Strategies, 10
  RAVE-O and, 27, 28
  Sound Partners, 13, 15
Computer-assisted instruction (CAI), 52
Computer-mediated instruction (CMI), 52
Concrete-representational-abstract (CRA)
    instructional sequence, 65–66
Concrete-Semiconcrete-Abstract (CSA)
    instructional sequence, 66–67
Confidence, illusions of, 1–2
Constant Time Delay, 62, 64
Content areas
  challenges for all students, 95–96
  content enhancement routines, 100–112
  co-teaching and, 114, 118–120
  intervention approaches, 98–100
  theoretical framework, 96–98
  word analysis and, 51, 57
Content Enhancement Routines (CERs)
  evaluation of, 110–112
  group accommodations and, 98
  learning supports, 100